Exodus!

✳

Exodus!

✦

Religion, Race, and Nation in
Early Nineteenth-Century Black America

EDDIE S. GLAUDE, JR.

The University of Chicago Press   Chicago and London

EDDIE S. GLAUDE, JR., is assistant professor of religion and Africana studies at Bowdoin College.

The University of Chicago Press, Chicago 60637
The University of Chicago Press, Ltd., London
© 2000 by The University of Chicago
All rights reserved. Published 2000
Printed in the United States of America
09 08 07 06 05 04 03 02 01 00   1 2 3 4 5

ISBN: 0-226-29819-1 (CLOTH)
ISBN: 0-226-29820-5 (PAPER)

An earlier version of chapter 1 appeared in Judith Jackson Fossett and Jeffrey A. Tucker, eds., *Race Consciousness: African-American Studies for the New Century* (New York: New York University Press, 1997), 115–35. Reprinted by permission of New York University Press and the volume editors.

Library of Congress Cataloging-in-Publication Data

Glaude, Eddie S., 1968–
    Exodus! : religion, race, and nation in early nineteenth-century Black America / Eddie S. Glaude, Jr.
        p.   cm.
    Includes bibliographical references and index.
    ISBN 0-226-29819-1 (hardcover : alk. paper)—ISBN 0-226-29820-5 (pbk. : alk. paper)
    1. Black nationalism—United States—History—19th century. 2. Black nationalism—Religious aspects—Christianity. 3. Afro-Americans—Race identity. 4. Afro-Americans—Politics and government—19th century. 5. Afro-Americans—Religion. 6. Afro-American churches—History—19th century. 7. Exodus, The—Typology. I. Title.

E185.18.G57 2000
973′.0496073—dc21
                                                                        99-049076

To the loving memory of my great-grandparents,

Ruby Wilson (1908–1990) and Russell Wilson (1915–1989),

whose wisdom and love continue to sustain me.

Contents

Acknowledgments

This book began as my dissertation for the Department of Religion at Princeton University, where many teachers and fellow graduate students supported the work in its initial stages. I am especially indebted to my dissertation committee; it was in Professor Albert J. Raboteau's work that I found the idea for this book. His essay "African-Americans, Exodus, and the American Israel" offered me a new way to make sense of my political commitments without the trappings of the ideology of black nationalism. He helped clarify my thinking about the relationship between black Christianity and black politics in the nineteenth century. Jeffrey Stout's meticulous reading of the dissertation and his demand for precision were invaluable. I have come to realize that his way of thinking informs a lot of what I do and how I do it. Cornel West was and remains the inspiration for most of my work. He is my mentor, and in some ways I will always be his student.

For their friendship and dialogue during this process, I am especially indebted to Raphael Allen, Kimberly Benston, William Hart, Paul Jefferson, Wahneema Lubiano, Lucius Outlaw, Fasaha Traylor, Howard Winant, Paul Gilroy, Stuart Hall, Orlando Brown, Nathaniel Norment, Daniel Black, Rodney Patterson, Farah Jasmine Griffin, Kevin Gaines, Willie Walker, my colleagues in the religion department and Africana Studies Program at Bowdoin College—Burke Long, John Holt, Elizabeth Pritchard, Randy Stakeman, Lelia DeAndrade, Patrick Rael, and Patricia Saunders—and the students in my classes at Bowdoin, particularly Kevin

Wolfe, NeEddra James, and Melvin Rogers. Special thanks go to Professor Will Gravely, who read the manuscript closely and provided detailed commentary on each of the chapters. The book is much better because of him.

Thanks also to Alan Thomas, my editor at Chicago, for his extraordinary compassion and guiding encouragement throughout this project (thanks for being patient with all of my insecurities); to Leslie Keros and the other folks who assisted the production; and to Jane Zanichkowsky, my thoughtful copyeditor.

Whatever I do is made possible by my family: my mother and father, Eddie and Juanita Glaude; my grandmothers, Delores Cox and Bernice Glaude; my two sisters, Bonita Glaude and Angela Glaude-Hosch; and my brother, Alvin Jones. I love them dearly. Thanks also to my special friends, Mark Jefferson and Paul Taylor, who are always available when I need to bounce an idea off someone. Finally, I want to thank the "love of my life," Winnifred Brown-Glaude—without whom my life would be empty and meaningless—and our beautiful son, Langston Ellis Glaude, who knew when daddy needed a break from work.

PART ONE

Exodus History

You shall not oppress a stranger. You know the heart of a stranger, for you were strangers in the land of Egypt.

EXODUS 23:9

Canaan land is the land for me,
And let God's saints come in.
There was a wicked man,
He kept them children in Egypt land.
Canaan land is the land for me,
And let God's saints come in.
God did say to Moses one day,
Say, Moses, go to Egypt land,
And tell him to let my people go.
Canaan land is the land for me,
And let God's saints come in.

SLAVE SPIRITUAL

1

"Bent Twigs and Broken Backs"

An Introduction

"STRANGERS IN A STRANGE LAND"

No other story in the Bible has quite captured the imagination of African Americans like that of Exodus. The story's account of bondage, the trials of the wilderness, and the final entrance into the promised land resonated with those who experienced the hardships of slavery and racial discrimination. Indeed, the story demonstrated God active in history and his willingness to intervene on behalf of his chosen people. But my interest in the Exodus story is not so much to provide an account of conceptions of deliverance or liberation in religious terms—even though the story is obviously about an act of God. My intention is to explore the ways the story became a source for a particular use of nation language among African Americans as well as a metaphorical framework for understanding the middle passage, enslavement, and quests for emancipation, for although Exodus was a sacred text, it was not understood only in religious terms. The history of the story and its broad application across a disparate field of political engagements suggest that it was also interpreted in this-worldly and historical terms as a model for resistance and, perhaps, revolution.

To be sure, the political efficacy of Exodus in the early nineteenth century rests in the socioreligious imagination of African American Christians. Through dramatic reenactments and ritual activity—preaching,

singing, and praying—black congregations collapsed the distance between the slaves of Egypt and the slaves of the United States. The slave
would sing:

Gwine to write to Massa Jesus,
To send some Valiant soldier,
To turn back Pharaoh's Army, Hallelu!

As time and distance folded in on each other, these peculiar subjects of
American slavery literally became the children of Israel and the chosen
people of God, forming communities and conceptions of freedom linked
to this biblical narrative.[1]

Yet to locate the idea of freedom among African Americans within a
religious space blurs the distinction between the sacred and the secular
and suggests that each infects the other. I emphasize the "secular" character of Exodus only to redirect our attention to the political value of the
story. Beyond that the distinction does not make much sense, for the idea
of political freedom was constructed, to some extent, within a language
that linked biblical figures to postbiblical persons, places, and events.[2] If
we only read the story of Exodus and its analogical application as examples of a community of faith awaiting an act of God, then we miss, I
believe, the full significance of this mimetic act and its powerful hold on
the black political imagination. Specifically, we miss the role and import
of salvific history, that is, accounts of the experiences of African Americans viewed from the perspective of the Bible that make sense of their
conditions of living.

Most efforts toward liberation in African American history have been
articulated as reenactments of Israel's exodus from Egypt. In the context
of slavery, the story empowered Christian slaves and free persons to look
beyond their condition and envision a future in which they were truly free.
The events of the Civil War and the mass migrations of the late 1870s and
1880s were also described as reenactments of the Exodus story. The Union
armies were scripted as the armies of God who came to deliver Israel from
bondage. The mass migrations, the Exodusters as it were, envisioned
Canaan, a territory of freedom, in Kansas and Oklahoma. This biblical
figuralism—always grounded in the urtext of the slave experience—articulated a sense of common history and a shared future. These events
affected a people, and the uses of the Exodus story solidified that sense of
communality needed for conjoint action. In short, the brutality of the

peculiar institution and of American racism was blunted as the sacred history of God's deliverance of his chosen people was transformed into an account of black liberation.

The major components of this account consisted in the long suffering of the middle passage, the evil of enslavement, and the mournful cries for emancipation: the beginning, the middle, and the end. The movement from beginning to end is central to the historical significance of the Exodus story,[3] particularly when we consider the fact that the end is quite different from the beginning. The journey forward—the promise that where we are going is radically different from where we are—marks the transformative aspect of the narrative. Unlike ancient tales in which the journey begins and ends at home, the narrative structure of Exodus describes a progression, the transformation of people as they journey forward to a promised land. Bondage in Egypt is replaced by the freedom promised in Canaan. Once the Israelites leave, there is no turning back. Egypt remains only as a possibility, a sign for the consequences of moral and civic transgression.

The journey transforms the community of Israel; the men and women who leave Egypt are not the same as those who arrive at the banks of the Jordan. The narrative structure of the story accounts for this transformation, for its subject is not a disparate group of individuals but the people of Israel. Exodus, then, is not only the story of these people but their history—a political history about slavery and freedom, law and rebellion.[4] And like the march, this political history has a determinate aim: to continuously retell the story of bondage, the march toward liberation, and the discipline necessary to remain free.

The march, with its linear progression, its movement from beginning to end, provides a key to understanding the historical and political significance of African American dramatic reenactments of the story. The stubbornness of slavery and the persistence of racism warranted recognition that the abolition of slavery did not guarantee freedom (as evidenced in the North). Vigilance of the first order was required of blacks to prevent their return to physical slavery. A moral alertness and a willingness to remember the horrors of bondage were necessary to secure freedom. The story had to be retold in the shifting context of America's racial landscape.

The journey in the Exodus story also provided a crucial source for the construction of a national identity for African Americans. The story concerns not only heroic individuals who escaped the persecution of Pharaoh but also the people of Israel as they journeyed toward moral renewal and self-determination. I refer to Exodus, then, not only for its historical relevance to any account of the emergence of nation language in the United States but also as a metaphor for a particular style of imagining the nation in early nineteenth-century black America. Exodus is a metaphor for a conception of nation that begins with the common social heritage of slavery and the insult of discrimination—the psychical and physical violence of white supremacy in the United States—and evolves into a set of responses on the part of a people acting for themselves to alleviate their condition. What sets it apart from the ideas of nation that have come to dominate black political debate is its moral component; that is, the nation is imagined not alongside religion but precisely through the precepts of black Christianity (I examine this issue in chapter 2).

Following Eugene Genovese, while desperately holding his paternalism thesis at bay, I argue that out of black religious life emerged a conception of black national identity. Genovese states that black-American Christianity

> made possible a universal statement because it made possible a national statement. [This] national statement expressed a duality as something both black and American, not in the mechanical sense of being an ethnic component in a pluralistic society, but in the dialectical sense of simultaneously being itself and the other, both separately and together, and of developing as a religion within a religion in a nation within a nation.[5]

Such was the case because of the racial basis of slavery, for the stain of slavery not only marked as the same black individuals who may have lived quite different lives—blacks in the South as opposed to blacks in the North and in the West—it also enabled them to view themselves as bound together, as in communion with one another.[6] This racial solidarity "forced slaves [and free persons] out of themselves—forced them to glimpse the possibility of nationality rather than class."[7]

Of course, in Genovese's view, the potential revolutionary impulses of this solidarity were attenuated by the moral precepts of Christianity. In spite of the slave's separation from the master, his creation of a distinctive style of worship, and a context-specific theology, the slave was bound to the master in Christian fellowship. As such, most slaves, or free black Christians, for that matter, saw their oppressors not as demons but as fellow sinners before God: they despised the peculiar institution and racism but not the individuals. Such an orientation, for Genovese, made it difficult "to hammer a revolutionary commitment . . . and even harder to raise a cry for holy war."[8]

Christianity also brought to the fore the tension between individual aspirations and collective aims. Although black Christianity gave the slave a sense of her own worth before God and others and enabled her to act as a self-determining agent, its primary focus remained the spiritual emancipation of the individual, which constituted the necessary foundation for black collective action. If the slave or free person failed to give her life over to God, for example, then any effort to liberate black people would necessarily fall short. For Genovese, this focus on individual salvation came at the expense of black collective action.[9]

In spite of these tensions and, in some ways, because of them, Genovese maintains that black religion was propelled "forward to the creation of collective identity and pride. The black variant of Christianity laid the foundations of protonational consciousness and at the same time stretched a universalist offer of forgiveness and ultimate reconciliation to white America."[10] Black Christianity also provided the slave and the free person with the languages to understand themselves apart from their experiences of humiliation, as well as the tools to construct forms of solidarity that would sustain them in the violence of America's racist culture. This occurred, in Genovese's view, despite Christianity's tendency to block the development of a black political consciousness and to impede a willingness to create what he calls a legitimate black authority (a black nation-state).

Genovese makes a mistake here. He is right to recognize the beginnings of a black national identity in the confines of black Christianity. He is also correct in his account of the moral underpinnings of that identity. But Genovese misses the mark when he claims that acceptance of Christianity blocked the way to the development of political consciousness. On the contrary, it may have impeded the emergence of a certain kind of political awareness but not political consciousness altogether. African Americans' uses of nation language (at least in the early nineteenth century) stand as a peculiar expression of their ambivalent relation to America. Its religious underpinnings make that expression an argument for (and about) the soul of America: it is a soul-craft politics. Acceptance of the "hegemony of the oppressor," then, does not necessarily end political consciousness as such. It merely locates the battle on a different terrain: inside the dominant culture, in which new ideas emerge from old ones by way of interpretation and revision.[11] (Chapters 3 and 4 take this issue up in more detail.)

Why use the language of nation to express this sentiment? Because it captures the sense of peoplehood that emerged in the face of practices that distinguished blacks as a separate people and their efforts to find resources, particularly their use of biblical typology, to make sense of those practices. Here *nation* is understood as a cultural artifact of a particular kind. That is to say, it bears the marks of a cultural identity shaped and constituted in a space made separate (initially) by the actions of others. It is not so much a political ideology, at least in the early nineteenth century, as it is a set of experiences and a moral outlook that aroused deep attachments.

To help elaborate this particular view I turn to the political theorist Michael Walzer. In *Exodus and Revolution* Walzer sets forth a vision of radical politics and democratic community through a close reading of the Exodus story. I take his account to be not only a vision of radical politics but also an attempt to imagine a nationalist politics without the baggage of political messianism, that is to say, without the desire for the apocalypse, a readiness to force the End, and claims of the unconditionality of the national mission. Ironically, Walzer begins the book with a description of a black preacher in Montgomery, Alabama, delivering a sermon on the black freedom struggle and the Book of Exodus. He recounts the preacher's rendering of the going out from Egypt: the cringe under the lash, the challenge of Pharaoh, the acceptance of the covenant.[12] The sermon inspired Walzer to pursue more seriously the centrality of Exodus in the political history of the West. He does not mention black folk again in the book, but the basic components of his account are helpful in understanding the relation of Exodus and nation language in early nineteenth-century black America.

For my purposes, three features of Walzer's account are important.[13] First, in his view, the nation is formed out of a remembrance of oppression and liberation. The brutality of bondage and the euphoria of freedom are kept in "living memory" to remind the people whence they came, to serve as conceptual tools for problem-solving, and to combat injustice not only from the outside but also in the internal arrangements of the group (this is a central issue in chapter 5). Second, the nation, if it is to be democratic, must be constituted through the consent of its members and through their ongoing political education. This amounts to a covenant, an agreement among fellows that serves as a regulative ideal against which to judge the group and others. Moreover, this covenant requires that the members of the community understand themselves as active agents, not simply as former slaves. They must overcome, through education, the legacies of Egyptian bondage in order to maintain the covenant (I examine these issues more closely in part 2).

Finally, the nation must have some sense of itself in relation to other nations. It must embrace the specificity of its own experience and understanding of liberation, but cultural or racial chauvinism is not allowed.[14] That would compromise the covenant. In the end, Walzer's reading of Exodus offers an understanding of nation and obligation that draws on the moral resources contained in the story (a story that is central to the Western political imagination), while holding at arm's length some of the more pernicious ways the story has been used. It is in this light that I examine the complicated relation of religion, race, and nation in early nineteenth-century black America.

In examining this relation during a period when an American identity was forming, the ideology of race was developing, and racial violence was a part of everyday life, I argue that the idea of nation was, first, neither conceived on analogy with a biological organism nor premised on the assumption that biologically inherited racial characteristics served as the basis for national identity. Second, the idea of nation was not conceived in terms of geographical territory or the creation of an independent nation-state. Instead, nation language emerged out of the common insult of slavery, the persistence and entrenchment of white supremacist beliefs in the social and political fabric of early nineteenth-century America (a set of practices and a period of time shadowed by the specter of racial violence), and the need to keep alive the memory of these realities. What Isaiah Berlin clearly saw as the constitutive element of nationalisms generally, collective humiliation, was the principal element of African American uses of nation language in the early nineteenth century: the reality of pain, suffering, and collective humiliation caused by a violently racist nation. This humiliation yielded a response, like the bent twig of the poet Schiller's theory, of a lashing back and a refusal to accept these conditions of living.[15]

African Americans turned to their faith in this effort. By appropriating Exodus, they articulated their own sense of peoplehood and secured for themselves a common history and destiny[16] as they elevated their experiences to biblical drama. This analogical reasoning provided many black activists with the vocabularies to condemn the practices of the United States and to talk of emancipation. Maria Stewart in 1831 cried out: "America, America, foul and indelible is thy stain! For the cruel wrongs and injuries to the fallen sons of Africa. The blood of her murdered ones cries to heaven for vengeance against Thee."[17] Because of its transgressions America was not symbolized as a promised land in the wilderness of North America. Rather, it was Egypt, the enslaver of the black Israel, God's chosen people. Stewart continued: "You may kill, tyrannize, and oppress as much as you choose, until our cry shall come up before the throne of God; for I am firmly persuaded, that he will not suffer you to quell the proud, fearless and undaunted spirits of the Africans forever; for in his own time, he is able to plead our cause against you, and to pour out upon you the ten plagues of Egypt."[18] The appropriation of the Exodus story not only gave an account of the circumstances of black lives, offering a regulative ideal to guide action and to define the nation, it ensured retribution for the continued suffering of God's people.

EXODUS AND RACIAL SOLIDARITY

My reading of Exodus extends a basic insight made more than twenty years ago. The editors of the anthology *Black Nationalism in America* wrote that the simplest expression of black nationalism was racial solidarity. "It generally has no ideological or programmatic implications beyond the desire that black people organize themselves on the basis of their common color and oppressed condition to move in some way to alleviate their situation."[19] This form of solidarity, they maintain, is essential to all forms of black nationalism, and its earliest expression is found in the formation of mutual aid societies and separate black churches in the late eighteenth and early nineteenth centuries. A simple idea: black people caught in the violence of a racist culture, struggling to find and generate meaning (possibility) for themselves, turn to religious narrative to make sense of the absurdity of their condition, to cultivate solidarity with similarly situated selves, and to develop a self-consciousness essential for problem-solving. No grand ideological or programmatic pronouncements: simply the conviction that African Americans must take the responsibility for liberating themselves.

Of course, this is not that simple. What exactly this self-liberation entails remains a critical issue. Moreover, the organization of black people on the basis of a common condition and color presents several worrisome problems. First, many have concluded that African Americans acting for themselves must translate, if such actions are to be described as nationalist, into efforts to form a black nation-state. This view maintains that the desire for a state stands as the basis for black nationalism. As such, absolute control of a specific geographical territory, the ability to defend that territory militarily, and the capacity to sustain its citizenry economically become the goals. Second, the idea of a common condition has lead many to elide the differences within black communities. Class and gender differences, for example, are subordinated to what are perceived as our common interests (interests that grow out of our common condition). Finally, the idea of a common color often, though not necessarily, assumes a biological basis to the nation rooted in race. Race binds us to one another and grounds the archeological work of cultural recovery. Such a view adds force to the proposition, often attributed to black nationalists, that we are or ought to be members of a single moral and political community: that our allegiances to the black nation should not waver because of our sexuality, gender, or class or some other value.

The first two problems can be dispensed with rather easily. I take it that a number of different political positions with very different aims assume the need for African Americans to take responsibility for their liberation. The students in the early stages of the Student Non-violent Coordinating Committee presented this very argument to black folk in the rural South as they urged them to register to vote. And I take it that Justice Clarence Thomas's urgings to end all forms of racial preferences stem from what he sees as the necessity of black folk acting for themselves (however misguided such a view may be). The notion of racial solidarity leaves unspecified how we ought to organize ourselves; this evades the trappings of certain ideological formations and opens up what can be described as expressions of national sentiment. To be sure, the plurality of voices within African American communities has led and will continue to lead to a plurality of responses as to what acting for ourselves will entail.

The idea of a common condition and by extension a common interest, however, is another concern. A problem may be a shared one for black individuals. We may all agree that slavery is wrong or that lynching is evil. But that fact does not lead to the conclusion that we have identical interests or that we will agree on a course of action. Some may pursue a moral or a legal means to end both practices: they may appeal to a broader moral law or simply to the stated principles of American democracy. Others may pursue a more violent course of action: they may call for insurrection or even outright revolution. In either case, the desired aims could very well be different. Proponents of moral argument alone or some form of legal redress might have as their goal the wholesale inclusion of African Ameri-

cans in American society. Those pursuing violent means to end the practices of slavery and lynching might want a complete separation of whites
and blacks. The issue is not common interests or an agreed-on course of
action. Rather, it is the common problem that necessitates conjoint action, actions that may vary, given the different conceptions of the good
that animate them, but are nevertheless connected by their efforts to respond to a palpably shared problem.

The goal of defining the interests of African Americans seems to me
impossible. What matters here again is the force of some meddlesome
circumstance or problematic—the need to move in some way to alleviate
the situation. I am reminded of Du Bois's famous account of race: if you
want to know the meaning of race look in the back of a Jim Crow car.[20]
This account does not define the interests of those who experience Jim
Crow as identical, nor does it demand that all those who can experience
Jim Crow pursue the same course of action. Rather, it simply isolates a
problem that confronts some of us in such a way as to lead to a subordination of some values and the superordination of others (choosing to speak
at that moment to the issue of race as opposed to that of gender or class).
The aim is to allow for a plurality of action and to build forms of overlap-
ping consensus with an eye toward problem-solving and not with the view
that there is but one conception of the good to be recognized by all black
people precisely because they are black.

Some theorists, let's call them cultural nationalists, hold the view that
there is a specific form of life that binds black people to one another in
the United States and throughout the world. This form of life is distinct
from that of white people or European peoples: different in conceptions
of knowledge and in its understanding of beauty, as well as in its formulation of the moral and ethical norms that ought to guide action in the
world. Africa is crucial. The vast continent is the Archimedean point for
this distinctive form of life. So, in spite of the perceived rupture caused
by the transatlantic slave trade and the subsequent creation of an African
diaspora, we can still discern, according to this view, the cultural legacy
of Africa in the New World—which, in the end, sets us off from white
people. Such a distinct form of life constitutes a nation and a national
identity: something to be retrieved in light of the desires and effects of
white supremacy and something to be preserved for posterity (its conception of the good). In short, racial solidarity and self-determination are
attained through, broadly speaking, culture, defined in terms of common

history, memories, beliefs, artistic and religious expression, and racial characteristics.

I do think that there are weak and strong versions of this view. The weak version simply points to our history and claims some superior status because of Europe's penchant for brutality. The strong version wants to claim an ontological status of superiority of black people: that we stand above other groups because of our genetic makeup or, perhaps, because of chauvinistic interpretations of religious ideas. Each version, however, takes as its point of departure a notion of collective identity bound by a common color and a deep-rooted, if not biologically grounded, form of life.

Wilson Moses contends, for example, that ideas of the nation-state necessarily cloak a sinister notion: that they are "accompanied by a belief in consanguinity, a commitment to the conservation of racial or genetic purity, a myth of commonality and purity of 'blood.'" He goes on to say that "the nation is seen as an organic segment of humanity, and like the family, an ordinance of God, whose members own a common ancestry and ties of ethnic kinship."[21] When we consider nationalism among black Americans, then, it is precisely in the concept of the racial self (how we understand common color) that we see, if we follow Moses's claim, the most sinister feature of black nationalism.

This bald formulation extends an earlier account of the importance of race or what Moses calls racial chauvinism in his conception of black nationalism. I want to focus on one particular feature of this account because it helps us see the different ways we can think about race, and it places in stark relief the central differences between Moses' and my views of the use of nation language among black Americans during the early nineteenth century. Moses contends that one of the ideas central to nineteenth-century black nationalism was that of a mystical racial chauvinism.[22] In this view the major proponents of classical black nationalism believed that the hand of God directed their movement. These religious sentiments were found in the rhetorical use of the biblical verse "Princes shall come out of Egypt; Ethiopia shall soon stretch forth her hands unto God" and in the convention of comparing the condition of African Americans to that of the Israelites in Egypt. Moses contends that the chauvinistic elements of such analogies were evidenced in the claim that "blacks are the chosen people of God who works not only in the hereafter, but in human history, his wonders to perform."[23] He likens such religious analogies to their secular counterpart: the adaptation of European racial theory, in which races were defined as types with innate characteristics.[24]

I will assume, with Anthony Appiah and others, that any account of race resting on bad biology is untenable and that those accounts that eventually fall back on such biological notions provide their own reductio.[25] But is it the case that any use of these religious stories by African Americans in the nineteenth century was necessarily chauvinistic? or, better, racially chauvinistic? This becomes a historical question and takes us to the heart of the problem of Moses' account. Moses moves too quickly to condemn the use of Psalms 68:31 and Exodus as chauvinistic appeals to racial destiny. In *Black Messiahs and Uncle Toms,* he rightly recognizes that this use of religious narrative was a typical American phenomenon. The American nation considered itself a "redeemer nation," a city on the hill, or the fulfillment of prophecy. This was the common vocabulary to describe its mission and people. And, to some extent, Moses helps us when he distinguishes two strands within America's messianic tradition: (1) a hard-line messianism that eventually developed into the doctrine of white supremacy and (2) a soft-line messianism based on Jeffersonian ideals and the American enlightenment that came to emphasize America's mission to preserve the inalienable rights of man.[26] But how African Americans came to this tradition is of critical importance. Did they embrace a soft-line version in order to criticize the prevalence of a hard-line use of messianism? To what extent did they draw on the prevailing vocabularies of the American nation to imagine their own in the face of widespread oppression? If they drew on these vocabularies, what did they take and what did they discard? Moses fails to provide any kind of account of this process. Moreover, he fails to historicize the development of biological conceptions of race among African Americans in the nineteenth century and attributes a form of racial thinking to them that might not necessarily hold given the prevailing issues and themes of the period. I agree with Moses that by the 1850s a form of biological racialism acquired common currency among many African Americans. But this was certainly not the case at the end of the eighteenth century and as late as the early 1840s. People were still debating these issues; they had not settled yet into common sense. Nation language developed as a crucial feature of black political rhetoric during the 1840s, and the "organic" conceptions of the nation that appeared in the 1850s represent a second phase in the development of the nation language still in use among African Americans.

The problem resides in Moses' understanding of the use of such language among early nineteenth-century black Americans and, consequently, in his periodization of the development of this language based on this account. In his view classical black nationalism has gone through several phases. The first phase occurred at the end of the eighteenth century when a number of African Americans expressed an impulse of self-determination. Although he locates the beginnings of nation language here, he qualifies it by terming the period protonationalistic because most African Americans at this time did not conceive of their efforts in terms of national destiny or the creation of a nation-state with a distinctive national culture.[27] This phase ended, however, in the 1830s, and black nationalism did not enter its second phase until its flourishing in the 1850s. It was eclipsed again in the 1870s, reemerged at the end of the nineteenth century, and reached its apex in its third phase, with the Garvey movement.[28]

What is of interest to me are the intermediate periods between each phase, particularly the 1830s and 1840s. I contend that a conception of a black nation was formulated during this period that differs quite starkly from Moses'—an idea of nation not predicated on a biological conception of race (particularly since such ideas had not yet settled into common usage!). Instead, race language captured the distinctiveness of the oppressed condition of African Americans; the language did not extend beyond the social and political relations that gave it meaning; it merely expressed the solidarity necessary to confront the realities of race in the United States. As Samuel Cornish, "Sidney," and Henry Highland Garnet made abundantly clear, race language was useful and relevant because of the explanation it made available to those engaged in the struggle against slavery and racism.[29]

RACIAL SOLIDARITY AND OBLIGATION

Racial and national identities constituted in the contexts of solidaristic efforts to resist violence and suffering shift the way we think about moral obligation to "the race" in antebellum black America. Here I am not thinking of moral obligation in the Kantian sense that moral deliberation must necessarily draw on general, nonempirical principles or, more specifically, that obligations to "the race" proceed from some general, nonempirical principles of race loyalty. Instead, following Richard Rorty and Wilfred Sellars, I want to think of moral obligation in terms of we-intentions—a sense of being one of us, the force of which is essentially contrastive in that it contrasts with a "they" that is made up of violent white human beings.[30]

As Rorty reads him, Sellars reconstructs the idea of obligation without recourse to an assumption of a central self or "the assumption that 'reason' is the name for a component present in other human beings, one whose recognition is the explanation of human solidarity."[31] Instead, Sellars views the notions of solidarity and obligation as historical productions. Obligations are made. They are constituted in the everyday doings and sufferings of ordinary people. Sellars identifies obligation with intersubjective validity, a validity that can refer to a range of different sorts of obligation, be they the west or the east coast in a regional rivalry in hip-hop culture, Bloods or Crips, AME or AMEZ, or the black race. For Rorty, "we can have obligations by virtue of our sense of solidarity with these groups. For we can have we-intentions, intentions which we express in sentences of the form 'We all want . . . ,' intentions which contrast with those expressed by sentences beginning with 'I want . . . ,' by virtue of our membership in any of them, large or small."[32] In the case of early nineteenth-century black America, solidarity and obligation are not thought of as a general recognition of biological similarity—the recognition of an essential racial self. Rather, both are thought of in the context of slavery and racial violence, realities that result in the subordination of differences in relation to the commonality of particular problems—not all problems, for racial solidarity and obligation are local phenomena. Both are located, bound up even, in the context in which they take form: an America where black skin renders one a slave, a second-class citizen, and an inferior human being in the eyes of the majority.

This book attempts to show that a concept of nation or peoplehood or "we-ness"—what can be generally called racial solidarity—informed all forms of black politics in the early nineteenth century. Evidence of this countertradition suggests that those who became nationalist ideologues in the 1850s did not have a monopoly on the use of the term. By arguing that all forms of black politics in the early nineteenth century employed this admittedly peculiar conception of nation language, I draw attention to the "in but not of" status of African Americans in this country—to the fact that we have always had an uneasy relation to this democratic experiment and that this relation colors our politics. Rather than seeking to construct an abstract theoretical language for dealing with these issues, this book seeks to unsettle our settled accounts of nation and nationalism by showing how complicated the language of nation has been, even within the discourse of a single historical community.

Part I, Exodus History, examines the relation between the construction of black identity and American identity (both of which are national). The chapters look at the different uses of Exodus by black and white Americans and the concepts of nation the story generates in each instance. As an archaeology of sorts, the chapters examine the extent to which the use of the Exodus story among African Americans of this period was mediated by broader uses of the story in the imagining of the American nation. I suggest that in the case of black Americans the story bears a family resemblance with the narrative used in the construction of American nationalism. Such a claim rejects any attempt to account for black nationalism or, better, for the use of nation language among African Americans in the early nineteenth century by appealing to a form of life entirely distinct from that of white people or European peoples.

Part II, Exodus Politics, moves beyond an account of the historical importance of Exodus and nation language to a more metaphorical use of the story to describe a particular style of imagining the nation. The chapters provide an extended examination of the National Negro Convention movement from 1830, the year of the first meeting, to 1843, when the convention was faced with a critical decision about the form of its political efforts. The idea of a black nation, from the late 1700s to the early 1900s, was dominated by the idea of progress and the doctrine of racial uplift. These ideas crystallized in the National Negro Convention movement. In a series of national meetings between 1830 and 1861, free blacks throughout the North gathered to deliberate issues facing their communities and to formulate responses to the wretched conditions of black Americans. The conventions extended the religious impulses of the independent black church movement into a quasi-secular domain. They addressed the policies of the nation-state as well as the inner social and ethical life of the black community. Their responses were often debated in the pages of the black press, combining, as it were, two distinctive forums for national conversation.

In some respects, these conventions represent the first national forum for civic activity among African Americans. The conventions were not sectarian. They were opened, at least in principle, to every black person in the nation. And, most important, they provided, along with the black newspaper, a national public forum for civil debate about the well-being of the community. During the eleven meetings between its inauguration and its demise, the convention, drawing on the resources of its members, generated a cultural and political conception of the black nation. The cultural idea of the nation evolved out the convention's focus on moral reform and social uplift. The political conception emerged as the convention confronted directly the practices of white supremacy of the American nation-state.

I hope the framework offered within can help us better understand the vibrancy of nation language in black America. We continue to listen to the chatter of nationalist ideologues, and we continue to fail to hear the voices of ordinary black folk. Figures such as Louis Farrakhan do not have their fingers on the pulse of black America. They simply articulate, oddly I must admit, long-standing sentiments in the black community, something like what my great-grandmother, Ruby Wilson, used to say to me: "You know white folks ain't gon' change, so you need to stop worrin' about them, cause dwellin' on 'em will eat you up." This commonsensical sensibility was and is, I maintain, a way of getting on in the world that recognizes fully the reality of race in the United States. It has close affinities to the sentiment that led to the formation of black civil society, and it avoids the trap of the essential black subject.

I believe that my great-grandmother understood that no matter how you slice it "America" was and is fundamentally a racial ideology. She understood in her own way that notions of white supremacy saturate the nation's principles, or as Ralph Ellison put it, that racism is "like a boil bursting forth from impurities in the bloodstream of democracy."[33] But she was thoroughly American, and she often reminded me that I was too. As she faced the potential terror of domestic service in the houses of white folk on the coast of Mississippi, her humiliation, continued insult and, more important, her endurance translated into a cultural logic passed onto her children and their children's children. Her words echoed the voice of Toni Morrison's Baby Suggs as she spoke to Denver: "Know it, but go on out of the yard."[34] This sentiment is where we must begin.

2

>‹‹

Of the Black Church and the
Making of a Black Public

In his seminal work *The Negro Church in America*, E. Franklin Frazier
declared that the black church in the United States was a nation within
a nation. For Frazier, this phrase captured the role of the church in the
lives of African Americans, how it circumscribed social activity and provided vocabularies for moral and ethical judgments. The black church was
in fact the primary vehicle for the exercise of black agency, a place where
the humanity of America's darker "citizens" was acknowledged and basic
human aspirations for self-determination were achieved.

The role Frazier assigned the black church harkened back to 1849,
when in describing black religious practices Martin Delany stated that
"among our people generally, the church is the Alpha and Omega of all
things. It is their only source of information—their only acknowledged
public body—their state legislature . . . their only acknowledged advi-
sor."[1] Delany went on to criticize the black church in particular and Christianity in general for teaching what he perceived as subservience in the
face of oppression. He wanted to break the hold that a certain reading of
Christianity had on the minds and lives of African Americans: a naive
pacifism or quietism when confronted with the evil of white supremacy.
Yet Delany recognized within this institution the workings of black civil
society. He acknowledged the importance and centrality of black religious

practices, in spite of their obvious limitations, in the social and political lives of African Americans.

We can see the statelike function of the black church in Delany's characterization. Just as modern nation-states provide a lens through which their citizens can view themselves and others, the black church in the nineteenth century provided "vocabularies of agency" for its members and nonmembers, tools needed to make choices with regard to their fellows and environs. These vocabularies, ways of describing, evaluating, and acting, contributed to talk about what constituted justice, the good life, and communal flourishing, and as such provided the terms for social and political critique.

Drawing on these vocabularies, Theodore Wright in 1836 proclaimed that "the slave has a friend in heaven, though he may have none here." Wright, a black pastor of a Presbyterian church in New York City, went on to say:

> There the chains of the slave will be knocked off, and he shall enjoy the liberty of the sons of God. We know that the influence of prejudice, and the love of power and avarice will oppress us here, and exclude us from privileges, on account of our color; but we know it will not exclude us from heaven, for God is no respecter of persons. Though we must be despised here, we know that our Redeemer liveth. We trust in God, who is able to save all that come unto him. God speed you on! Go forward in his name, and you will prosper.[2]

Wright seemingly falls into the trap of a glib hope for a pie-in-the-sky heaven. But he draws on a fundamental precept of black Christianity, "God is no respecter of persons," and he locates God's transforming power—all are equal before his eyes—in the lives of black people: "I listen, and I think I hear the trumpet of jubilee sounding—I hear the voice of emancipation proclaiming to my down-trodden brethren, to stand up and be free!"[3]

Like the modern state, black churches also helped organize the resources of the life of the community through their institutional mechanisms and administration. We need only think of the numerous activities occurring under their roofs to get a sense of the churches' function in the lives of antebellum blacks. Schools, mutual aid societies, athletic clubs, libraries, insurance companies, and general social events were housed in black churches and captured by the churches' commitments to the Christian gospel as well as by the institutional arrangements of those commitments. Such activities aided in the construction of common ideological and cultural beliefs that were incorporated in the everyday doings and sufferings of its members and, to a great extent, its nonmembers.

As W. E. B. Du Bois noted in his classic text *Souls of Black Folk,* the black church stood as "peculiarly the expression of the inner ethical life of a people in a sense seldom true elsewhere."[4] That is to say, the black church was more than an institutional reflection of a community of the faithful. Rather, it embodied a basic reality: sustained black cultural solidarity in the context of a racist culture. Black Christians attended church not only to worship God but also to commune with similarly situated selves, "to share and expand together the rich heritage they have inherited,"[5] and to continue the development of a self-consciousness vital to potential problem-solving activity. In other words, black churches were not confined simply to their formal roles. Instead, their institutional boundaries were quite "elusive, porous, and mobile,"[6] such that the churches' sphere of influence extended well beyond their institutional walls to the public imaginings of antebellum black America.

PUBLICS AND THE BLACK CHURCH

But the analogy with the modern state only takes us so far. The church stood not only as the institutional organization of the community's resources and a kind of ideological and cultural common ground for everyday interaction or association among antebellum blacks. These institutions, as Evelyn Brooks Higginbotham rightly notes, were also "mediating structures,"[7] standing between black individuals and the racial state. As the U.S. nation-state, through its institutions, policies, conditions, and rules, as well as the social relations in which each of these were embedded, circumscribed the lives of black individuals and communities,[8] black religious institutions, through their ability to sustain numerous newspapers and other activities as well as their ability to render black experiences in the dramatic terms of the Bible, rearticulated the racial practices of the U.S. racial state and helped construct a collective identity.

These churches were organized publics consisting of "all those who [were] affected by the indirect consequences of transactions to such an extent that it [was] deemed necessary to have those consequences systematically cared for."[9] Black religious institutions were, to a large extent, the consequences of the efforts of members of the community to address their

common ills. They resulted from the organization of publics for the protection of the interests shared by their members. The first edition of the
African Methodist Episcopal discipline (1817), particularly the historical
preface, suggests this point:

> We have deemed it expedient to have a form of Discipline, whereby
> we may guide our people in the fear of God, in the unity of the
> Spirit, and in the bonds of peace, and preserve us from that spiritual
> despotism which we have so recently experienced—remembering,
> that we are not to Lord it over God's heritage, as greedy dogs, that
> can never have enough; but with long suffering, and bowels of com-
> passion, to bear each other's burdens, and so fulfill the law of Christ.[10]

My description of black religious institutions as publics follows Higginbotham's brilliant analysis in *Righteous Discontent.* Higginbotham stresses
"the public dimension of the black church, not the religious dimension of
the public realm."[11] This reversal shifts the emphasis from the prevalence
of religious symbols and values in the organization of our social lives and
in our political languages to the different ways public spaces have been
"interpolated within black religious institutions."[12] For example, in the
preface to the AME discipline, the reality of race and its consequences
were accounted for within the very effort to formulate rules and structure
for the new church; the two went hand-in-hand. Such riffs (interpolating
activity) on white Christianity (in this instance, white Methodism) and its
complicity with slavery and white supremacy signaled a particular manner
of engagement in public spaces in that black publicity always entailed the
real possibility of personal humiliation or group sanction, since the organization of public spaces in the United States reflected the nation's racial
attitudes. Black churches, then, were the sites for a public discourse critical of white supremacy and the American nation-state as well as the spaces
for identity construction. Here African Americans engaged in public deliberation free of humiliation (at least by whites). They also spoke in a
self-determining voice, defining a cultural identity through a particular
idiom and style.

Unlike Higginbotham's, however, my understanding of publics draws
on the work of John Dewey, not Jürgen Habermas. I am suspicious of
Habermas's reliance on the Kantian picture of enlightened public opinion, and more inclined to favor beginning with what Dewey sees as characteristic forms of human action and their consequences. For Dewey, hu-

man beings, like all natural objects, exist in association with their kind. But unlike other objects, human beings act with intelligence, that is, they act in light of perceived consequences and efforts to control how those consequences might affect them.

The consequences of actions are thought of, in this view, in two ways: (1) those that affect only the individuals directly engaged in a particular transaction—these are private transactions—and (2) those with indirect consequences, that is, consequences affecting individuals not immediately concerned with the transaction. These are public only in the sense that the indirect consequences are "extensive, enduring, and serious."[13] A public, then, is formed when some association perceives a common interest in an effort to avoid some consequences and secure others; it "is created through an act of shared practical judgment."[14]

In this light, the actions of American whites in relation to African Americans had far-reaching consequences—extensive, enduring, and serious consequences indirectly affecting individuals not immediately concerned in the "transaction." Put simply, the existence of slavery and the reality of race affected all persons physically marked as black, slave or free! These realities led to the organization of African Americans, specifically those in the North who were "free," to deal with the indirect consequences of this associated activity. As such, publics were formed, particularly independent black churches, to respond to the conjoint action of white supremacists with state and ecclesiastical power.

I hasten to qualify this point. I do not want to image the independent black church movement as a complete reaction to white proscription. This would certainly obscure the more positive role it has had in the formation of black communities. I am merely suggesting that the cooperation among black individuals to address the common ills of their lives contributed to the construction of what would become a "national" community, for the conjoint activity of African Americans would not remain simply a reaction to white proscription. "Wherever there is conjoint activity whose consequences are appreciated as good by all singular persons who take part in it," John Dewey writes, "and where the realization of the good is such as to effect an energetic desire and effort to sustain it in being just because it is a good shared by all, there is in so far a community."[15]

With this formulation I am able to evade choosing between two related historiographical tendencies regarding the rise of independent black churches. The emphasis has been either on the story of white proscription, "the conscious exclusion from positions of power of black members

in biracial congregations and denominations,"[16] or on the coming-of-age
of black communities, that is, black communities becoming fully aware of
themselves as distinctive collectivities with particular interests and needs
(with separate churches as key components of their infrastructure). Both
factors, in my view, are crucial to any adequate understanding of the role
of black churches in the development of a national communal and political consciousness among antebellum blacks. We must keep track of both
simultaneously, for without both factors at work in our interpretative activity we can lose sight of two important points.

First, if our focus remains only on white proscription, we tend to reduce the importance of the more proactive dimensions of black activism
and community-building in the early nineteenth century. In one sense,
this view can easily lead to the position that if racism ends, black communities and, in this case, specifically black churches, are no longer justified.
Some such argument was made by William Whipper and members of the
American Moral Reform Society in the mid-1830s. Here the idea that
African Americans view as their responsibility the conservation, transmis-
sion, rectification, and expansion of the heritage of values they have received in order that succeeding generations may be assured of a better,
more secure future gives way to a preoccupation with the practices of
white racists and, in some cases, a facile form of humanism.

Second, if we focus only on a celebration of black cultural independence, then we have a tendency to reify the tools used only in attempts to
solve specific social problems. That is, we fail to grasp that the functional
adequacy of our concepts must be evaluated in the context of their particular situations. We tend to read too much in the deployment of the language of race and talk of national community. As a result, some theorists
find the early nineteenth century filled with black ideologues of nationalism or racial essentialism—both odd descriptions in light of the historical context.

It remains important that we give a full account of the role of white
discrimination in the formation of separate black churches, and some very
good work has been done in this area.[17] Most of these accounts begin
with the November 1787[18] incident in St. George's Methodist Episcopal
Church in Philadelphia when several black members and local preachers
were pulled from their knees during prayer and told to go to the seats
designated for blacks. This incident precipitated the formation of the first
two African congregations in the city in 1794, St. Thomas Episcopal

Church and Bethel African Methodist Episcopal Church. Richard Allen, one of the key figures in this episode, would later help found the first *national* black denomination,[19] the African Methodist Episcopal Church. This moment, in some ways, is paradigmatic of the formation of separate African churches. We see similar incidents repeated throughout the major cities in the Northeast and along the Atlantic seaboard. As whites refused to share authority with their black members and continued to subject them to various forms of public humiliation (for example, refusing to christen black babies, serving blacks communion only after all whites were served, and denying blacks access to church burial grounds),[20] many African Americans sought to create institutions where they could worship and have fellowship without the burden of white Christian racism. Hence, they organized publics to secure consequences that enabled the possibility of the good life.

In New York City, for example, black Methodists, led by James Varick and Abraham Thompson, formed what came to be known as the African Methodist Episcopal Zion Church after continued conflict over the ordination of black preachers. In a letter to the bishops and preachers of the Philadelphia and New York Conferences, Varick and George Collins listed the major reasons for the formation of the new denomination; most important was the failure of the white church to extend the privileges necessary for black preachers to sustain a "ministry amongst our coloured brethren."[21]

Like the black Methodists, black Baptists faced the insult of white Christian proscription. In Boston, with the support of the predominantly white First and Second Baptist Churches, black Baptists organized the African Baptist Church in 1805 and appointed their pastor, the reverend Thomas Paul, in 1806. Paul also helped organize the Abyssinian Baptist Church in New York City. Although these churches maintained active relations with white Baptist churches—and, in the case of the Boston congregation, joined the Boston Baptist Association in 1812—they nevertheless came into existence, for the most part, because of the prevalence of discriminatory practices. Elias Smith, a white Baptist minister, wrote of Paul in 1804, "When Thomas Paul came to Boston the Dr. [Samuel Stillman, a Baptist minister] told him it was Boston, and they did not mix colours."[22] This reality of white racial proscription and its consequences compelled African Americans to seek out a space for the free and autonomous worship of God and to secure an institutional setting for the social activity of solving problems confronting their community. To state the point baldly, God and community became by force of circumstance the objects of black Christian commitment in the early nineteenth century.

In one sense, my use of the conjunction *and* understates the extent to which faith in God and obligation to community were inextricably bound together in early nineteenth-century black America. Even as the infrastructures of newly emerging black communities began to settle in places such as Philadelphia and Boston, they were "always already" connected to an enduring and prophetic faith. Prior to the incident in St. George's Church, members of the black community in Philadelphia, with the leadership of Absalom Jones and Richard Allen, had formed a benevolent voluntary association called the Free African Society. Although written in the latter part of the eighteenth century, the society's preamble sheds light on the complex relation between faith and community among antebellum blacks generally.

> Whereas Absalom Jones and Richard Allen, two men of the African race, who, for their religious life and conversation have obtained a good report among men, these persons, from a love to the people of their complexion who they beheld with sorrow, because of their irreligious and uncivilized state, often communed together upon this painful and important subject in order to form some kind of religious society, but there being too few to be found under the like concern, and those who were, differed in their religious sentiments; with those circumstances labored for some time, till it was proposed, after a serious communication of sentiments, that a society should be formed, without regard to religious tenets, provided the persons live an orderly and sober life, in order to support one another in sickness, and for the benefit of their widows and fatherless children.[23]

The "secular" aims of the society were framed by the religious faith of its members, however varied their denominational commitments. The organization not only hoped to provide social services and aid for "people of African descent," but the society also offered a moral or normative vision, based in its members' religious faith, for the community itself.[24]

This moral vision can be seen in the work of the African Union Society in Newport, Rhode Island, and similar organizations in Boston, New Haven, or Providence. In these organizations religious commitment and secular aims were rarely thought of separately. The Newport African Union

Society, organized in 1780, "by the end of the decade sponsored a unified scheme of emigration with comparable organizations in Boston, Providence and Philadelphia."[25] The society also held religious services in the homes of its members. These societies passed resolutions to regulate the moral behavior of their members, visiting them regularly that they might increase in grace and knowledge and every Christian virtue. They also provided basic services for members and nonmembers. Because most white communities denied African Americans access to cemeteries, many societies owned their own cemetery properties. Some, like the Free African Society in Philadelphia, petitioned the city to designate land for a black cemetery. This social focus stood alongside the religious faith of the membership. Both provided the terms for the moral sense of community and established what Gayraud Wilmore describes as "a pattern of religious commitment that had a double focus: free and autonomous worship in the Afro-American tradition, and the solidarity and social welfare of the black community."[26]

David Walker's address in December 1828 before the General Colored Association in Boston brilliantly exploited this double focus. Walker understood the need for "forming societies, opening, extending, and keeping up correspondences" as a means "to ameliorate our miserable condition,"[27] for the violence of America's racist culture necessitated conjoint action. As Walker put it: "Do not two hundred and eight years of very intolerable sufferings teach us the actual necessity of a general union among us? Do we not know indeed, the horrid dilemma into which we are, and from which, we must exert ourselves, to be extricated?"[28]

The reality or evil of racist violence required faith in God and ourselves. Walker wrote: "It is our duty to try every scheme that we think will have a tendency to facilitate our salvation, and leave the final result to that God, who holds the destinies of people in the hollow of his hand, and who ever has, and will, repay every nation according to its works."[29] Here Walker simultaneously warns white America of its impending judgment and urges black America to action, for God's judgment of nations extends not only to acts of evil but also to submissiveness in the face of evils. African Americans must extricate themselves from their oppression—no one else. Even as some white Americans argue on their behalf, Walker maintained, "we should cooperate with them, as far as we are able by uniting and cultivating a spirit of friendship and of love among us."[30] A crass form of individualism gives way to a communitarian ethic: our duty is not only to ourselves but to the well-being of the community and those like us.

Only with this orientation and the will of God, Walker claimed, will the "dejected, degraded, and now enslaved children of Africa . . . take their stand among the nations of the earth."[31]

As the demographics of antebellum black communities changed—with inmigration, the abolition of slavery in the northern states between 1777 and 1818, and the rise of an indigenous black leadership class—the timbre and tone of black self-assertion changed. These communities, by the late 1820s, "resting on a settled infrastructure of numerous benevolent organizations, black churches, residential proximity, and a deep-seated ethos of mutual assistance,"[32] had organized themselves (as evidenced in Walker's address) to speak directly to their circumstances and to envision the good life for all African Americans. Localities attempted to connect with other local communities, and a national imagined community began to take form. Samuel Cornish, a Presbyterian minister in New York City and co-editor of *Freedom's Journal* and editor of its short-lived successor, *The Rights of All*, wrote feverishly in 1829 of such an effort:

> Our general agent whose duty it shall be to continue travelling from one extremity of our country to the other, forming associations communicating with our people and the public generally, on all subjects of interest, collecting monies, and delivering stated lectures on industry, frugality, enterprise, etc. thereby [might link] together, by one solid claim, the whole free population, so as to make them think and feel and act, as one solid body, devoted to education and improvement.[33]

Such remarks exhibited an energetic desire and effort to sustain the consequences of a certain conjoint activity because this activity constituted a good shared by all.

Independent black churches stood as the primary institutional representation of this maturation. Through its conception of God, black religious life and its institutions provided support in the face of uncertainty as well as the languages to resist dread and despair. These institutions "embodied an ecstatic celebration of human existence without affirming prevailing reality: rejoicing in the mere fact of being alive yet maintaining a critical disposition toward the way the world is."[34] Black religious life enabled its participants, through faith, to see beyond the opaqueness of their condition in order to create room for the exercise of agency.[35]

The worship ceremonies within most of these institutions—the liturgies, the singing and dancing—invented, maintained, and renewed senses of communal identification that celebrated, even reveled in the uniqueness of black people and their relation to God. We see this most clearly, I believe, in the uses of biblical imagery to explicate the condition of black people in the United States and in the world. Daniel Coker, speaking before an excited congregation on January 21, 1816, about the recent Supreme Court decision in Pennsylvania that freed Bethel Church from Methodist Episcopal control, likened the plight of African American Methodists to that of Jews in Babylon. "The Jews in Babylon were held against their will. So were our brethren," Coker preached. "Those Jews as above stated, had not equal privileges with the Babylonians, although they were governed by the same laws and suffered the same penalties. So our brethren were governed."[36]

This analogy with the Jews of the Old Testament occupied the religious and political imagination of antebellum blacks. The Exodus story, for example, provided a hermeneutic lens to account for their condition and to articulate a faith that God was active in history. The slaves sang:

God did say to Moses one day,
Say, Moses, go to Egypt land,
And tell him to let my people go.
Canaan land is the land for me,
And let God's saints come in.

These lines collapsed the past with the present in order that a future might be imagined, for God's activity in history assured African Americans freedom if they comported to his will.

To be sure, black churches provided in the nineteenth century the standards of judgment by which forms of life were critically examined and found wanting. We can think of this as their prophetic dimension. This dimension extended, as I suggested earlier, well beyond the community of the faithful into the social and political domains. Indeed black religious life provided vocabularies for political argument: the images of Exodus, Psalms 68:31, the suffering servant, a grace-centered piety, a concern with human fallenness, rituals of conversion, a persistent focus on evil—all are preoccupations of black religious life and are, subsequently, tools in black political life.

In the South, this biblical language made possible a hope among slaves that God would deliver his chosen people once again and that the evil of

slavery would be no more. This sustaining faith, however, evaded or de-
ferred the critical question of the existence of evil: Why did God allow us
to suffer? In the North, these vocabularies were tools in the active fight
against slavery and racism, providing a language to envision a moral community beholden to certain precepts and a particular way of being in the
world. In the case of the slave evangelical in the South, Albert Raboteau
suggests, the essence of Christian life was principally liturgical—the ecstatic experience of God's presence, singing, dancing, and shouting were
central—whereas the essence of Christian life in the North was ethical,
with a stress on education and moral reform.[37] Both nevertheless presupposed a moral community, a certain kind of associated activity intent on
securing certain consequences and sustaining them for future generations.

W. E. B. DU BOIS AND THE PROBLEM OF DESCRIPTION

Raboteau's distinction helps elucidate the differences in the tone of black
evangelical piety in the South and in the North. In some ways, he amends
Du Bois's earlier characterization in *Souls of Black Folk,* in which "the inner ethical life" of the church is rendered in rather schematic terms. For
Du Bois, Christianity reinforces the passive submission of the slave; it
becomes, in light of the persistence of the slave's condition, a form of
religious fatalism, and is only transformed with the emergence of a free
class of blacks who identified with "the dream of Abolition, until that
which was a radical fad in the white North and an anarchistic plot in the
white South had become a religion to the black world."[38] In Du Bois's
view, black religious life oscillated between a form of deep religious fatalism and a pragmatically driven social ethic, that is, an other-worldly escapism and a this-worldly sense of racial advocacy.

Raboteau's use of liturgy to describe the essence of Christianity in the
black South avoids the temptation to characterize black slave piety as necessarily escapist. The context of the slave South constrained certain kinds
of actions, particularly open rebellions against the peculiar institution. It
does not follow, however, that accommodation to such a brutal context
necessarily entailed an internal acceptance of oppression. Indeed, Christian slaves turned to their faith and to biblical narrative to assure themselves of possibility. The slave would sing:

He delivered Daniel from de lion's den
Jonah from de belly ob de whale,

and de Hebrew children from the fiery furnace,
and why not every man?

Their internal attitudes, as Raboteau puts it, must be distinguished from their external actions, for "the inner world of slaves was the fundamental battleground and there evangelical Christianity served as an important weapon in the slave's defense of his psychological, emotional, and moral freedom from white domination."[39] And if that freedom found its most successful and eloquent expression in the frenzy of black religious practice, then so be it!

We must not conclude, however, that such frenzied action failed to include an ethics. Even as the slaves drew on the story of Exodus to account for their condition and found in Moses' words to the Israelites, "Stand still and see the salvation of God," assurance of eventual freedom, they knew that God's deliverance depended on their actions—how they comported themselves to his will. Put simply, liturgies always entail an ethics: they presuppose a certain way of being in the world and seek to impart that to participants and their activity. Liturgies, of course, do much more than this. My only intention here is to collapse a dichotomy that only takes us so far in understanding black religious practices. The emphasis on ethics *or* liturgy, however useful the word may be in avoiding bad descriptions, obscures the fact that both play a central role in the South and in the North,[40] that liturgies and other rituals—just as explicit forms of racial activism—articulated early conceptions of the moral community among northern blacks as well as southern.

Raboteau's subtle correction of Du Bois remains important, however, for Du Bois redeployed his use of fatalism and racial advocacy in his analysis of black religion in the post-Reconstruction era. After abolition waned and the "Age of Reaction" swept over the nation, Du Bois maintained, the role of black religion entered a critical stage. First, the close proximity with the values of American democracy, what Du Bois called the "soul-life of the nation," and the tremendous religious and ethical forces moving throughout the nation necessarily affected African Americans. This proximity was overshadowed by the reality of race and its consequences. Black folk, despite America's rapid development, continued to confront the "Negro problem." They had to "live, move and have their being in it, and interpret all else in its light and darkness."[41]

This preoccupation with the problem of race was compounded by the growing pains of the community, that is, problems of family, of the status of women, of the accumulation of wealth, and of developing responses to forms of social deviance. The combination of these concerns, Du Bois wrote, meant "a time of intense ethical ferment, of religious heart-searching and intellectual unrest." He went on to say: "From the double life every American Negro must live, as a Negro and as an American, as swept on by the current of the nineteenth while yet struggling in the eddies of the fifteenth century,—from this must arise a painful self-consciousness, an almost morbid sense of personality and a moral hesitancy which is fatal to self-confidence."[42] The rapidly changing world and the increasing complexity of the black community itself produced what Du Bois believed to be a wrenching of the soul and a sense of bewilderment. He wrote that "such a double life, with double thoughts, double duties, and double social classes, must give rise to double worlds and double ideals, and tempt the mind to pretence or to revolt, to hypocrisy or to radicalism."[43]

An ethical paradox, then, marked the lives of black folk, Christian or not, in the late nineteenth century. Forced to confront the persistence of racial violence, the psychic torment and physical threat, the continued infringement on their rights and ideals, and a public conscience deaf to righteous appeal, African Americans' faith wavered between a sneer, a wail, and mere casuistry. As Du Bois wrote: "The danger of the one lies in anarchy, that of the other in hypocrisy. The one type of Negro stands almost ready to curse God and die, and the other is too often found a traitor to right and coward before force; the one is wedded to ideals remote, whimsical, perhaps impossible of realization; the other forgets that life is more than meat and the body more than raiment."[44] Du Bois mapped this distinction onto the South and the North. Just as the piety of the slave yielded a deep religious fatalism and forms of escapism, the slave's religious commitments and circumstances produced a "culture of dissemblance" and a way of being in the world that nurtured submissiveness and passivity. The North, on the other hand, because of the difficulties of quasi freedom, wallowed in "radical complaint, radical remedies, bitter denunciation or angry silence."[45]

Sometimes ideal types are useful. They help us organize a crowded conceptual terrain. They tidy things up for us. But, sometimes, ideal types can be too successful; they make things too neat for us. As such, we lose sight of the messiness of human action, the ambiguity that surrounds the moments that most concern us. Du Bois rightly noted that between his two ideal types "wavers the mass of the millions of Negroes," moving from pretence to revolt, from hypocrisy to radicalism and back again. Rigid either-or formulations rarely help us capture this kind of ambiguity and ambivalence. In short, religious feeling in the black South was not simply liturgical or hypocritical, nor was the piety of the North merely ethical or tending toward anarchy. Ambivalence (about America, about themselves), what Du Bois provocatively described as a double life, was definitive of the religious and social experience of antebellum blacks even before the late nineteenth century.

I prefer the phrase "structure of ambivalence"[46] to Du Bois's use of "double life." I am more inclined to think about the ambiguities and ambivalences surrounding African American life in the United States in ways that extend beyond the psychic torment of black individuals. Instead, my use of structures of ambivalence references ambivalence "as a set, with specific internal relations, at once interlocking and in tension." The phrase also refers to a quality of experience, something heartfelt that has the enduring effect of defining a particular moment or period. Adapting Raymond Williams's apt description of structures of feelings, structures of ambivalence can be thought of as "social experiences in solution."[47] As an analytic tool, then, the phrase helps account for the tortuous relation of African Americans to American culture: their lingering sense of being in but not of a nation ambivalent about its own identity.[48]

The relation of black Christianity to Christianity broadly speaking is a case in point. Black evangelicals had to come to terms with the fact that early Christian evangelicalism was, to some extent, complicitous with slavery and white supremacy. Many of its proponents assumed the inferiority of black people. Such beliefs and actions confronted black Christians with a basic dilemma: what meaning could Christianity have for them if the religion was, as it was assumed, a white man's religion? Moreover, black Christians, in reckoning with the dominant form of evil in their lives, had to ask why a just God allowed them to suffer. As African Americans attempted to respond to these heart-wrenching questions, they "developed a distinctive evangelical tradition in which they established meaning and identity for themselves as individuals and as a people."[49] They were Christian but with a difference. American but not quite. Ambivalence marked their relation to a tradition within which they were ensconced and in tension.

This leads me to the first half of the nineteenth century, a period of intense ethical ferment. During this period, African Americans etched in vague outline the parameters of black Christianity, denying "the doctrinal basis of slaveholding Christianity by refusing to believe that God had made them inferior to whites."[50] Moreover, these peculiar Christians elevated their experience to biblical drama, and since God works his wonders in human history, constructed a salvific history in which God was on their side. Daniel Coker in 1810 offered such an account in the appendix of *A Dialogue Between a Virginian and an African Minister.* He drew on 1 Peter 2:9–10: "But ye are a chosen generation, a royal priesthood, and an holy nation, a peculiar people; that ye should shew forth the praise of him who hath called you out of darkness into his marvellous light: which in time past were not a people, but are now the people of God: which had not obtained mercy, but now have obtained mercy."[51] Although Coker and other black Christians concerned themselves with free and autonomous worship, they knew that their efforts extended well beyond the desire for ecclesiastical freedom. Black people were chosen. They were a holy nation, a peculiar people, and God's mercy brought some of them out of the darkness into the light. Those who were free were charged, then, with the moral responsibility to uplift those who were still bound. Independent black churches institutionalized this sensibility, and new figures, forms, and conventions gave it voice.

DAVID WALKER'S APPEAL

David Walker's *Appeal to the Coloured Citizens of the World* (1829) stands as a critical indication that new ways of thinking and acting among antebellum northern blacks were forming in the late 1820s. Not only the content of the document but its form heralded a dramatic change in the nature of black public engagement in the North. Walker explicitly called for armed black resistance against the sinful institution of slavery (resistance sanctified by the grace of God) and prophesied America's fall and destruction unless the nation repented for this evil. Walker's *Appeal,* then, was a black jeremiad, that is, a rhetoric of indignation urgently challenging the nation to turn back to the ideals of its covenant. Walker wrote:

> Oh Americans! let me tell you, in the name of the Lord, it will be good for you, if you listen to the voice of the Holy Ghost, but if you do not; you are ruined!!! Some of you are good men; but the will of God must be done. Those avaricious and ungodly tyrants among you, I am awfully afraid will drag down the vengeance of God upon you. When God almighty commences his battle on the continent of America for the oppression of his people, tyrants will wish they never were born.[52]

Wilson Moses suggests that such uses of the jeremiad often represent an early expression of black nationalism, for within the rhetorical form African Americans like Walker "revealed a conception of themselves as a chosen people"[53] (Remember: "the oppression of his people.") Yet the black jeremiad grew out of an ambivalent relation with white evangelical Christianity in the sense that African American uses of the form simultaneously rejected white America and participated in one of the nation's most sacred traditions. The black jeremiad as a rhetorical form ought to be understood as a paradigm of the structure of ambivalence that constitutes African Americans' relation to American culture.

I am particularly interested in the different ways ideas of peoplehood and community obligation are constructed within the rhetoric. Walker, for example, imaged African Americans as a chosen people, but he went beyond the analogy to provide ways to forge a committed and intelligent solidarity to respond to the reality of racism and its consequences. Walker's *Appeal* not only prophesied God's wrath (its particular linkage with the American tradition of the jeremiad), it also proposed to awaken a spirit of inquiry and investigation among antebellum blacks, offered a radically different way of engaging in public deliberation—one grounded in the pain and suffering of experience—and appealed for the moral responsibility of self-determination (if freedom was truly to be acquired and enjoyed). Walker's use of the jeremiad not only urged the nation to turn from sin; he also exhorted African Americans to act intelligently for themselves.

Walker aimed to cultivate among a downtrodden people the ability to ask appropriate questions and to seek answers to them intelligently. The preamble to the *Appeal* states: "But against all accusations which may or can be preferred against me, I appeal to Heaven for my motive in writing—who knows that my object is, if possible, to awaken in the hearts of my afflicted, degraded and slumbering brethren, a spirit of inquiry and investigation respecting our miseries and wretchedness in this Republican Land of Liberty!!!"[54] A critical examination of the experiences of African Americans was necessary for articulating an intelligent course of action in light of the specific realities of race and its consequences. For Walker, blacks were to respond appropriately to what was going on around them in order to secure certain outcomes and avoid others. He aimed to instill in blacks what can be called critical intelligence: an intelligence that was the sum of impulses, habits, emotions, and discoveries that indicated what was desirable and undesirable in future possibilities and that worked ingeniously on behalf of an imagined good for people of African descent.[55]

The first task of the *Appeal*, then, was to make sense of the prevailing discourse of race, which dehumanized African peoples. Walker counted American slavery as one of the most brutal forms of bondage in human history. What distinguished American slavery from all other historical examples was the ideological justification of the institution, which argued that African peoples were not a part of the human family—that somehow these organisms stood between man and ape. Walker wrote:

> I call upon the professing Christian, I call upon the philanthropist, I call upon the very tyrant himself, to show me a page of history either sacred or profane, on which a verse can be found, which maintains, that the Egyptians heaped the insupportable insult upon the children of Israel, by telling them that they were not of the human family. Can the whites deny this charge? Have they not, after having reduced us to the deplorable condition of slaves under their feet, held us up as descending originally from the tribes of Monkeys or Orang-Outangs! O! my God! I appeal to every man of feeling— is not this insupportable? Is it not heaping the most gross insult upon our miseries, because they have got us under their feet and we cannot help ourselves? Oh! pity us we pray thee, Lord Jesus, Master.—Has Mr. Jefferson declared to the world, that we are inferior to the whites, both in the endowments of our bodies and our minds?[56]

Walker understood the need to challenge this notion head-on, and his invocation of Jefferson served to focus his efforts to assess the very peculiar arena within which African Americans were to exercise critical intelligence.

Thomas Jefferson's speculations on black inferiority in the *Notes on Virginia* signaled the beginnings of a significant shift in the racial sentiments of the new nation. The ideological fervor of the American Revolution, which led to widespread condemnation of the institution of slavery, was giving way to the calcification of racial categories. These categories helped defined who belonged and who did not. The Naturalization Act of 1790, for example, aided in the effort to consolidate an American national identity as European immigrants were transformed (through national legislation) into free "white" persons. We also begin to see efforts to define the African American slave more clearly as a "living tool, property with a soul."[57] American national identity by the end of the eighteenth century, then, was fast becoming associated with whiteness. And by the time of Walker's *Appeal,* such racial attitudes had hardened, often drawing on Jefferson for their justification.

In 1784 Jefferson wrote that "the blacks whether originally a distinct race, or made distinct by time and circumstances, are inferior to whites both in body and mind." For Jefferson, African Americans had never "uttered a thought above the level of plain narration." He also refused to accept environmental accounts of the differences between the races. Citing the harshness of slavery in classical Greece and Rome, Jefferson maintained that ancient slaves "excelled in science, insomuch as to be usually employed as tutors to their masters," and those who had "were of the race of whites." The condition of slavery, then, was not the determining factor in the present status of African slaves. As Jefferson wrote, "It is not their condition, . . . but nature, which has produced the distinction."[58]

Despite the seeming certainty of this conclusion, Jefferson hesitated. He claimed that such an opinion had to be made with great diffidence. Jefferson realized that his conclusion could easily lead to the degradation of an entire race. So, he concluded that such matters had to be decided by scientific investigation, requiring, as Jefferson put it, "many observations, even where the subject may be submitted to the Anatomical knife, to Optical glasses, to analysis by fire, or by solvents. How much more then where it is a faculty, not a substance, we are examining; where it eludes the research of all senses; where the conditions of its existence are various and variously combined; where the effects of those which are present or absent bid defiance to calculation."[59] Until conclusive evidence could be marshaled, African American inferiority, Jefferson maintained, had to be held as only a "suspicion" rather than a factual proposition.

Walker refused to accept the grounds on which Jefferson and others argued for black inferiority, for the appeal to science or rational deliberation emptied the issue of its moral significance. African Americans could respond to Jefferson on logical grounds, and many did so, but, for Walker, the psychic and physical horror of the consequences of such ideas required a different kind of response: one grounded in the pain and suffering of African Americans. Peter Hinks in his wonderful text *To Awaken My Afflicted Brethren* describes this move as Walker's strategy of emotionalism. On one hand, Walker holds the view that "the hypothesis of black inferiority was first and foremost a moral abomination founded on a vicious racial hatred of blacks by whites and on a desire to make the exploitation of the labor of an already subject people more perfect."[60] The terror of black subordination and its emotional expression was deployed as a counter to the "rational" arguments of white racists. On the other hand, this strategy aimed to affirm the experience of African Americans—to give voice to the terror, Hinks maintains, in order to move black individuals from the psychic havoc an oppressive situation "wrought on them to some new posture of internal coherency and self-respect."[61]

"Emotionalism" is a bad description here. It lends itself perhaps too easily to the idea that Walker's *Appeal* was unreasonably emotive. It is better to read Walker's strategy as an attempt to offer African Americans a new way of engaging in public conversation. Walker refused to believed that public deliberation always proceeded as rational discussion among enlightened subjects, particularly when the discussion had such deadly consequences. For him, rational deliberation about the inferiority of African people was on its face an absurdity. How could one argue rationally with someone who claimed that one lacked reason? Walker's response was not to assume the irrationality of the claim and then proceed to enlightened his mistaken interlocutor. No. A reasonable and appropriate counter, Walker maintained, was an outpouring that called attention to the absurdity of the utterance. Such a response gave powerful voice to matters otherwise considered private and to the fact that African Americans were not dim-witted beasts of burden but rather human beings capable of genuine feeling and of discerning their own interests. As Walker wrote, "You are not astonished at my saying we hate you, for if we are men, we cannot but hate you, while you are treating us like dogs."[62]

Just as Walker rejected a certain way of engaging in public conversation about race, he empowered African Americans to draw on their experience when engaging in public deliberation. The simultaneous doings and sufferings of black folk, for Walker, ought to determine the manner in which they deliberate about their common ills. In other words, the pain and suffering of their experience ought to mark their point of entry in public conversation about matters of race and its consequences. Walker believed that any discussion about race required that the interlocutors confront the true terror the subject called forth, not only the physical pain but the psychic violence of slavery and racial discrimination, both of which, in his view, necessitated conjoint action among black individuals. Walker's *Appeal,* then, belligerently gave voice to a range of emotions and impulses, habits and discoveries that characterized a people experiencing the brutality of slavery and white proscription. Such experiences, he maintained, could be the only basis for argument against the likes of Jefferson (or Henry Clay) and the insidious power of the "American ideology."

Walker believed that one of the real tragedies of slavery and racial discrimination was the extent to which these practices cultivated habits of servility among African Americans. In some ways, the problem Walker confronted was not so much the failure of African Americans to strike the first blow for freedom but, rather, their submission to racial hierarchies and "their consequent belief that they owed all whites certain respectful duties, that they were prevented from perceiving themselves as entitled to freedom and personal empowerment, and thereby seizing it when it was before them."[63] Walker's *Appeal* concerned itself with personality and provocation: a desperate attempt to convince African Americans that they were self-determining agents and that white Americans were not the bearers of freedom (only God assumed this role), and that as agents they must act for themselves and take the responsibility for their lives and their futures.

William James wrote that habits were "the enormous fly-wheel of society, its most precious conservative force." Habits forestalled revolutions, prevented "the hardest and most repulsive walks of life from being deserted by those brought up to tread therein."[64] Habits sanctioned conduct. They reinforced traditional ways of doing things and provided what John Dewey called "the center of gravity in morality" in the sense that our actions are often justified through conformity with "ancestral habit."[65] Walker understood this. The brutality of slavery and life as a humiliated and degraded people left African Americans doubting their worth and dignity. The force of their circumstances cultivated a "death-like apathy" and a habit of "abject servility." Walker's account of the story of the slave woman who helped capture a band of sixty escaped slaves demonstrated the degree to which slavery savaged the black personality.[66] In his view, this woman could not act as a self-determining agent, for she failed to understand herself outside of her relation to white masters. Walker described such actions as a form of servile deceit, born in the entrails of an evil form of life that dehumanized and betrayed African peoples. Such circumstances highlighted "the force of degraded ignorance" and made customary "deceit among us."[67] He aimed to shift the center of gravity from that of abject servility to that of critical intelligence and action. African Americans could not begin to change their condition until "they could acknowledge and describe the conditions and system under which they existed,"[68] and such an effort, in Walker's view, did not "consist in protecting devils."[69]

Walker hoped through his demonization of white slaveholders and racists to provoke blacks to think of freedom apart from white people and
to define themselves not by their standards but by the laws of God. He
understood, however, that ridding ourselves of the habit of servility required much more. Walker, as Peter Hinks rightly notes, believed that
every African American had to experience metanoia, a radical transformation of heart and disposition. Of course, God's presence would precipitate such an event, but Walker went even further. This conversion would
begin only when blacks unleashed their anger and expressed in public
rage. Walker wrote: "There is an unconquerable disposition in the breast
of the blacks which, when it is fully awakened and put in motion, will be
subdued, only with the destruction of the animal existence. Get the blacks
started, and if you do not have a gang of tigers and lions to deal with, I
am a deceiver of the blacks and of the whites."[70] This radical rage would
lead to a transvaluation of values. No longer would African Americans
define themselves by the standards of whites, and no longer would they
"meanly submit to their murderous lashes." Instead, their experience
would ground their public conversation; they would speak events unspo-
ken regardless of the feelings of whites. It is important to note that Walker
was not advocating a destructive expression of anger. Not at all. His intent
was to shift the center of gravity in our morality to a place where our
justification for action emanates not from custom or habit but from conscience or some principle of thought. If African Americans were not rage-
ful about their conditions, Walker maintained, then they obviously had
failed to analyze and understand the problems of race and its consequences. Expression of rage, then, began the process of purging blacks of
the habit of servility (if I can express rage at my tormentor's action, I
can rise up against him) and of clarifying the particulars of their miseries
and wretchedness.

Walker recognized, however, the tremendous obstacles blocking the
way to such a transformation in consciousness. Years of brutal subordination left many African Americans believing that their station in life was to
serve white people. Moreover, many white Americans had seemingly lost
their capacity to recognize the evil of their actions. As Walker noted, the
"avaricious spirit [of white men] and the natural love in them, to be called
masters . . . bring them to the resolve that they will keep us in ignorance
and wretchedness as long as they possibly can."[71] Radical rage served only
to jump-start action in light of the moral imperative to respond to the evil
of white supremacy—an evil that often shook the foundations of Walker's

faith: "I aver, that when I look over these United States of America, and the world, and see the ignorant deceptions and consequent wretchedness of my brethren, I am brought ofttimes solemnly to a stand, and in the midst of my reflections I exclaim to my God, 'Lord didst thou make us to be slaves to our brethren, the whites?' "[72] Here Walker confronted head-on the particular problem of evil facing African Americans: how to reconcile our present circumstances with our faith in a just God.

His answer drew on the distinctive evangelical tradition of black America and his faith in the capacity of blacks to confront their condition courageously: "When I reflect that God is just, and that millions of my wretched brethren would meet death with glory . . . in preference to a mean submission to the lash of tyrants, I am with streaming eyes, compelled to shrink back into nothingness before my Maker, and exclaim again, thy will be done, O Lord God Almighty."[73] Rage might precipitate a transvaluation of values, but only the will of God could secure the victory. For Walker, the two went hand-in-hand: African Americans could not wait for God to liberate them; they had to act for themselves. But such actions had to emanate from him:

> *We believe that, for thy glory's sake,*
> *Thou wilt deliver us;*
> *But that thou may'st effect these things,*
> *Thy glory must be sought.*[74]

The great sin of Walker's contemporaries, in his view, was their failure to act intelligently for themselves, and insofar as they failed to do this they failed to act on what God had promised them. Walker stated the point quite directly:

> If you commence, make sure work—do not trifle, for they will not trifle with you—they want us for their slaves, and think nothing of murdering us in order to subject us to that wretched condition— therefore, if there is an attempt made by us, kill or be killed. . . . Look upon your mother, wife and children, and answer God Almighty! and believe this, that it is no more harm for you to kill a man, who is trying to kill you than it is for you to take a drink of water when thirsty; in fact, the man who will stand still and let another man murder him, is worse than an infidel.[75]

In short, Walker believed it was the duty of every black Christian to fight (even if it meant death) against the scourge of slavery and racial discrimination because submission to such evils was tantamount to a sin against God.

Walker's *Appeal* illustrates the inseparable linkage between black religious life and black political activity. He even dedicated a number of pages to extolling the virtues of Bishop Richard Allen, the primary symbol of the independent black church movement. Walker wrote of Allen "that he [had] done more in a spiritual sense for his ignorant and wretched brethren than any other man of colour, since the world began."[76] Like Allen, he drew on the distinctive tradition of black Christianity and found the vocabularies to exhort African Americans to freedom. He wrote: "Though our cruel oppressors and murderers, may (if possible) treat us more cruel [*sic*] as Pharaoh did the Children of Israel, yet the God of the Ethiopians, has been pleased to hear our moans in consequence of oppression, and the day of our redemption from abject wretchedness draweth near, when we shall be enabled, in the most extended sense of the word, to stretch forth our hand to the Lord our God."[77] This is salvific history at its best,[78] for the brutalities of African American life are read in relation to biblical narrative, and African Americans are made over in the image of Hebrew slaves. Walker wrote: "How cunning slave-holders think they are!!!—How much like the king of Egypt who, after he saw plainly that God was determined to bring out his people, in spite of him and his, as powerful as they were. He was willing that Moses, Aaron and the Elders of Israel, but not all the people should go and serve the Lord. But God deceived him as he will Christian Americans, unless they are very cautious how they move."[79] American structures of oppression are understood in relation to the dispositions of a people who have constituted themselves as a community of the faithful, the chosen people of God. This sense of being chosen aided in the development of a national consciousness (a sense of being obligated to others who are similarly situated) and a national mission (the effort to secure some consequences for us and avoid others).

It also imposed certain constraints on the nature of black associated activity. The conjoint action of African Americans (and its reliance on black Christianity) had to offer a moral vision not only for the black nation but for those against whom they struggled. Violent resistance remained a last resort; it was inevitable only if white America failed to live up to the principles of its covenant. In the form of a typical jeremiad, Walker wrote:

I say let us reason. . . . I speak Americans for your good. . . . And wo, wo, to you if we have to obtain our freedom by fighting. Throw away your fears and prejudices then, and enlighten us and treat us like men and we will like you more than we now hate you. . . . Treat us like men, and there is no danger but we will live in peace and happiness together. For we are not like you, hard-hearted, unmerciful, and unforgiving. . . . Treat us then like men, and we will be your friends. And there is no doubt in my mind, but that the whole of the past will be sunk into oblivion, and we yet, under God, will become a united and happy people.[80]

Walker called on white Americans to humble themselves before God and to live up to the nation's promise. His efforts to exhort African Americans to see their worth and dignity, his aims to provoke this wretched class to act intelligently for themselves remained, in spite of the venom of the *Appeal,* ambivalently tied to "the values of liberty and equality that actually formed the hope that was America."[81] As Walker put it, "This country is as much ours as it is the whites, whether they will admit it now or not, they will see and believe it by and by."[82] For him, African Americans, remade in the image of the Hebrew slaves crying for freedom in Egypt, called the nation back to its principles and in the process defined themselves as a distinct people who were distinctly American.

3

✦

Exodus, Race,
and the Politics of Nation

A frican American appropriations of the Exodus story designated the
God of Israel as the God of oppressed blacks in the United States.
This designation was important in the processes of self-identification,
which stood over and against white Christian claims that God intended
Africans to be slaves. It not only enabled black individuals to make themselves over in the image of God and thereby escape the debilitating relation of master and slave, it also offered the terms to imagine a national
community—to constitute a collective identity.[1] Werner Sollors, in *Beyond
Ethnicity: Consent and Descent in American Culture,* describes these processes as typological ethnogenesis: the sense of peoplehood that emerged
through the hermeneutic of biblical typology.[2]

Typological ethnogenesis refers to ways biblical figuralism has influenced
and shaped American culture. Since the New England Puritans, Americans, with the help of typology, have rhetorically elevated and transformed
American history into biblical drama, interpreting "their transatlantic
voyage as a new exodus, their mission as an errand in the wilderness, and
their role as that of a chosen people."[3] Sollors goes as far as to argue that
different groups of people in the United States employ the terms and
characters of the Exodus story in the construction of their own group
identities. Through figural participation in the narrative they become biblical antitypes of ancient Israel. This not only indicated the Americaniza-

tion of the groups who used it but also served, in some cases, "to define a new [sense] of peoplehood in contradistinction to a general American identity."[4]

My focus on the story of Exodus tries to unearth the manifold ways in which the conscious or unconscious uses of the narrative among early nineteenth-century African Americans generated a distinctive sense of peoplehood—what I see as black America's particular use of nation language. The endless repetition of the story in black life established the narrative as paradigmatic in the developing black political culture of the North. Northern blacks were constantly entering into covenants; the promised land was continuously reimagined; and in African American pulpits across the country, God's deliverance was often read along an axis of political and economic victories. Of course, the ubiquity of the story in the early Republic affected its use. In many respects, African American interpretations of Exodus cannot be understood apart from the broader cultural pattern that informed the construction of the American nation. The task, then, is to examine how this typological rhetoric served to define a distinct or new black nation and at the same time indicated its implication within this broader process of American identity construction.

SACVAN BERCOVITCH AND THE LANGUAGE OF NATION

Particular attention must be given to the alternative ways in which a concept of nation is constructed within the ritualized activity of reading, interpreting, and performing the Exodus narrative. Within early African American politics the idea of nation grounded conjoint action and associated activity in an understanding of America's racial order. The concept as constructed through analogical readings of the Exodus story empowered African Americans (although in limited and highly negotiated ways) as they struggled against slavery and racism. Richard Allen, for example, drew on the images of Exodus as he informed slaveholders and the nation that God would act to end the evil of slavery:

> I do not wish to make you angry, but excite your attention to consider how hateful slavery is in the sight of God who hath destroyed kings and princes for their oppression of the poor slaves. Pharaoh and princes, with the posterity of King Saul were destroyed by the protector and avenger of slaves. . . . When you are pleaded with, do not you reply as Pharaoh did, "Wherefore do ye, Moses and Aaron,

let the people from their work, behold the people of the land now are many, and you make them rest from their burden." We wish you to consider God himself was the first pleader of the cause of slaves. . . . If you love your children, if you love your country, if you love the God of love, clear your hands of slavery.[5]

Allen's use of Exodus not only warned the nation but also, like good salvific accounts, assured African Americans that God would act again on behalf of his chosen people.

Of course, broader conceptions of nation in the early Republic provided, to some degree, the vocabularies of African American constructions of nation, for the story of Exodus was central to the imagining of the American nation. The American Revolution was viewed by the colonists as the culmination of a political Exodus—a rhetoric inherited, in large measure, from colonial New England, Puritans who imagined their migration from the Old World as an exodus to a New Canaan and an errand into the wilderness. I want to think about these two typological motifs together even though they reference different biblical passages. Both illustrate the dynamic way in which typology became a critical tool to account for drastic changes in the lives of the New Englanders. Moreover, each type shares the image of the other: the wilderness, in both cases, represents an intermediate phase, a preparatory moment for the second coming of Christ or the attainment of the promised land.

According to Sacvan Bercovitch, the idea of errand among the Puritans of New England entailed notions of migration, pilgrimage, and progress. Each of these was an element in an ideological mode of consensus used to fill the needs of a certain social order. Migration suggested not simply the movement from one place to another but the journey from the Old World to a New Canaan. Migration was prophetic. It signaled the coming of the new millennium in the bounty that was America, for the Puritans' claim to the New World had been sanctioned in the promises of the Bible.

The errand as pilgrimage was broadly conceived as an inward journey, a march through the wilderness of one's soul to God, or as Bercovitch puts it, "the believer's pilgrimage through the world's wilderness to redemption."[6] This aspect of the errand linked individual action to a broader community of concern. Thus, the concept of pilgrimage promoted individualism without the possibility of anarchy by grounding the community in the private acts of the will and rooting personal identities in social enterprise.[7] Finally, errand as progress referred to the teleology inherent in these biblical dramas. Colonial New England "was movement from sacred past to sacred future, a shifting point between migration and millennium."[8]

Two major events, according to Bercovitch, expanded this rhetoric beyond the narrow confines of Puritan New England. First, the Great Awakening opened the analogy of America as the New Canaan to any evangelical, North or South, such that between 1740 and 1760 the rhetoric of errand as migration, pilgrimage, and progress was extended to every Protestant American. Second, the French and Indian War expanded this rhetoric even further to mobilize the colonist, evangelical or not, to fight against an outside threat and to fortify civic institutions. Both of these events involved what Bercovitch sees as a general redefinition of the self. On one hand, the revivals of the Great Awakening loosened and enlarged the Puritan concept of representative selfhood (as expressed in the concept of errand as pilgrimage) by joining private enterprise with incentives for self-assertion, self-interest, and self-love. On the other, the French and Indian War "appealed to conscience and self-interest, only to make these synonymous with Protestant patriotism, and the Protestant cause inseparable from the rising glory of America."[9] In both cases, as in the Puritan use of the rhetoric of errand in New England, revivalism and war were means to create a social order; they ushered in the first rituals of intercolonial unity by binding the rights of personal ascent to the rites of social assent.[10]

In emphasizing these historical developments and transformations in the rhetoric of errand, Bercovitch details what he considers to be a developing ideological mode, the "American ideology." The Great Awakening marked not only an expansion of a biblical vocabulary to all Anglo-American settlers but also helped direct the energies of economic growth.[11] The French and Indian War created a kind of Protestant patriotism as it solidified the newly created civic institutions of the colonists. Both contributed to the rhetoric of the American Revolution.

In their efforts to control the egalitarian impulses unleashed by the Revolution, patriotic Whigs used this "ideology of errand" as a vehicle for social control. They characterized other revolutions as dangerous or anarchic or as threats to society while describing the American Revolution as the fulfillment of prophecy or the unfolding of a divine plan. The idea of independence within this context gave full sanction to an ideology of consensus; independence in any other context threatened the stability of society. In the United States, the idea of independence "gave a distinctive national shape to the idea of progress"[12] because the Revolution provided ample evidence of biblical prophecy: America's independence was the shifting point between migration and millennium. The Puritan rhetoric of errand was thus transformed, for the American Revolution marked the complete separation of the Old Canaan from the New,[13] and the mechanisms of control that the leaders of the New England faithful created were now translated into "a rhetoric of continuing revolution"—what Bercovitch sees as an enduring ideology for a liberal middle-class society.[14]

The transformation of the Puritan rhetoric of errand into a rhetoric of continuing revolution is the source of this ideology's power. The symbology of America contained the act of migration, the progress from theocracy to republic, and the evidence of prophecy in the pilgrimage of the representative American.[15] It represented the complete break from Old Israel and the fulfillment of prophecy with the creation of the New Israel: "With the Revolution, God has shown that 'the United States of America are to be His vineyard'—'the principal Seat of [His] glorious kingdom'—wherein the promises of the past 'are to be brought to harvest,' for 'the benefit of the whole world.' "[16] One of the obvious points here is that biblical typology, particularly Exodus, is an important part of the cultural and political beginnings (ideology, if you will) of the United States, so much so that most political events are captured and understood within the terms of the narrative. We all know the story. And, in some significant sense, it is our story. We are the New Israelites. That is, unless you are black.

The image of America as the New Canaan is reversed within African American reenactments of the Exodus story. We are still the New Israelites, but the United States is Egypt, and the seat of Pharaoh is in Washington, D.C. As Vincent Harding notes, "one of the abiding and tragic ironies of our history [is that] the nation's claim to be the New Israel was contradicted by the Old Israel still enslaved in her midst."[17] For Bercovitch, though, more general uses of the narrative in the United States sidestepped the problem of race.

The Enlightenment rhetoric of the "people," although central in other nation-building efforts, was recast within the rhetoric of the continuing revolution. The "people" were distinct from the "chosen people." This distinction allowed for an embrace of the universal impulses implicit in the leveling concept of the people[18] and simultaneously enabled an erasure of the contradiction of that impulse with the presence of slavery and servitude. The contradiction was ameliorated "[t]hrough the rituals of continuing revolution [in which] the middle-class leaders of the republic recast the Declaration to read, 'all propertied, white, Anglo-Saxon males are created equal.'"[19] These men were the chosen people, and they were representative Americans—not members of the people. Exodus history, then, provided the words for the imagining of the United States as a peculiar nation comprised of ordinary and chosen people.

Although implicit in the story of Exodus is a national ambition in which the Israelites are in search of a definite land base, a place where they can exercise self-determination, the uses of the symbols of Exodus within the American context, according to Bercovitch, are deployed for other ends, most important of which is the construction of cultural continuity, or a mode of consensus. The ritualization of Exodus in the United States sought to consolidate a highly stratified society:

> It served . . . as always, to blur . . . discrepancies. . . . It locates the sources of social revitalization and integration. It helps explain how the majority of people kept the faith despite their day-by-day experiences. It reminds us that although the concept of hegemony involves the dialectics of change, the direction of change are in turn crucially affected by the terms of hegemonic constraint. And in this case the effect was demonstrable in the way the rhetoric of consensus molded what was to all appearances the most heterogeneous "people" in the world into the most monolithic of modern cultures.[20]

As seen outside of this consensus, however, mid-nineteenth-century America was fraught with differences and conflicts. Racial and ethnic strife and economic disparities were glaring divisions that posed a serious threat to society. Hence the importance of the rhetoric of consensus. It was a way to constrain differences and conflicts, a means to shackle dissent through this dominant pattern of discourse. Bercovitch suggests that the hegemony of "America" converts dissent into restraint and collapses all political expression into an articulation of consensus or simply a debate as to the meaning of America.

Several problems present themselves when we push Bercovitch's arguments. First, although he claims to view ideology as a rhetorical battleground in which sometimes contradictory positions coexist, Bercovitch tends to conclude, more often than not, that ideology compresses dissent and difference into cultural continuity: its main function in the United States is the production of consensus. In this view the hegemony of the rhetoric of errand is too strong for cultural dissent to seep beyond its bounds. Thus, in most of his examples cultural and political dissent merely reinforce the values that they supposedly speak against.

Second, Bercovitch's view limits the scope of his analysis. He argues that the "American was not (like the Frenchmen or the Latin American) a member of 'the people.' He stood for a mission that was limitless in effect, because it was limited in fact to a 'peculiar' nation."[21] The view that the experiences of African Americans are central to what it means to be American, then, is never taken seriously. These people are part of "the people," maybe, but not members of the chosen people. Finally, Bercovitch understands ritual only in terms of forms or strategies of cultural continuity. The ultimate goal of ritual in the context of the United States is that of conflict resolution and the instilling of a dominant ideology. What gets lost in this view is any sense of ritual activity as an arena for the negotiation of power, that is, the negotiation of particular relations of domination, consent, and resistance.

Bercovitch contends, for example, that the ways in which the symbology of Exodus functioned within mid-nineteenth-century America suggest that the rhetoric of errand was more cultural than national. Unlike biblical Hebrews, genealogy, geographic boundaries, and a certain form of religious faith were not constitutive elements of the American national community. America was simply an extension of the idea of mission, and her frontiers were open to unlimited expansion. I want to make clear that for Bercovitch all of this is problematic. His project aims to disclose the different ways the American ideology and its utopian wishes undermine radical or progressive critique. But each of the problems mentioned earlier can be readily seen in his historical formulations.

Bercovitch understands ideology as the means by which consensus is produced, as a system of ideas that provides the terms for identification and national cohesion. The primary function of ideology is the disciplining of dissent and the production of cultural continuity. In mid-nineteenth-century America, in his view, the main source of dissent among U.S. renaissance writers was the guiding ideology of the early Republic. These texts represent the strategies of liberal hegemony. Although they may have intended to subvert the status quo, nineteenth-century U.S. renaissance writers attest to the capacity of the American ideology to absorb critique. As Bercovitch states:

[t]hese classic writers had no quarrel with America, but that they seem to have had nothing but that to quarrel about. Having adopted

the culture's controlling metaphor—"America" as a synonym for human possibility—and having made this tenet of consensus the ground of radical dissent, they redefined radicalism as an affirmation of cultural values. For the metaphor, thus universalized, does not transcend ideology. It portrays the American ideology . . . in the transcendent colors of utopia.[22]

The hegemony of "the American ideology," for Bercovitch, is so strong that any attempt to engage in social criticism within its frame reasserts the hegemony of the ideology. Such a position discounts the counterideological (at least in the United States), for all social and cultural critique necessarily emanates from a broader system of ideas that provides the terms of dissent. And, more important, these critiques cannot "engage in processes of reflection on the values that generate them without at the same time being subsumed by those values."[23] Serious social and cultural criticism is effectively trivialized. If we agree with Bercovitch, we are left asking: Since we cannot escape the "American ideology," what then becomes the point of social criticism? And, How do we engage in the process of reflection necessary to create a language to dislodge the idea of America from the "transcendent colors of utopia" (without having to claim some other country as our place of birth!)?

Bercovitch's suggestion that the American rhetoric of errand is more cultural than national does not seem to me the best way of talking about the uses of Exodus: far better to see Exodus as both national and cultural, as a story that provides vocabularies for our beliefs as well as tools for the imagining of our nation. In some respects, Bercovitch makes this distinction to contrast the kind of nationalism found elsewhere in the world during this period with that of the United States. In the case of the former, we have examples of nationalisms attempting to unify communities alongside and, in some cases, through archaic myths of a communal past. He cites French, German, and Russian nationalisms and the conflicts that were generated as efforts to modernize these states clashed with antimodern sentiments.

With respect to America, however, no such conflicts or appeals were necessary. Bercovitch makes this claim by arguing that the leaders of the American nation sidestepped the Enlightenment rhetoric of "the people." By defining themselves and consolidating power ideologically—through the mobilization and deployment of the rhetoric of errand—middle-class, white males were able to marginalize groups of people and create, in the process, a conformist spirit that foreign observers termed a tyranny of the majority, or what Bercovitch considers a tyranny of liberal-symbolic thought. As such, "nation meant Americans, Americans meant the people, and the people meant those who, thanks to the Revolution, enjoyed a commonplace prosperity: the simply sunny rewards of American middle-class life."[24]

For him, it is beside the point that this account evades the fissures and tensions of American society during this period. The rhetorical deployment of this powerful ideology of American middle-class life avoided the pitfalls of the Exodus story and modern nationalism. Unlike the task of the biblical Hebrews and other nation-building efforts, genealogy and geography were not constitutive elements of the American national community. Instead, the sacredness of the "continuing errand" was the central vehicle for the national consolidation of the community of the faithful. I quote him here at length:

> Genealogy and boundaries, and a certain form of religion were precisely what American nationhood has not meant. American genealogy was simply the mission brought up to date. As a community, New Israel was the heir of the ages; its representative citizen was independent, unbound by any public or personal ties, except the ties of culture that required him to be self-made. As for boundaries, political leaders dissolved that barrier to progress by reversing the meaning of frontier. Traditionally, a frontier was a border dividing one people from another. It implied differences between nations. In a sense, antebellum Americans recognized such differences—their frontier separated them from the Indians—but they could hardly accept the restriction as permanent. This was God's country, was it not? So they effected a decisive shift in the meaning of frontier, from barrier to threshold. Even as they spoke of their frontier as a meeting ground between two civilizations, Christian and pagan, they redefined it, in an inversion characteristic of the myth-making imagination, to mean a figural outpost, the outskirts of the advancing kingdom of God.[25]

But surely the presence of enslaved black bodies and the "ominous" threat of native Americans make genealogy and geography central elements in the construction of consensus, for the word *white* acquires significance only within the context of America's racial order, and the frontier becomes all the more important with the threat of native Americans, different nations on the borders of America.

Genealogy and geography disappear only when Bercovitch brackets these realities of antebellum America. He is able to do this because the rhetoric of errand, in his view, contains such exclusions by way of a strategy of absorption. Blacks and native Americans, although considered pariahs in antebellum America, may one day be considered true Americans if they adopt America's ideals. But this grossly underestimates the entrenched nature of America's racial beliefs, particularly the fact that the idea of chosenness was racialized such that members of the chosen people were all white men delineated or distinguished from those who were not chosen on the basis of race.

But Bercovitch's point is well taken: the extraordinary cultural continuity that is America sets it apart from most nations. What holds all of this together is the ritual of consensus. In this view ritual functions solely as a matter of transmitting shared beliefs or instilling a dominant ideology. Ritual activity cannot be limited to the maintenance of hegemony, however, for ritual symbols are too indeterminate and flexible to lend themselves to any simple process of instilling fixed ideas. They entail too many qualifications of the complexity of relations of power.

For Bercovitch, in his less careful moments, most American acts of criticism conform to a ritual of consensus in that the issues of debate are restricted, symbolically and substantially, to the meaning of America.[26] What gets lost in this view is any sense that ideologies are fought over and that these battles are waged in different ways and under different circumstances. Little room exists in Bercovitch's account for understanding ritual activity as an arena in which resistance actually occurs (although in highly limited and mediated ways). As ritualized agents we are merely caught within the webs of our ideological beliefs, so much so that utterances from persons as radically different as John C. Calhoun and Frederick Douglass end up accomplishing the same aim: institutional stability.

RACE AND THE LANGUAGE OF NATION

The different ways ideology functions in the United States are best illustrated, I believe, in African American uses of Exodus. In the early nineteenth century, for example, a concept of a black nation was used in the political rhetoric of many black leaders. The existence of this "national community" was imagined in the characters and events found in the Exodus story, such that the national quest of Israel became an analog for the aspirations and aims of African Americans. This community—a result of conjoint activity whose consequences were considered good—stood as a form of critique of American society for betraying its ideals as well as evidence of positive self-identification among blacks.

Although the terms of this dissent drew on a broader rhetoric of chosenness and even continuing revolution, they functioned differently in the context of the struggle against slavery and racial discrimination. Unlike the "white" leaders of the early Republic, African American users of Exodus in the early nineteenth century were not primarily concerned with marking out the racial (blood) ties of fellows or the acquisition of land. The construction of a national community of persons with certain moral and civic obligations (to that community) was more important in efforts to respond to particular problems. To be sure, the Exodus story lends itself to chauvinistic and territorialist readings. The idea that God has singled us out as special can easily lead to forms of self-righteousness that sanction all sorts of action. Moreover, acquisition of the promised land can be understood as the principal aim of the journey: "merely living on the land itself is a good thing and guarantees blessings."[27] However, because of the moral underpinnings of African American political action—its relation to black Christianity—the aim was not so much to gain land as to guarantee blessings through righteousness. Exodus read in ethical terms, then, mandated ongoing struggle, for the promise was temporally uncertain. "Its achievement [was] not a matter of where we plant[ed] our feet but of how we cultivate[d] our spirits."[28]

Race, of course, was important for African Americans in the early nineteenth century. In some respects, an idea of racial solidarity among black individuals was impossible without the experiences and relationships of race that these individuals held in common. But race understood as a biological category was not the basis of this solidarity. Instead, race as experienced by blacks was a sociological category, a consequence of a set of practices that demanded conjoint action on the part of persons similarly situated. It merely singled out those who were prone to be treated a certain way or vulnerable to certain kinds of experiences. In light of this, nation language emerged in African American political discourse as a synonym for peoplehood, a way of grounding solidaristic efforts in an understanding of America's racial, hegemonic order. From about 1800 to the early 1840s blacks generally understood nation language in these terms: the sense of peoplehood that emerged as persons drew on biblical typology, particularly the Exodus story, to make sense of and to struggle against the racist practices of white America. The ethical reading of Exodus aided this construction of a national identity and based it in the religious imagination of black Christians.

Nathaniel Paul, the venerable pastor of the African Baptist Church in Albany, New York, illustrated the convergence of these themes in his July 5, 1827, address to a freedom celebration. Paul began by characterizing the effort of commemoration itself as a kind of work common to all nations.

> And as the nations which have already passed away have been careful to select the most important events, peculiar to themselves, and have recorded them for the good of the people that they should succeed them, so will we place it upon our history; and we will tell the good story to our children and to our children's children, down to the latest posterity, that on the Fourth Day of July, in the year of our Lord 1827, slavery was abolished in the state of New York.[29]

The story of slavery and freedom, for Paul, constituted the narrative of the black nation, defining its contours and imposing certain obligations on those who identified with it. Paul went on to talk about the horrors of slavery and the duties necessary to remain free. He stated that "this day commences a new era in our history; new scenes, new prospects open before us, and it follows as a necessary consequence that new duties devolve upon us."[30] Contending that these duties result in the black nation's moral improvement, Paul proclaimed, "it is righteousness alone that exalteth a nation, and sin is a reproach to any people."[31] But what is most striking about his address is the way he imagined the future:

> The God of Nature has endowed our children with intellectual powers surpassed by none; nor is there anything wanting but their careful cultivation in order to fit them for stations the most honorable, sacred, or useful. And may we not, without becoming vain in our imaginations, indulge the pleasing anticipation that within the little circle of those connected with our families there may hereafter be found the scholar, the statesman, or the herald of the cross of Christ. Is it too much to say that among that little number there shall yet be one found like the wise legislator to Israel, who shall take his brethren by the hand and lead them forth from worse than Egyptian bondage to the happy Canaan of civil and religious liberty[?][32]

Here Exodus functions as a narrative of political history, a way to narrate the past as well as imagine a future in order to call forth a certain kind of conjoint action (action that finds its motivation in righteousness).[33]

By the mid-1840s the metaphors of Exodus had indeed sedimented as the predominate political language of African Americans. The analogy had been diffused into the popular consciousness of black America. The ritual emplotment of bondage, liberation, and nationhood had been elaborated: the middle passage, slavery, and efforts to achieve freedom were understood within the narrative frame of Egyptian bondage, the wilderness, and the promised land. Exodus, in effect, was no longer the story of Israel but an account of African American slavery and eventual deliverance—the taken-for-granted context for any discussion of slavery and freedom. Several events led to this broad diffusion of the symbology of Exodus throughout early nineteenth-century black America. Here I want to note briefly the historical events and transformations, specifically the Second Great Awakening (1770–1820), the development of independent black churches (1816), and the forming of the first "race" newspaper (1827), which deepened, in my view, these vocabularies of Exodus.

The sedimentation of the symbology of Exodus among African Americans occurred against the backdrop of broader processes of expansion: the historical transformations that extended the symbology of Exodus to everyone in the United States. The far-reaching consequences of the Great Awakening and the French and Indian War provided a civic base for religion and a religious base for liberalism in America.[33] All of this contributed to the development of "the rhetoric of continuing revolution," in which ideas of liberty and brotherhood became "controlling" metaphors for national identity. The Great Awakening between 1740 and 1760 extended the metaphors of Exodus to any evangelical in the North or the South. This included blacks who embraced Christian doctrine, for the evangelical revivals of this period were attended by white and black alike. More important, however, the revivals between 1770 and 1820, the Second Great Awakening, yielded a more extensive embrace of Christian doctrine among black populations. The emphasis on immediate conversion and the familiarity of worship in these revivals, coupled with an initial condemnation of slavery among Baptists and Methodists, led to an unprecedented number of conversions to Christianity among blacks.[34]

Also, within these evangelical movements, churches were conceptualized as societies of people who were capable of changing their own lives. As such, revivalism, to some degree, provided its participants with the means to assert control over their lives and, for those who were lost, the means to regain some sense of direction. Within the context of American slavery and racial discrimination, this view, for blacks, proved significant in the development of a corporate identity and a political culture. In particular, the willingness of evangelical churches to license black men to exhort and preach resulted in black preachers' pastoring to their own and laid the foundations for independent black churches, institutions that provided the core of free black communities. These institutions or, better, publics provided African Americans with a formal basis to assert a cultural and national identity, and one of the main vocabularies for its expression was found in the symbology of Exodus.

Although independent black churches emerged in the South before 1800 and influenced the social and cultural lives of black slaves, my focus is primarily on the development of independent black churches in the North. The African Methodist Episcopal (AME) Church, founded in 1816 after a series of conflicts with white Methodists in Philadelphia, played a crucial role in the process of political and social self-definition among African Americans. As I noted in chapter 2, the gallery incident was paradigmatic for the emergence of the independent black church movement. The subsequent achievement of institutional independence and the effort toward ecclesiastical self-definition among black Methodists carried over into the political sphere and marked the first effective stride toward freedom among African Americans[35]—what I want to call the first covenantal convening of the nation.

The efforts of black Methodists were understood not as evidence of doctrinal differences among Methodists but as a commentary on the ubiquity of racism in American society. The initial impetus for ecclesiastical independence was not religious doctrine "but the offensiveness of racial segregation in the churches and the alarming inconsistencies between the teachings and the expression of the faith."[36] The complicity of white churches with the policies that justified slavery and racism necessitated a response, one that would dislodge Christianity from the evil of men, and "the Black Church emerged as the symbol and the substance of their rebellion."[37] Independent black churches were the main sites for debate over the problems facing black communities and the crucial vehicles for the construction of a national sense of identity. The fact that their struggles for institutional independence emerged out of struggles against racism in general connected their specific achievements with broader quests for freedom and liberty.

If we briefly glance at the way the leaders of the AME Church related their beginnings, we can see the process by which the efforts toward institutional and ecclesiastical independence carried over into the political arena. We can also see one of the ways the Exodus story underlies black religious and political discourses. At the centennial of the AME in 1887, members of the church celebrated what was described as the exodus from St. George's in Philadelphia. According to David Wills, the subsequent celebrations and accounts of this historical moment amounted to "Church Patriotism." But this patriotism extended beyond the confines of AME history, for the story of the beginnings of the church became, in a sense, a historical account of black self-determination in the United States.

During the centennial meeting, the Council of Bishops of the AME Church adopted a resolution prepared by John Mifflin Brown recounting the gallery incident in St. George's Methodist Episcopal Church and the subsequent exodus that led to the founding of the AME. Brown went on to analogize this event with the historical transformations wrought by the Haitian Revolution and likened Richard Allen to Toussaint Louverture. According to David Wills:

> This linking of the creation of a black church with the creation of a revolutionary black nation-state makes clear that . . . [the] call for . . . "Church patriotism" was an apt phrase. Religion and a sense of nationality, so often associated in the experience of white Protestants—and other American religious and ethnic groups—were here combined with specific reference to African American experience. What was to be celebrated in November of 1887 was not simply an incident in ecclesiastical history, but the emergence of a self-determining black people in the Americas.[38]

Although this account can be seen as a description of late nineteenth-century thinking among the AME leadership, it also suggests the central role the church played in the construction of a black national identity in the early republic, for the exodus from St. George's and the subsequent founding of the AME Church resulted in the first formal basis of that identity.

Between 1770 and 1820 African Americans in the North, as evidenced in their participation in the Second Great Awakening and the formation of independent black churches, imbibed the symbology of Exodus primarily through religious experiences. During this period a distinctive sense of group consciousness took shape among northern blacks, situating independent black churches at the center of a developing political culture. In the late 1820s, though, the formation of the first black newspaper gave added impetus to the national formation of African Americans. The combination of technological advances and increased literacy among African Americans made printing cheap and the newspaper a practical means for disseminating information to a growing public. As James and Lois Horton note, "the increase in the number of newspapers, particularly the growth in the number of specialized publications . . . reflected both the formal participation of working men in the political process and more widespread opportunities for education in the northern states."[39] Despite the racial restrictions imposed on them, African Americans in the North attempted to exploit this medium in order to forge a national network of activism and to provide an arena for deliberation about matters confronting the community.

Samuel E. Cornish, a black Presbyterian clergyman, and John Russwurm, the first black graduate of Bowdoin College, founded *Freedom's Journal* in 1827 to address the problems that blacks in the North faced as well as to oppose misrepresentations of their community by whites. It was their goal "to make [the] Journal a medium of intercourse between our brethren in the different states of this great confederacy; that through the columns an expression of our sentiments, on many interesting subjects which concern us, may be offered to the publick; that plans which apparently are beneficial may be candidly discussed and properly weighed; if worthy, received our cordial approbation; if not, our marked disapprobation."[40] This effort also included serious attention to those who were in bondage. Cornish and Russwurm viewed blacks in the South as kindred souls and offered the columns in the *Freedom's Journal* to promote sympathy and action for those held in slavery. They (and many others)[41] also understood that the idea of conjoint action required that something become the object of desire and effort and that to move black individuals from sentences that began with "I want" to those that began with "We want" demanded ongoing conversation in order that certain consequences were esteemed and sought after.

What is interesting about Cornish's and Russwurm's effort was not the success of the *Freedom's Journal* (the newspaper was short-lived) but, rather, the possibility of a national community that the convention of the race newspaper enabled. The editors intended the newspaper to be a vehicle for debate and conversation among fellows about the problems of the community. They included in the paper various events from different parts of the country and the world. What connected these events? What allowed their juxtaposition? Following Benedict Anderson, I would say that the inclusion of a variety of events does not merely demonstrate sheer capriciousness on the part of the editors but, instead, shows that the linkage between these events is imagined.[42]

This imagined linkage derives from two related sources: calendrical coincidence and the relation between the newspaper and the market. The idea of calendrical time allows the events to be talked about simultaneously. The date at the top of the newspaper suggests a commonality between the events and the steady progression of modern time. Even as the race newspaper prints pieces about the problems of racism and slavery in the United States on a set date in the year, these occurrences continue even when the paper no longer reports about them. "The novelistic format of the newspaper assures [us] that somewhere out there the 'character' . . . moves along quietly, awaiting its next appearance in the plot."[43]

The newspapers' relation to the market calls our attention to the fact that newspapers are, in Anderson's words, extreme forms of the book. They are books sold on a colossal scale. The mass production of the newspaper enables the mass consumption of the events organized within the newspaper: "The significance of this mass ceremony—Hegel observed that newspapers serve modern man as a substitute for morning prayers— is paradoxical. It is performed in silent privacy, in the lair of the skull. Yet each communicant is well aware that the ceremony he performs is being replicated simultaneously by thousands (or millions) of others of whose existence he is confident, yet of whose identity he has not the slightest notion. Furthermore, this ceremony is incessantly repeated at daily or half-daily intervals throughout the calendar. What more vivid figure for the secular, historically clocked, imagined community can be envisioned[?]"[44] The daily consumption of the newspaper produces a genuine sense of community among fellows who would otherwise know nothing about one another, particularly when all of the events reported concern those most vulnerable to certain experiences.

The race newspaper aided in the broad diffusion of the symbology of Exodus among African Americans. Such papers printed sermons, political treatises, debates over emigration, and even accounts of festivals that used metaphors as rhetorical devices to struggle against racial discrimination in the North and the institution of slavery in the South. Reprinted sermons that drew on the symbology of Exodus—emphasizing the narrative structure of the story and its movement from beginning to end—spoke of freedom promised in Canaan and deployed the image of Egypt as a caution for moral and civic backsliding. In a striking moment on October 20, 1838, the editors of the *Colored American* printed a dialogue between Moses, Pharaoh, and others. Resembling exegesis in the midrashic tradition, an early form of rabbinic exegesis that imaginatively interpreted scripture for contemporary moral and edifying purposes, the exchange recounted the events of the story in ways that approximated the contemporary context. Pharaoh argues that freeing the slaves was impractical because "they cannot take care of themselves." His secretary talks about the threat of insurrection, and his friend fears the possibility of amalgamation. "Oh King, there would be an amalgamation of the Egyptians and Hebrews, utterly destructive of honor and happiness. We never can come upon such grounds of equality with them. The question is settled." Moses counters with the often-quoted passage from Acts 17, "hath God made of one blood all nations."[45] He also talks of liberty and rights, emphasizing all along that the slaves are God's people. The column ends simply with God ordering Moses, "Go tell Pharaoh to let my people go." With no explanation, the column presupposed a prior knowledge of the story and its application to the experiences of African Americans. Of course, the fact that this imaginative interpretation occurred on the front page of the *Colored American* made that point quite clear. Readers knew who Moses spoke for and on whose behalf God acted. Moments like these and their mass consumption by literate African Americans allowed for a fellowship in anonymity and a participation, psychical or physical, in the ritualization of the Exodus story. This effect of the race newspaper—its dissemination of the images of Exodus—along with the events of the Second Great Awakening and the formation of independent black churches laid the foundation for the use of nation language in early nineteenth-century black political culture.

The 1840s, however, marked the beginnings of a decisive shift in the political language of African Americans. The discordant waves of Jacksonian democracy, which had already made its way into black enclaves in the North, joined with the new science of race.[46] Environmental and biblical accounts of racial differences were under constant attack. African Americans, through the findings of phrenology and ethnology, were increasingly seen as intrinsically different and, for some, inherently lacking in certain moral and mental capacities. These beliefs were fast becoming commonplace. Although blacks responded to these findings with their own ethnological and biblical accounts,[47] by the 1850s many assumed the validity of the claim that race had intrinsic value.

The different ways the language of race was embraced affected the conception and use of the word *nation*. The idea of nation among African Americans in the early nineteenth century differed greatly from that of the mid–nineteenth century. The word was not used to indicate something that actually existed in the world, a sort of nonmoral, descriptive statement about a thing that could be true or false. Instead, nation language grounded a set of common experiences and relations in an effort to combat American racism, and race was merely an explanation that helped account for the specificity of those experiences. The broader cultural pattern of Exodus symbology in the United States provided some of the vocabulary for these efforts. As such, the idea of a black nation was imagined through the prevailing symbology of the American nation. But African American dramatic reenactments of the deliverance of the nation of Israel were inversions of America's national community—the New Israel was Egypt, and blacks were demanding that Pharaoh (white Americans) let God's people go.

4
>‹‹

Race, Nation, and
the Ideology of Chosenness

In the nineteenth century a number of significant words in present-day black political rhetoric acquired new and important meanings. Among them were *culture, tradition, nationality, civilization,* and *nationalism.* The different careers of these words enable us to assess broad transformations in black life and thought during this decisive period. We can in fact use them as a way to reconnoiter the ever-changing political landscape of early nineteenth-century black America. Two words in particular that direct our attention to the complex developments of this period are *nation* and *race.* The changes in their use among black and white Americans suggest significant changes in our ways of thinking about our society and our fellows, particularly if we understand these words as intimately related.

The new historical consciousness of the period aided in the transformation of these terms. This awareness, of course, was linked to profound transformations in the West. The rising influence of science and the new technologies it created, the impact of large-scale industry, the rise of new states, and the waning authority of Christianity all contributed to a different sort of preoccupation with the search for origins. Spurred on perhaps by the homogeneity imposed by these new forces, many recognized that the function of history was to provide a specific temporal dimension to man's awareness of himself.[1] And, for some, the critical tools for this new historical work were race and nation.

Nation and *race* were often viewed as interchangeable. The *Oxford English Dictionary* defines *nation* as an aggregate of persons with a common ancestry as to form a race or people. In fact, the Latin *nationem* means "breed, stock, or race." *Race,* at least in one of OED's many definitions, is described as a tribe or nation with a common descent.[2] The term entered the English language in the sixteenth century and, like early uses of *nation,* referred to common features present because of shared descent.[3]

Both words can be used to give an account of cultural and physical differences among human beings. To belong to one nation or race is not to be a member of another; using the term can be a way of calling attention to different historical experiences, languages, stories that only some of us share, and, perhaps, biological inheritance. The two terms obviously overlapped, so much so that in the nineteenth century changes in the general use of one word were evidenced in the use of the other.

The different uses of *race* are significant, then, if we are to understand the distinction between early and late uses of *nation* in nineteenth-century black political culture. How do we distinguish, for example, between African American uses of *nation* in utterances such as "I shall endeavor by divine assistance to enlighten the minds of my brethren; for we are a poor despised nation"(1782)[4] or "Let us conduct ourselves in such a manner as to furnish no cause of regret to the deliverers of our nation"(1808)[5] and "We have native hearts and virtues, just as other nations" (1852)?[6]

We could easily read these sentences as examples of speakers who have the competence to use the word *nation* at anytime and in any place. Such a view of language would seem to block the way to the broader transformations in our lives and thinking that changes in our language inevitably reflect.[7] Our competence does not lie in our capacity to say anything at any time but, rather, in our capacity to say something when it is appropriate to do so.[8] Each utterance is made within a given context, with prevailing conventions governing its use, such that the use of the word *nation* in 1782 can be very different from its use in 1852. This difference is crucial to our ability as social critics to analyze "sentences a propos": speech-acts that are germane to particular situations and attuned to the relations of power that characterize those situations.[9]

I suggested at the end of chapter 3 that the different ways the language of race was embraced by African Americans in the nineteenth century affected the use of *nation* in black political discourse of that time. Absalom Jones's use of *nation* in 1808 was different, in my view, from Martin Delany's use of the word in 1852. The source of this difference resides not only

in the texts themselves but in the prevailing issues and themes with which
the texts are in conversation, the most important of which are the specific
changes in the meaning of race.

In the early nineteenth century, race was publicly understood in one of
two ways: as part of God's design or as caused by environmental conditions. But three significant shifts in considerations about race had occurred or were occurring: (1) the importance of classification, observa-
tion, and evidence, which ordered human beings in terms of physiological
and mental criteria, challenged monogenetic accounts of human origins.
Natural history was dividing and subdividing human beings into general
categories; (2) the new relation seen between the body and the mind—
the subjectivist turn—had a direct bearing on what was called national
character; and (3) the relations among physical anthropology, history, and
classical aesthetics heightened awareness of physical features in order to
distinguish national character. In other words, we have already in place
the ingredients for the modern discourse of white supremacy—particularly with the joining of the Enlightenment passion for the new sciences
and the authority of Greek antiquity. This fusion led to the classification
and judgment of African peoples as inferior, because "whatever the physical measurement or comparisons made, in the last resort the resemblance
to ancient beauty and proportions determined the value of man."[10] The
practices of black subordination and the assumptions of black inferiority
had wide currency.

Prior to the 1830s, however, or at least from 1776 until the 1830s, open
assertions of permanent inferiority were rare in the United States. The
Genesis account of human beginnings stood alongside the beliefs and passions of the revolutionary generation.[11] Biblical accounts represented all
human beings as children of Adam and Eve and, therefore, as descendants of a common stock. Defenses of slavery and racial subordination,
then, were not based on polygenetic accounts of human origins but often
justified by St. Paul's insistence that Onesimus return to his master, or as
Richard Nisbet, a former West Indian planter, suggested, by the decree
given to Moses in Lev. 25:44–45: "Both thy bond-men and thy bond-
maids, which thou shalt have, shall be of the heathen that are round about
you: of them shall ye buy bond-men and bond-maids. Moreover, of the
children of the strangers that do sojourn among you, of them shall ye
buy . . ."[12] Moreover, the ideas of republicanism and the philosophical
views of the Enlightenment often lent themselves to arguments against
slavery. Many colonists used the ideas of natural rights and the equality

of men to defend themselves against the intrusions of England and to condemn the practice of slavery in the United States.

James Otis, in his pamphlet *Rights of the British Colonies Asserted and Proved* (1764), used a natural rights argument to deride the institution of slavery. He asserted that the "Colonists are by the law of nature free born, as indeed all men are, white or black. . . . Does it follow that 'tis right to enslave a man because he is black? Will short curl'd hair like wool, instead of christian hair, as 'tis called by those whose hearts are as hard as the nether millstone, help the argument? Can any logical inference in favour of slavery be drawn from a flat nose, a long or a short face?"[13] For Otis and many others, the arguments directed against England turned on the British colonists, for "freedom [was] unquestionably the birth-right of all mankind, of Africans as well as Europeans, [and] to keep the former in a State of slavery [was] a constant violation of that right, and therefore of Justice."[14] These writers, aware of the relation of science and aesthetics, also rejected the aesthetic assumptions that led to the claim that blackness was a justification for slavery.

The Reverend Samuel Stanhope Smith published in 1787 and revised in 1810 the first major work on racial differences in America. Smith's *Essay on the Causes of the Variety of Complexion and Figure in the Human Species* accounted for the abject condition and the lack of "genius" among the darker peoples of the country. Smith noted:

> I am inclined . . . to ascribe the apparent dullness of the negro principally to the wretched state of his existence first in his original country, where he is at once a poor and abject savage, and subjected to an atrocious despotism; and afterwards in those regions to which he is transported to finish his days in slavery, and toil. Genius, in order to its cultivation, and the advantageous display of its powers, requires freedom: it requires reward, the reward at least of praise, to call it forth. . . . The abject servitude of the negro in America, condemned to the drudgery of perpetual labor, cut off from every means of improvement . . . must condemn him, while these circumstances remain, to perpetual sterility of genius.[15]

In Smith's view three factors accounted for the differences among the races: climate, state of society, and manner of living. Variations among the races, then, were not suggestive of any inherent or biological difference

among human beings. We were all part of the same species, and any no-
ticeable variation was the result of environment.

Smith echoed the general public sentiment of revolutionary America.
Most educated persons of the period agreed with the notion that "the
earth was peopled by a single race of men"[16] and that evident differences
between talents and achievements were the result of climate and social
conditions. I am not suggesting that the prevailing attitudes of race in
the early republic consisted of only benevolent environmental accounts of
racial differences. Even though American intellectuals generally accepted
the environmental view of race in the eighteenth and early nineteenth centuries, the setting was ripe for the development of scientific accounts of
the innate inferiority of blacks and native Americans—a view that would
begin to acquire widespread acceptance by the 1830s. The existence of
slavery and racial discrimination cultivated an environment in which
blacks were not considered different simply in complexion and condition.
Jefferson's remarks in the *Notes on Virginia* clearly suggest otherwise. However, remnants of these sentiments are also evidenced in the writings of
Rush and Stanhope Smith, individuals opposed to slavery.

In his "Address on Slavery of the Negroes" (1773) Benjamin Rush,
maintaining an environmentalist position, assumed the inferiority of some
blacks in the United States. "I shall allow . . . that many of them are inferior in Virtue, Knowledge, and the love of Liberty to the Inhabitants
of other parts of the World: but this may be explained from Physical
causes."[17] Although Rush did not account for the lack of virtue and knowledge among blacks by reference to a natural state of inferiority, he still
viewed them as inferior. He argued later that the burden of this race could
be lifted with the elimination of black skin. In his paper "Observations
Intended to Favour a Supposition That the Black Color (as It Is Called)
of the Negroes Is Derived from the Leprosy," Rush claimed that scientists
and the nation should devote their attention to developing a remedy for
the disease of black skin.[18]

Underlying Rush's position was an assumption of radical otherness. In
his eyes, black people embodied an unsettling difference within American
society, a difference that was becoming the mainstay of America's preoccupations and desires.[19] The exclusion of black people from the body
politic (their enslavement and disenfranchisement) called attention to the
chasm between an ideology of equality and entrenched practices of violent
rejection of groups of other human beings. Rush's assumptions of black
inferiority and his remedies for the disease of black skin aided in the ob-

jectification of black people in the United States (in spite of his opposition to slavery). His environmentalism indeed blunted the sharp edges of this radical distinction. Nevertheless, Rush's view of blacks as significantly different maintained the distinction, and such a position was not unusual. John Adams, during the struggle for independence, drew on this sense of otherness to solidify commitment to the revolutionary struggle. "[W]e won't be their [Britain's] negroes. Providence never designed us for negroes. I know, for if it had it would have given us black hides and thick lips . . . which it hasn't done, and therefore never intended us for slaves."[20] Two interrelated factors other than slavery, disenfranchisement, the new science, and classical aesthetics grounded this sense of the radical otherness of blacks in the early nineteenth century: the ambivalence of proponents of antislavery regarding the integration of blacks into U.S. society and the fear of black insurrection. The question of how to integrate newly freed blacks into the fabric of American society developed as antislavery arguments drew on the ideology of the Revolution. The fervor of many early abolitionists diminished when faced with this question. For most proponents of antislavery, the prospect of living with blacks was simply horrifying. They condemned slavery as a contradiction of the philosophies of the Revolution, but they had no desire to live with former slaves. Some argued for colonization: send them to the western territories or back to Africa. Others suggested their complete disenfranchisement: they would not be enslaved but would be forever denied access to the tools of citizenry.

These sentiments were fueled by the threat of black insurrection. The French Revolution in 1789 and, more important, the success of the Haitian Revolution terrified the leaders of the new nation. These fears were substantiated by the attempted slave revolts of Gabriel Prosser in 1800 and Denmark Vesey in 1822. Edwin Holland, after the Vesey plot was discovered, described blacks as America's Jacobins: "Let it never be forgotten, that our Negroes are truly the Jacobins of the country; that they are the anarchists and the domestic enemy; the common enemy of civilized society, and the barbarians who would, if they could, become the destroyers of our race."[21] The idea that blacks could ever be incorporated into society seemed an illusion for many white Americans and, by the 1830s, an impossibility.

African American leaders were well aware of these sentiments. Richard Allen and Absalom Jones, in their *Narrative of the Proceedings of the Black*

People, During the Late Awful Calamity (1794), addressed in candid language arguments about the innate inferiority of blacks.

> The judicious part of mankind will think it unreasonable, that a superior good conduct is looked for, from our race, by those who stigmatize us as men, whose baseness is incurable, and may therefore be held in a state of servitude, that a merciful man would not doom a beast to; yet you try what you can to prevent our rising from the state of barbarism, you represent us to be in, but we can tell you, from a degree of experience, that a black man, although reduced to the most abject state human nature is capable of, short of real madness, can think, reflect, and feel injuries.[22]

Jones and Allen challenged directly the presumption of innate racial differences and thus revealed the troubling presence of these sentiments in the day-to-day social life of northern whites as well as in the development of public policy with regard to free blacks.

James Forten, a leading black businessman in Philadelphia, recognized these beliefs in Pennsylvania's effort to stop the migration of blacks into the state. He argued that "all men are born equally free and independent and have certain inherent and indefeasible rights, among which are those of enjoying life and liberty."[23] Along with other black leaders of the period, Forten understood the lingering effects of slavery and racial discrimination on the postulates of human equality and natural rights that characterized the thinking of the American Revolution. Apparently, Forten quipped, supporters of the Pennsylvania bill did not consider the ideals of the Revolution applicable to black individuals because they did "not consider us men." Forten countered with a series of condemning questions: "Why are we not to be considered as men? Has the God who made the white man and the black, left any record declaring us a different species? Are we not sustained by the same power, supported by the same food, hurt by the same wounds, wounded by the same wrongs . . . ? And should we not then enjoy the same liberty, and be protected by the same laws?"[24] Forten and other leaders exploited the explicit connection between the unity of human beings and the political ideology of the Revolution.[25] They contended that there was no biological basis for a distinction between the races; extant differences were the result of environmental and social conditions. Thus, the claims of natural rights and equality, they argued, extended to all men.

But the critical linkage between environmental explanation and the ideology of the Revolution was challenged early on. Charles Caldwell in an essay published in 1811 in response to Samuel Stanhope Smith argued that climate could not account for the differences between races because environment could not significantly alter our racial makeup.

> Although the combined influence of climate, the state of society, and the manner of living may, and we believe does, produce varieties in the same race, it is incapable of altering the distinctive characters of the race—incapable of breaking down those substantial partitions of feature, figure, complexion and stature, which exist between the different races of men, and which the wisdom of the Deity has erected, though in a manner unknown to us, yet no doubt for purposes the most bounteous and beneficent.[26]

This position challenged biblical accounts of racial differences: if different races were not the result of environmental effects, then the races must have different origins.

Caldwell argued vehemently, however, that such a position posed no threat to Revelation but simply exceeded the bounds of its explanatory power. The origins of racial differences were a question for science, not religion. The rhetorical thrust of the argument emphasized the importance of sound reasoning and empirical validation of conclusions about racial differences, neither of which, in Caldwell's view, threatened the sanctity of religion and revelation: "for the former will remain the same incomparable [book] of moral truth and the same immaculate system of divine instruction, and the latter will retain the incontrovertible marks which now possesses of its heavenly origin, unshaken alike by the success or failure . . . of the present hypothesis."[27]

Caldwell's position was not widely accepted because of the intellectual climate of the Revolutionary age.[28] But there was a persistent undercurrent of doubt. The presence of large numbers of enslaved blacks and the growing view that blacks were radically and permanently different "clearly made many Americans extremely receptive to theories of inherent racial difference; indeed it helped create a scientific attitude of mind that was willing, even anxious, to develop such theories."[29] These beliefs did not acquire widespread public acceptance until the 1830s and 1840s, when the issues of origins and difference continued to be muddled as white Americans accounted for the obvious differences between them and their black subordinates.

Although as late as 1856 Noah Webster's *American English Dictionary* defined *race* in biblical terms (we are all members of the race of Adam),[30] by the mid–nineteenth century the definition of *race* as "subspecies" had acquired wide currency in the United States. Like inhabitants of the natural world, we were of different types, and these differences were permanent. Theological explanations of human origins came under attack in early and mid-nineteenth-century America, for the authority of science had reared its head and begun to replace theological and moral accounts of physical and cultural differences.[31] *Race,* before this period, was a name for common descent or bloodline, and this sense of the word continued well into the nineteenth century. But, by the middle decades of the century, race came also to mean something else. It described human beings' moral and mental capacities and their potential for civilization. *Race* was a word not only for designating sameness but also a word for radical Others. And science offered accounts of these separate human types and different species or races, all with inbuilt biological characteristics arranged in a hierarchy.[32]

Likewise, from the 1830s the idea of nation changed. Prior to this period *nation* designated the inhabitants of a province, a country, or a kingdom, foreigners, or students attending the University of Paris.[33] As early as the thirteenth century *nation* was used to describe a sense of collective identity, a shared heritage, or common descent. The word often alternated with other forms of collective identification such as *people, community,* or *race.* Its distinctive modern meaning emerged in England in the sixteenth century, when the word was applied to the population of the country and made synonymous with "the people."[34] The connection between the nation and people was further established in the American and French Revolutions as ideas of the sovereignty of the state were explicitly equated with the doctrine of popular freedom.

Yet, these uses of *nation* were distinctive from those that followed in the 1830s. Unlike notions of nation that assumed the importance of language, ethnicity, and territory in defining the boundaries of "the people," *nation* in the era of the Revolutions represented a set of common interests over and against a set of opposing interests. I am not suggesting a complete discontinuity between uses of the word during this period and uses after 1830. Elements of nineteenth-century notions of *nation* were in fact present during the Age of Revolution.

In the case of France, a linguistic criterion helped define the boundaries of the nation: Individuals within the territorial confines of the nation who did not speak French were suspect. But as Eric Hobsbawn notes, "in theory it was not the native use of the French language that made a person French—how could it when the Revolution itself spent so much of its time proving how few people in France actually used it?—but the willingness to acquire this, among the other liberties, laws and common characteristics of the free people of France."[35] You did not have to be born in a context that provided you with an opportunity to speak French; rather, you had only to be willing to learn the language (among other things) to be considered a full French citizen.

In this view the idea of nation was open-ended and informed, at least in theory, by voluntarist principles. The notion of a unique identity, one acquired by inheritance, was not necessary for membership in the nation. Membership could and sometimes had to be acquired. Nevertheless, the requirement of speaking French signaled the use of stronger terms of national belonging in the nineteenth century—a view that predicated national identity on the particular ethnic characteristics of the people, characteristics that could not be acquired or changed. As such, uses of *nation* during the Age of Revolution brought together the central aspects of nation language in the modern world: self-determination and self-government, group unity, and, eventually, unique and authentic identity.

In the case of America, ideas of uniqueness were lodged in an ideology of chosenness. The democratic ideas of the sovereignty of "the people" were confined to a certain group of individuals. There was "the people" and then there was the "chosen people." This ideology was inherited in large part from the Puritan rhetoric of errand: the sense that the migration and pilgrimage to the New World constituted the fulfillment of divine prophecy and progress toward the millennium.

The Puritan rhetoric of errand was transformed after the success of the American Revolution. The ideology of chosenness was a way of interpreting the time and space of America. "[I]t belonged to the peculiar fusion of providential and republican ideology that took place after the Revolution, a most dynamic combination of sacred and secular concepts. Visions of the United States as a sacred space providentially selected for divine purposes found a counterpart in the secular idea of the new nation of liberty as a privileged 'stage' for the exhibition of a new world order, a great 'experiment' for the benefit of humankind as a whole."[36] Scripture provided the vocabulary to talk of America's greatness. The parallel drawn between the election and persecution of the children of Israel and America's struggle for freedom gave way to the imagining of the former colonies as a "Providential Nation" and its people as the chosen children of God. Directed (inwardly) toward the recognized citizens of the new nation, this ideology enabled a sense of solidarity and provided a vocabulary for what Sacvan Bercovitch calls a rhetoric of consensus.

The ideology of chosenness was also aimed (outwardly) in at least two other directions. It differentiated the colonists in the New World from the English in the Old and rhetorically identified radical otherness. On one hand, America stood as the fulfillment of democratic ideas born in but betrayed by England. On the other, it was a nation in which all and only white, propertied males were created equal—a place where a doctrine of racial election thrived.

A sense of the force of the ideology of chosenness is seen in Samuel Langdon's sermon *The Republic of the Israelites an Example to the American States* (1788). Here he likens America to the nation of Israel:

> The God of heaven hath not indeed visibly displayed the glory of his majesty and power before our eyes, as he came down in the sight of Israel on the burning mount; nor has he written with his own finger the laws of our civil polity. But the signal interpositions of divine providence in saving us from the vengeance of a powerful irritated nation from which we were unavoidably separated by their inadmissible claim of absolute parliamentary power over us; in giving us a WASHINGTON to be captain-general of our armies; . . . and finally giving us peace with a large territory and acknowledged independence; all these laid together fall little short of real miracles and an heavenly charter of liberty for these United States. . . . [W]e cannot but acknowledge that God hath graciously patronized our cause and taken us under his special care, as he did his ancient covenant people.[37]

The divine care of God was not extended to all nations. America and its people were special, chosen in fact, as evidenced in the success of their strivings toward independence, and such ideas laid the foundation for the notion of an American racial destiny.

In spite of these chauvinistic elements, the language of nation during the Age of Revolution was grounded, at least in principle, in the idea that "the people" were sovereign and free from external constraint. The criteria of language, ethnicity, and, to some degree, territory so common in nineteenth-century discussions of national belonging were not necessary and sufficient evidence of what constituted the people. "[T]here was no logical connection between the body of citizens of a territorial state on one hand, and the identification of a 'nation' on ethnic, linguistic or other grounds or of other characteristics which allowed collective recognition of group membership."[38] What connected groups of individuals was not primarily these elements, although they could indicate collective membership, but instead a set of common and related interests poised over and against a set of particular interests: a community in which individuals understood themselves in communion with other like-minded and similarly situated persons, perhaps woven into the weft of a collective narrative.

Put crudely: The American colonists came to national consciousness in their battle against King George. England's betrayal of democratic ideas in its parliamentary tyranny over its colonial citizens generated ideas of the common good and the community in America. Language and ethnicity were beside the point. "There was no linguistic identity to claim, for it was shared with the British. There was no specific territory to claim, for it was growing and indeterminate in size and, besides, the status of the individual states and their relation toward each other remained unclear. Aside from the Puritan genealogy, there was no readily available mythology of ethnogenesis to which one could appeal."[39] The American nation, or people, were the defenders of liberty and equality, which in turn defined the contours of the nation. Thus, the use of *nation* in the United States stressed the equality and liberty of individuals. It was neither ethnically based nor derived from an all-consuming hatred of another country. Instead, nation language in the United States arose from the uplifting, dignifying effects of ideas of liberty and equality developed in the entrails of its mother country, England, and enshrined in a sacred constitution.

But . . . the community, or common good, was also established with the ideology of chosenness. As the common good was articulated, as disparate groups of individuals saw themselves in common cause, a stronger claim of difference was made. The colonists accounted for the true difference between them and the mother country by turning to the legacy of the Puritans and the rhetoric of errand. England represented the Old World and America the New Canaan.

With the Revolution, the Puritan vision flowered into the myth of America. For the errand was rooted in biblical myth. However eccentric their interpretations, the Puritans had relied on the authority of scripture. . . . The Revolutionary Whigs took the justification, rather than the tradition behind it, as their authority. No matter how piously they invoked scripture they were appealing not to Christian tradition, but to the series of recent events through which they defined the American experience. Their symbology centered on the act of migration; their text was the progress from theocracy to republic; their source of prophecy was the pilgrimage of the representative American.[40]

What distinguished the Americans from the English and all nations was not language or ethnicity but the idea of chosenness. We were the chosen people—read nation—of God. Even the state and its governing documents, once formally organized, were understood in this way: the community recognized itself in the institution of the state and inscribed its aspirations for the fulfillment of biblical prophecy within the state's horizon. This recognition and inscription presupposed a specific ideological form of chosenness. The colonists recognized themselves in communion as "Americans" and, through the story of their struggles for freedom, lived on and within a divinely sanctioned future. This sense of chosenness was the condition for the communion among fellows and served as the primary means for differentiating friends and enemies, us and them.

The ideology of chosenness also allowed the leaders of the American nation to sidestep the Enlightenment rhetoric of "the people." White males were the chosen people. All others were merely ordinary individuals (although the Exodus story and the idea of chosenness can be read to include slaves). This difference, more so than the contrast with England, directs us to the complicated imbrication of languages of race, religion, and nation in the United States, for the vocabularies of America's imagining of itself as chosen were overlaid with practices that constituted a parallel image of the nation, one that was (and is) thoroughly racialized.[41]

The idea of the nation involved the sense of the sacred—as Samuel Langdon stated, "God hath . . . taken us under his special care"—which, to some extent, consolidated national sentiment. Yet, this consolidation occurred alongside or, perhaps, within the construction of an American racial identity. Here freedom was understood over and against the unfreedom of black slaves; divine election was read along racial lines; and

America was fast becoming a white man's nation! National identity was grounded, then, in the construction of a racialized, collective identity that derived its effectiveness from everyday practices that structured the lives of individuals, practices that included slavery, disenfranchisement, and an entrenched racial prejudice.

The reality of race and the ideology of chosenness in American society defined, to a great extent, the texture of the new nation. As Barbara Fields notes, "American racial ideology is as original an invention to the Founders as is the United States itself. Those holding liberty to be inalienable and holding Afro-Americans as slaves were bound to end by holding race to be a self-evident truth."[42] As such, the overwhelming presence of slavery and racial discrimination helped define American culture. Race, whether based in environment or biology, truly mattered.

This is a significant point if we are to understand the relation between America's ideology of chosenness, the reality of race, and the use of nation in nineteenth-century America. With the success of the Revolution Americans came to see their endeavor as providential and themselves as chosen. This sense of chosenness was a way of differentiating themselves from others and consolidating their own identities. At the heart of this effort lies the process of negation: garden versus wilderness, chosen people versus the nations of the earth,[43] and white versus black. So, even when the postulates of the Revolution led to a condemnation of slavery and a dissociation of blackness from servility, the sense of radical otherness remained. Its construction made possible the expression of a prior unity among otherwise different individuals; it was a difference that enabled the interplay of religious and national identity in the United States.

This view of the development of American national consciousness differs slightly from Etienne Balibar's general account of national identity formation. Balibar argues that a model of collective unity must anticipate the constitution of that union. Some ideological form enables the process of unification, the effectiveness of which can be measured by the willingness of individuals to sacrifice their lives for that union or, better, confront death collectively. Most, in Balibar's view, turn to an analogy with religion to account for this ideological form: nationalisms, like religious commitments, inspire people who would otherwise not know one another or, perhaps, not care about the well-being of perceived strangers to mobilize collectively and confront death.

And, to some extent, Balibar suggests that this view has merit, not only because religious commitments institute various forms of community and different sorts of social or societal obligation, but also because most nations imagine themselves as chosen at one point or another. In other words, the languages of religious communities offer themselves as tools in the sacralization of the state, "which make it possible for a bond of sacrifice to be created between individuals, and for the stamp of truth and law to be conferred upon the rules of the legal system."[44] But for Balibar, this is only a transitory moment in the formation of national ideologies, for religious discourses and nationalist ones inevitably come into conflict (a clashing of the universalist pretenses of both).

Balibar argues that indeed national ideology involves ideal signifiers that inspire love, respect, and sacrifice—sentiments often associated with religious communities—but the transfer of these sentiments from religious communities to the state is made possible only because of a more fundamental difference: the racial community, or what Balibar calls fictive ethnicity. The racial community makes possible the expression of a prior unity seen in the state, and it provides the terms to judge the state and its role in the fulfillment of the nation's mission. For Balibar, then, the term *fictive ethnicity* captures the process by which local communities are nationalized, that is, the process by which social formations are "represented in the past and in the future as if they formed a natural community, possessing of itself an identity of origins, culture, and interests which transcends individual and social conditions."[45]

Historically this form of community has been naturalized through two competing routes: language and race. Often the two work together, aiding in the construction of "the people" and in expressing an idea of national character. Both constitute ways of rooting historical populations in a fact of nature. Language, however, remains too malleable. Although we do not choose our "native" tongues, the possibility of appropriating other languages and thereby transforming oneself into a "different kind of bearer of discourse" is always available. As Balibar contends, "the linguistic community induces a terribly constraining ethnic memory, but it is one which nonetheless possesses a strange plasticity: it immediately naturalizes new acquisitions."[46] We need only think of the complicated appropriation of the French language by those in the (former) French colonies to get a sense of this point. These marginal populations inhabit the national language as a mother tongue. Their use is as spontaneous and hereditary as the speech of those we consider to be "really" French. The language community, then, is too open; it is a "community in the present, which produces the feeling that it has always existed, but which lays down no destiny for the successive generations."[47]

Race, however, anchors the community in an extra degree of particularity. Unlike linguistically formed communities, racial communities are not open. They are based on exclusions and are predicated on definitions of sameness and otherness grounded in nature. As such, race acquires its effectiveness in the everyday activities of individuals as they differentiate themselves from others. Moreover, the race community collapses differences within the group into an ambivalent similarity by defining what is of genuine national concern for us and what is not.

What's at the heart of the concept of race is the schema of genealogy: "the idea that the filiation of individuals transmits from generation to generation a substance both biological and spiritual and thereby inscribes them in a temporal community known as kinship."[48] For Balibar, it is precisely when this sense of kinship dissolves at the local level (the level of clan, neighborhood, and social class), only to be transferred to what he calls the threshold of nationality, that we have the racial community (when nothing prevents marriage between one's fellows)—that deeper difference which binds the national community.

Balibar's account of national identity formation is convincing. But he dichotomizes the process a bit too much. He argues that the sentiments of love, respect, and sacrifice that cement religious communities are transferred to the nation and state only because of the racial community. This view, in some significant ways, turns most traditional accounts of nationalism on their heads: for nationalism and the willingness of people to die in defense of it are often made sense of through an analogy with religion. In Balibar's view, religious sentiments cannot be the vehicles that transfer the sense of the sacred to the state, because if they were, national identity would not inevitably replace forms of religious identity, forcing it itself to become nationalized.

Such an account is helpful in understanding American national identity formation insofar as it recognizes the centrality of the racial community in the construction of the nation, but the account falls short because it fails—at least when applied to the United States—to grasp the centrality of America's religious symbology. Here the complex interrelation of race and religion provided the terms for national belonging in that a racialized religious life (and the terms have to be thought about together) gave us the models for the idealization of the nation and the sacralization of the state.

The ideology of chosenness provided the religious base for America's political ideology and its national identity. The Puritan rhetoric of errand was translated into an idiom that gave America its national myth. It differentiated the Old from the New, the chosen from the ordinary. The

ideology also confined the success and meaning of America to God's chosen people who happened to be white men in the United States. Race,
then, was a constitutive part of the founding of the nation. The enslavement of black bodies stood in stark relief against a backdrop of claims
for liberty and natural rights. In spite of environmental accounts of racial
differences and the passions of the Revolution, this antimony remained a
part of the American landscape and structured the lives of the nation's
citizens, so much so that race through the American ideology was lived,
in the North and the South, as irreducible.

African American leaders in the early nineteenth century addressed
this antinomy by rearticulating the languages of race, religion, and nation
in the United States. The reality of race and the ideology of chosenness
were used to fight the battle against slavery and racial discrimination and,
subsequently, produced a language of nation peculiar to the circumstances of blacks in the United States. The slave experience stood as the
crucial event in the development of this language, for it left black individuals in the North and the South with experiences and assumptions quite
different from those of their white neighbors.[49] Every black person in the
nation was affected by the institution of slavery and the prejudices it
spawned. This continuity of experience yielded an effective ideological
form that enabled the construction of the "black community": in the battle against slavery and racism, the rhetorical movement from present to
future and back into the past produced a sense of continuity and an idea
of shared good, what Balibar terms the imaginary singularity of national
formation.

Such an imaginary was presented in a narrative form often drawn from
Biblical stories. Through the ritualization of these stories, particularly Exodus, and the reality of racism, the black individual was projected into a
collective narrative. The story provided an account of their present condition, promised freedom, but required a certain moral stance (one in line
with the laws of God). In 1808, for example, a member of the African
Society in Boston published a pamphlet addressed to a black and white
audience. Throughout the document, the condition of African Americans
and the state of America are likened to that of the Hebrews and to the
fate of the Egyptians and Babylonians. To reassure blacks that God would
act for them in spite of their debased condition, the writer noted:

> It is not a real sign that a man is rejected of God because he is en-
> slaved by man. The Israelites, after a long series of hardships by the
> oppressive hand of Pharaoh, were carried into captivity ten times.

Although, perhaps, they did not experience slavery in that awful se-
verity that their fathers did: yet they experienced it in such a manner, as in which, when they were delivered, it was so delightful a
thing that their mouths were filled with laughter and their tongues
broke forth in singing. . . . To know that the Lord reigneth, ought
and will afford the slave the greatest consolation of anything in this
world, if his heart is right with God.[50]

On one level, the community recognized itself in the Exodus story and,
later, in the institution of the church, inscribed its political struggles
within the narrative and the institution's horizons by formulating its aspirations for freedom and citizenship as divinely sanctioned ends. The idea
of the "black community" involved, then, the sense of the sacred that consolidated national sentiment. This consolidation occurred within the construction of a racial identity and made possible the expression of a prior
unity (as seen in the analogical reading of Exodus) among otherwise
different individuals.

The formulation is deliberately ambiguous. The idea that the black
community involved a sense of the sacred that consolidated national sentiment within the construction of a racial identity points in several possible
directions. First, it can yield a politics that emphasizes the covenant: a
focus on the moral obligations we have to one another and the choices we
make in light of our historical experiences. Second, this view can easily
lead to some form of chauvinism. The emphasis is not so much on one's
moral duty but, instead, on the idea of divine racial election. We are the
chosen ones and, thus, our actions—right or wrong—are sanctioned by
God. This view informs much of what many of us take to be nineteenth-
century forms of black nationalism. The last view, however, remains the
most important for my purposes. The idea that the black community involves a sense of the sacred can also lead to forms of propheticism that
ground political aims in deeply moralistic conceptions of the world. The
emphasis here is on ethical ideals and moral standards used to inform the
members of the community as they reflect with others on the conditions
of collective life. The law remains, racial chauvinism is held at arm's
length, and a premium is placed on "immanent criticism"—that is, the
internal conversation so critical to Exodus politics.

The ideology of chosenness (within the African American Christian
imagination) was central to this effort. The vocabularies were used not
merely to differentiate the group from a radical other but to account for

evil in the world and the inevitable triumph of good. Moreover, through the analogical reading of the Exodus story blacks not only constituted themselves as a nation but also created an interpretative framework in which hope could be sustained, for African American reappropriations of the ideology of chosenness relied on the authority of scripture: the God active in history who delivered Israel would surely deliver the oppressed in the United States. "African-American Christians believed they were a chosen people, not because they were black, nor because they suffered, but because their history fit the pattern of salvation revealed to them in the Bible. They saw themselves in Christ, the suffering servant. Their lives modeled the paradoxes of the gospel: in weakness lies strength, in loss, gain, in death, life."[51]

The language of nation in early nineteenth-century black political rhetoric derives, at least in part, from this rearticulation of the ideology of chosenness. African Americans reread the American version of Exodus to account for their circumstances in the United States. They became the nation of Israel, the chosen people of God. As such, the ritualization of the story in African American political culture represented a set of common interests arrayed against particular interests: their natural right of liberty and equality against the racial order of American society.

5

><

The Nation and Freedom Celebrations

On January 1, 1808, in Philadelphia, Absalom Jones delivered a sermon in thanksgiving for the end of the transatlantic slave trade. He began his speech with Exodus 3:7–8: "And the Lord said, I have surely seen the affliction of my people which are in Egypt, and have heard their cry by reason of their taskmasters; for I know their sorrows; and I am come down to deliver them out of the hand of the Egyptians."[1] Through an analogical reading of the story of Exodus, Jones adroitly directed his audience's attention to the affliction of slavery, to the favor of God, and to the eventual deliverance of a people in bondage. His invocation of Exodus emphasized a kind of radical voluntarism in which the telling and retelling of the story within the context of black American experiences encouraged each participant to imaginatively relive the moment of bondage and deliverance. They were to become the Israelites. America was to be seen as Egypt.

This communal performance had an ethical dimension, for in his reading of Exodus, Jones knew that the promise of deliverance was not certain; its fulfillment depended on the manner in which the people lived their lives in accordance with the laws of God. Thus, he suggested five duties to the community of listeners, and each duty emphasized thankfulness and remembrance. Jones encouraged participants to express gratitude to God throughout the year for his blessings and grace. He urged them to pray continuously for the complete abolition of slavery. He also warned the participants to conduct themselves in such a manner as not to cause regret for their deliverance. They were to be mindful of their former status—"the rock whence we were hewn, and the pit whence we were digged"—and their actions were to be in accordance with the laws of God. Jones ended by saying:

> Let the first of January, the day of abolition of the slave trade in our country, be set apart in every year, as a day of publick thanksgiving for that mercy. Let the history of the sufferings of our brethren, and of their deliverance, descend by this means to our children to the remotest generations; and when they shall ask, in time to come, saying, What mean the lessons, the psalms, the prayers and the praises in the worship of this day? let us answer them, by saying, the Lord, on the day of which this is the anniversary, abolished the trade which dragged your fathers from their native country, and sold them as bondmen in the United States of America.[2]

The act of remembering—the telling and retelling of the story—not only ensured the blessings of God but defined the contours and borders of the nation. For Jones, the memory of Egypt was a crucial feature of the new national consciousness.

Jones's use of Exodus was not that unusual. Black Christians in the North and the South drew on the story's metaphors as a source of inspiration and hope. The builders of the American nation also drew a parallel between the children of Israel and the English colonists. The story had wide currency. Jones read Exodus, however, in a different context. He was not huddled around a huge kettle-pot on the outskirts of a plantation reading or performing the story for fellow slaves. Nor was he reading the story within the context of a white Episcopalian church in the North, celebrating America as an example of God's will. Instead, Jones was preaching a sermon in St. Thomas African Episcopal Church in Philadelphia. He was preaching at a freedom celebration, a ritualized space in which the story of the black sojourn in the United States was retold and mobilized as countermemory, a story in which America was not figured as Canaan but instead as the home of Pharaoh.

By *countermemory* I mean the accounts of marginalized groups that call into question prevailing norms and stories of a society: an alternative narrative that directly or indirectly opposes—operating under and against—

the master narrative of the nation.[3] Through the commemorative activity
of local and, sometimes, national freedom celebrations, black Americans
in the North created, articulated, and came to share memories of experiences that challenged the collective memory (and forgetfulness) of the
nation. They told in effect a different story.

The celebrations focused on the group's identity and the events that
occasioned its historical formation. Africa, the middle passage, and the
brutality of slavery figured as crucial moments in the story line and provided significant moral lessons for the members of the group. Although
each celebration was called to commemorate a specific act, be it the end
of the transatlantic slave trade or the emancipation of slaves in the British
West Indies, they were structured by a broader account of the group's
history that provided each individual with a general notion of his or her
shared past. In this sense, the celebrations served as a crucible for the
formation of the nation, portraying it as a unified people moving through
history.[4]

It is also important, at least for my purposes, to understand this
broader story in relation to, or, better still, as an aspect of Exodus history,
particularly the ways significant events are recast within its story line:
where, through the central use of the text or by reiterative reference, black
Americans and the nation of Israel shade into one another. This is important precisely because it affects how we understand the use of nation language among early nineteenth-century black Americans, specifically the
way a certain religious story provided the terms for their imagining of
the nation.

The freedom celebrations, although rarely referring to Exodus explicitly, draw our attention to the story because of the importance of thanksgiving, remembrance, and duty in each individual act of commemoration,
reproducing, as it were, central themes of the Exodus story—what I
briefly described in chapter 4 as a form of covenant politics. Here *thanksgiving* turned the participants' attention away from themselves to the
blessings of God and reaffirmed that they were his chosen people; *remembrance* made history into living memories, a constant reminder of past
persecutions and present circumstances; and the emphasis on one's *duty*
kept before the group the binding obligation of the covenant and the consequences of failure to live in accordance with the laws of God, reminding
them that only in the practice of righteousness might they obtain deliverance and continued freedom. Each of these themes was framed by the
partial character of the celebrations. The reality of slavery in the South

rendered these gatherings partially proleptic. They were hope-laden gatherings, festive commemorations of freedom expected but not fully realized.

The conjunction of this narrative structure and the ritual activity of commemoration yielded a powerful paradigm for formulating the group's history and its future. It helped constitute a subversive countermemory hostile and, for some, opposed to the developing story of America. I want to focus on three dimensions of this activity: (1) the ritual features of the celebrations, (2) the rhetorical purpose of the celebrations, and finally, (3) the role of this activity in the making of a national tradition among black Americans.

There were three major commemorative celebrations among Northern free blacks prior to general emancipation. Each celebrated, in one form or another, the abolition of an element of slavery. The first of these gatherings was the New Year's Day celebration located primarily in New York and Philadelphia, commemorating the end of the foreign slave trade on January 1, 1808.[5] These celebrations set the pattern for subsequent commemorations. From the beginning, they were explicitly linked with black churches. The program of the events borrowed its form from the liturgies of black services: it included singing, reading of "sacred" texts, and sermons or speeches. More than likely, black preachers delivered the keynote addresses, which focused on the hardships of slavery and the memory of the brutality of the middle passage. The New Year's Day celebrations declined, however, after eight years or so. The trafficking of black bodies continued in spite of the law, and the slave trading of the border states replaced the brutality of the foreign slave trade.[6] The hopes that the end of the transatlantic slave trade had created subsequently diminished.

The second major commemoration centered around the end of slavery in the state of New York on July 4, 1827. This black holiday was celebrated more extensively than the January 1 gatherings. More than five states participated in the celebrations, and observances were held as late as 1859.[7] Like the New Year's Day celebrations, these commemorations were closely tied to black churches. They drew on the liturgies of church services, and black preachers were usually the keynote speakers. But unlike the January 1 commemorations, New York's Abolition Day consisted of extensive outdoor activities: gun salutes, picnics, and processions. The publicity of these observances was a central aspect of their symbolic and political meaning.[8] They were held on July 5,[9] apart from the national holiday, during a period in which Americans had begun to feel that their heroic past was slipping away from them.[10] The fact that African Americans walked through the major thoroughfares of cities in order to commemorate the end of slavery and to remember the brutality of their own experiences on July 5 as opposed to July 4 placed in stark relief the fundamental contradictions between the nation's commitment to democratic ideals and its practices of racial exclusion.

The July 5 festivals were eclipsed by the emancipation of 670,000 slaves in the British West Indies on August 1, 1834. August 1 became the most widely observed holiday among northern blacks prior to general emancipation.[11] Unlike the other commemorations, nearly all of these celebrations occurred outdoors. Because of the number of celebrants, the church building was pushed to the margins of the freedom holiday. Its presence remained, however, in the activities of temperance societies, which set up separate tables at the outdoor events or, in some cases, sponsored separate celebrations. But such efforts were overshadowed by the emancipation balls, the all-day cookouts, and the steamboat excursions. These activities enabled persons otherwise shackled by the debilitating effects of racism to enjoy, as Frederick Douglass noted, their "happiness in [their] own way, and without any very marked concern for the ordinary rules of decorum."[12] The cookouts and balls joined with the elements of thanksgiving and remembrance and, together, aided in the construction of a national community.

Each of the freedom celebrations was somewhat different because of the shifts in the political and social contexts that informed them. In each case these particular ritualized ways of acting functioned in their specific contexts to make strategic distinctions that defined both community and personal identity. In fact the ritualization of this activity, and the manner in which memories of Africa, the middle passage, slavery, and brave acts of overcoming hardships were mobilized, enabled the projection of a national community and the production of specific vocabularies to speak about and to argue for emancipation, citizenship, and self-determination.

CATHERINE BELL AND RITUALIZATION

Catherine Bell's use of ritualization is important to my understanding of the political effects of these public gatherings. Bell understands ritualization as fundamentally a strategy for the making and remaking of certain forms of power relationships effective within specific organizations.[13] Her emphasis is more on ritual as an activity—with particular emphasis on how this activity distinguishes itself from other ways of acting and what it accomplishes in doing so—than on ritual as a "natural" or "universal" category of human endeavor.

In contrast, some approaches tend to define ritual in one of two ways: either as a distinctive, autonomous set of activities with universal qualities or as an aspect of all human activity. The first view has resulted in a "plethora of ritual types,"[14] an attempt, as it were, to account for the activity that does not fit neatly into the established categories of rituals. The main concern here is determining, with a set of already established criteria, what is or is not ritual. The second view focuses on ritual's formal features rather than its symbolic and expressive ones. Yet, to view ritual as constitutive of all human activity makes it difficult to discern what is actually distinctive about it. As Meyer Fortes noted, "it is a short step from the proposition that everything is ritual to the practical reality that nothing is ritual."[15]

Bell claims that in order to avoid the pitfalls of both of these approaches ritual must be understood as a practical activity. That is, rather than impose categories of what is or is not ritual on certain actions or erase the distinctiveness of ritual by claiming it as a feature of all human activity, we should confront the act itself. We should refer to the specific contexts in which activities, in their doing, differentiate themselves (or don't) from other ways of acting.

Ritual acts, then, necessarily share four distinctive features of practical activity. First, rituals are always *situated*. They are embedded in certain social relations and are structured by macro- and micronetworks of power. As a consequence, not much can be said about rituals outside of the contexts in which they occur. We cannot understand, for example, the practice of gift-giving apart from its context, else we are bound to confuse very different ways of acting. Even the general exchange of items, an act consistent in every gift-giving situation, cannot be understood apart from the context that lends it its significance. If this is not the case then gift-giving would be no different from the routine trading of baseball cards between two bright-eyed boys, or gift-giving during an African American celebration of Kwanzaa[16] would be the same as that of a birthday celebration.

This is directly related to the second feature of activities. They are *strategic*. Rituals are always sizing up situations, detailing their various components, and orienting our attitudes toward contexts.[17] The strategies of a Kwanzaa celebration, for example, distinguish it from other African

American gatherings. African words describe the different days of the rite. Gifts must be inexpensive. The rite follows the Christmas holidays, and most participants are asked to wear traditional African clothing. Each strategy aims to immerse the celebrant in a certain version of history and a particular conception of community and personal identity.

Yet there is a sense of indeterminacy about ritual activity, a kind of blindness with regard to what it actually achieves. Bell understands this as a *misrecognition* (the third feature) of what ritual is doing, of its limits and constraints, of the relation between its ends and its means. Returning to the Kwanzaa example: the ritual was created by Ron Karenga, a self-described cultural nationalist and founder of the US movement during the 1960s. He envisioned the rite as a vehicle for the proliferation of certain political views and the creation of a shared sense of the reality of African Americans' political status. But persons from a variety of political perspectives participate in the ritual, shaping it through their own particular understanding of their situations. In short, not all celebrants of Kwanzaa are cultural nationalists.

This takes us to the fourth feature of ritual activity: the production of the terms of counterideological acts, what Bell calls *redemptive hegemony.* Our situations or contexts are ones of limits and constraints; we are caught, as it were, in webs of power and domination. But our situations are also ones of possibility, contexts for our actions. Redemptive hegemony denotes, then, "the way in which reality is experienced as a natural weave of constraint and possibility, the fabric of day-to-day dispositions and decisions experienced as a field of strategic action."[18] So even though we are conscripted into a set of relations (all Kwanzaa celebrants, regardless of their political commitments, participate in a rite created by a self-described cultural nationalist), we often accede in ways that effectively empower us, irrespective of the rites' intentions, to act.

These four features bring into focus Bell's use of ritualization. For her,

> [r]itualization draw[s] attention to the way in which certain social actions strategically distinguish themselves in relation to other actions. In a very preliminary sense, ritualization is a way of acting that is designed and orchestrated to distinguish and privilege what is being done in comparison to other usually more quotidian, activities. As such, ritualization is a matter of various culturally specific strategies for setting some activities off from others.[19]

Our task in confronting the act itself is to describe the manifold strategies used to distinguish some ways of acting from others. The focus is on (ritual) actions and how, through the strategic use of value-laden distinctions, they constitute themselves as different from other activities. Such ways of acting cannot be understood apart from situations or contexts that structure them, contexts that we reproduce, albeit in a misrecognized and transformed way. And it is through this misrecognition or our own limited and biased construal of the relations in which we find ourselves that we are able to act, however limited or constrained those actions may be.

Differentiation and privileging of certain practices are key strategies of ritual activity. Every ritualized act invokes and contrasts itself, in the form of a juxtaposition of opposites, to another act. Such oppositions yield sets of qualifications and various kinds of appropriations and rereadings that grant particular ways of acting a privileged status. Yet these privileged contrasts make sense only within a specific semantic field and, in some way, reproduce the constitutive relations to which they speak. In short, ritualized action involves differentiation that entails at least three basic dynamics: (1) the construction and deployment of oppositions, (2) the privileging of some ways of acting over others, and (3) the constant back-and-forth of practices that structure and are simultaneously structured by our contexts.

Freedom celebrations are distinguishable from ordinary public gatherings in the nineteenth century. They are differentiated in the very act (the doing) of celebration or commemoration and, to some extent, derive their significance from the contrast implicitly set up between their formality and periodicity and other informal and, perhaps, spontaneous public gatherings. The celebrations are understood as special, then, only in relation to similar actions that are not so special: we have the contrast and opposition, then the privileging and hierarchical arrangement of the activity. As Bell suggests, "this generates an endlessly circular run of oppositions that come to be loosely homologized to each other, deferring their significance to other oppositions so that the meaning of any one set of symbols or references depends upon the significance of the other."[20]

These homologous oppositions (for example, white-black, chosen-ordinary, true democrats-false ones) can come to organize what Bell calls taxonomic sets (for example, the set of white, Egypt, and slavery or the set of black, promised land, and freedom). The set is arranged such that a sense of identity or coherence is produced among its elements. Black people come to be identified with the Israelites in bondage and their quest for self-determination: Exodus. So, under particular circumstances—the freedom celebrations, for example—only one or two of the elements from a set need be invoked to imply a whole series of relations and implications, and this experience facilitates the emergence of some symbolic terms in a dominant relation to others.[21]

But all of this happens in context. We cannot grasp the significance of the "endless deferral" unless we understand ritual activity first in terms of what it shares with all activity, then in the manner in which it differentiates itself from other ways of acting; we can then only characterize ritual in particular because actions vary from context to context. So, when we venture to say something about ritual activity, we must understand it within a semantic framework, that is, as a way of acting that is dependent on its place within and relation to a specific context. What is assumed here is a set of contingent circumstances and conditions from which came the act.

Bell offers a useful approach for looking at the often ritualized ways we live in a world saturated with power: we manipulate it; we appropriate it; we differentiate within it. She avoids, as much as possible, the tendency to impose categorical definitions of ritual. We are to look at particular activities in contexts, and how these contexts are manipulated by the act itself. Her view of ritualization also rejects the idea that ritual only legitimates power relations or that it simply produces consensus among otherwise conflicting interests (remember Bercovitch's mistake).

She wants us to see that there is negotiation going on even as a reproduction of specific power relations occurs: that it is through ritual activity that macro- and micronetworks of power are appropriated and used in the fight against certain forces or problems. This kind of activity is most effective when power is hidden in indirect claims of authority as well as in efforts to render the hegemonic order socially redemptive in order for it be personally liberating,[22] for example, an ideology of chosenness or a doctrine of divine racial election that is manipulated and mobilized in the counterideological efforts of a pariah people.

RITUALIZATION AND THE FREEDOM CELEBRATIONS

From the beginning of the nineteenth century to well after the outbreak of the Civil War, northern blacks gathered in private and public spaces to tell the story of their experiences and struggles against prevailing forms of dehumanization and degradation. The celebrations were primarily concerned with problem-solving and with the expansion of a heritage of values in order that succeeding generations could be assured a better future. "If their purpose was to invent tradition, it was, one must emphasize, a tradition of struggle, jeremiad, and claim-staking. As such, these commemorations . . . contributed to the development of the collective memory—not just memory of past events but the memory of the future, in anticipation of action to come—and of the historical consciousness of a people who are often perceived as victims rather than as historical agents."[23] It is important to understand these events as ritualized activity—not in some sense to produce consensus among otherwise different individuals or to account for sudden social change but rather as an inaugural moment for the manner in which African Americans *acted* in political spaces: a way of acting that distinguished itself from other ways of acting precisely because traditional forms of political engagement were unavailable.

Early nineteenth-century celebrations in the North are distinctive in this regard. They stand as examples of the ritual activity that aided in the construction of a black political public in the North. Like the early petitions for freedom, these commemorations were inchoate forms of black abolitionism, for arguments against slavery and racial discrimination were made within the activity itself. Yet, these celebrations did not produce a resolution of the problems of slavery and racism. They stood instead as a mode of translation or redescription, a way of rereading the immediate concerns of the day in the dominant terms of the ritual—a means of reappropriating the prevailing ideals of the nation in the imagining of their own.[24] So we must understand them, first, as ritual acts.

The formalization and periodicity of the rites distinguished them from other kinds of celebratory gatherings among northern free blacks. The New Year's day commemoration, for example, had an internal structure. It included a solemn address to Almighty God, an appropriate anthem, the reading of the legislative act, an appropriate hymn, and another address to God[25] (and this was only the morning service!). This internal orchestration of the celebration contrasted the sacred character of the gatherings with more mundane activity and privileged it in relation to the latter. The celebrations were to trigger the perception that the images and values talked about and performed were special. Thus, there were specific people who participated, certain texts and objects designated as significant, and verbal and gestural combinations that evoked movement from present circumstances to future possibilities.

Moreover, important dates particular to black experiences in the North were set aside for commemoration. Indeed, the very existence of these celebrations juxtaposed the practice of racial discrimination and slavery and the ideals of American democracy within a semiformalized alternative calendar. These dates directed attention to the hardships of slavery and racism and the hope for true freedom. As such, a calendrical critique of the United States became a central part of the identity of African Americans, a way to set themselves off as a distinctive people.

The commemorative cycle also shaped the community's basic understanding of its past and future. As Yael Zerubavel notes: "The holiday cycle itself constitutes a traditional site of memory. . . . Historical holidays offer rituals of remembrance that create a shared network of practices around which clustered the common memories of the people as a whole."[26] The rituals, then, contribute to sustaining the group in the face of changing circumstances. They provide a sense of continuity as the nation continuously reshapes and remembers its past and projects its future.

Each freedom celebration involved at least three elements[27] that can be seen as a part of the commemorative cycle's framework for the representation of the past.[28] First, there was a sense of historicity with a focus on the *doing* of certain actions. The ritual called attention to an event in time: at one point, the transatlantic slave trade and, consistently, the institution of slavery. In the crowds at the January 1, 1808, celebrations, one could probably hear people speaking different African languages. The immediacy of the separation from their homelands was heard in the voices of the participants. Africa was a living memory. The rite focused, then, on this event in time along with slavery, the formation of the community, and the development of guidelines to ensure the community's longevity. In some cases the most definitive activity was an anamnesis, a reappropriated enactment of Christ or, in this case, the biblical story of Exodus. Within these rituals the middle passage and slavery were read as examples of Egyptian bondage and, eventually, God's deliverance. The transatlantic slave trade and the horrors of slavery were relived as they were experienced by each participant. They gave thanks for their deliverance, emplotted their experiences to pass on to others, and, by way of the rite, grounded the community in the lived experiences of the slave trade and slavery. Thus, this reappropriation provided the terms for communal identity and ethical obligation: what we, as a nation or people, must do in order to acquire freedom and remain free.

Second, the rites involved a sense of history as allegory with a focus on what was being *said*. After a period of years, the memories of Africa diminished as the transatlantic slave trade ended. The July 5 and August 1 celebrations did not have a large number of "fresh-water" African participants. Instead, the history of the slave trade was imaginatively relived through narrative accounts. Speakers *told* the stories. Here *rhetorical* contrasts and differentiation became all the more important. The dramatic accounts of the slave trade and the living memory of slavery stood alongside the ideals of American democracy. This glaring contradiction became the primary tool to argue for freedom and, for some, citizenship.

Finally, the rites involved *celebration* as an act of self-recognition by which the assembled group experienced itself as a national community. The ritualized activity itself became the basis for the expression of this community within each person. This was particularly evident in the outdoor activities. Here the group's identity expressed itself in the enthusiastic exchanges of fellows, the eating of barbecue, or in the celebratory use of alcohol. The emphasis was not so much on what was done or what was said, but, rather, on the *ritualized coming together* of fellows and the self-expression that activity allowed within the racialized spaces of the United States.

Each of these elements was a distinctive feature of early nineteenth-century freedom celebrations. At different moments one element could be emphasized more than another, yet each remained an essential feature of the rite. They combined with strategies of contrast and opposition to distinguish particular moments, events, and actions from others as well as to establish the inherent value of the distinctions themselves. One crucial contrast was between that of unconnected individuals and a nation of people of African descent.

The Reverend David Nickens took this distinction as his point of departure in his July 5 oration in Chillicothe, Ohio:

> I wish to address you on the important subject of cultivating a friendly union among ourselves as an oppressed people. . . . Let us . . . respect each other according to character and merit. . . . Let the good citizens of color arise, male and female, young and old, and give their aid, for the purpose of reconciling and consolidating society again, and set their faces against every person of color who dares to raise his puny arms to interrupt our peace or mar our heritage. Let this maxim be engraven on our memories: united, we stand— divided we fall.[29]

Nickens's call for unity derived its significance from the contrast implicitly set up between individuals and a community of fellows with memories and a heritage to bind them. His rhetorical performance evoked a sense of community, enabling the collapse of individual differences into a fuzzy similarity. Moreover, the rite itself, and the narrative it reproduced with its three distinctive features, emphasized the idea of a national community. The celebrations led participants to take the rite's aims as a straightforward communication of the group's most cherished values and of its unified movement through history. This happened whether the speaker spoke about it directly or not.

As the people congregated, coming from different backgrounds and situations to assemble at a specific place and time, the gathering generated a contrast between a dispersed population and that of a central community. The emphasis, say, on an event in time highlighted this initial opposition through the telling and retelling of narratives of loss, exile, and journey while, at the same time, it generated a kind of collectivizing trope (the slave experience) that enabled the communion among otherwise different and dispersed fellows. This general contrast, with different sorts of inflections depending on the political and social context of the rite, was then overlaid with other oppositions: chosen versus ordinary; true democrats versus false ones; black versus white.

Absalom Jones's analogical use of Exodus is an excellent example of this initial opposition. The rhetorical move presupposed (and simultaneously created) the corporate unity of the participants while reorganizing memories of Africa in the construction of an African American identity. The sermon began with an account of Exodus and the affliction of the nation of Israel. Jones conveyed to his audience that even though the nation of Israel experienced the brutality of slavery, God had not forgotten them, for he heard their cries and he, not angels, came down to deliver them out of the hands of the Egyptians.

Here God's activity in history (salvific history) becomes the basis for rereading the past and mobilizing memories in a dialectical relation with more secular accounts of history.[30] Africa is reread; the middle passage and slavery are reread; America is reread; and aspirations for freedom and citizenship are formulated as divinely sanctioned ends. Notice the rhetorical shifts in Jones's analogical account and the way communal aspirations are generated by his descriptions:

Yes, my brethren, the nations from which most of us have been descended, and the country in which some of us were born, have been visited by the tender mercy of the Common Father of the human race. He has seen the affliction of our countrymen, with an eye of pity. . . . He has seen the ships fitted out from different ports in Europe and America, and freighted with trinkets to be exchanged for the bodies and souls of men. . . . He has seen them exposed for sale, like horses and cattle, upon the wharves; or like bales of goods, in warehouses of West India and America sea ports. . . . He has seen all the different modes of torture, by means of the whip, the screw, the pincers, and the red-hot iron, which have been exercised upon their bodies, by inhuman overseers. . . . Yes: but not by these only. Our God has seen masters and mistresses, educated in fashionable life, sometimes take the instruments of torture into their own hands, and, deaf to the cries and shrieks of their agonizing slaves, exceed even their overseers in cruelty. Inhuman wretches! though You have been deaf to their cries and shrieks, they have been heard in heaven. The ears of Jehovah have been constantly open to them: He has heard the prayers that have ascended from the hearts of his people; and he has, as in the case of the his ancient and chosen people the Jews, come down to deliver our suffering countrymen from the hands of their oppressors.[31]

Jones refracted popular identities and histories through the telling and retelling of the horrors of slavery and the story of Exodus. Individuals were joined together as the story unfolded, for the participants were to assume a sort of consensus—all of them *knew* the horror of their affliction. But more important, the celebration turned their attention to that event in time. They were asked to relive the horrors of their experiences and to remember the event that occasioned the historical formation of the nation. Thus, during the rite they were not just individuals but a community of fellows and the faithful awaiting deliverance and freedom.

The contrast between a dispersed population and that of a central community was the consistent opposition to emerge in the early freedom celebrations. The public nature of the commemorations, however, overlaid this contrast with an external opposition in which individuals came to see themselves as a community opposed to racist practices directed toward them. Unlike the slave festivals that usually took place on the outskirts of the city, most of the freedom celebrations were held within the city's limits. Blacks and whites faced one another in public space as black Americans asserted their right to work out issues facing their community in the public domain.[32] No one failed to notice that this angered many northern whites and, in some cases, resulted in violence. The question then arose: How do we mobilize our *resources as a community* to fight against these practices? The contrasting and subsequent privileging of the community offered a response. But this opposition was overlaid by the external practices themselves, the contradiction of the state's ideals: America was supposed to be a land of liberty and freedom for individuals yet it denied these rights to black Americans. Ultimately this last opposition became a crucial part of the commemorations, for black Americans within the context of the celebrations became the true defenders of America's ideals: the true democrats as opposed to the false ones.

William Hamilton's July 5, 1827, address illustrates these sets of oppositions. He began his speech by delivering a boisterous thanks to the heavens for freeing "the sons of Afric[a]," and then proceeded to give a brief account of the horrors of the slave experience, culminating in a charge, in the form of duties, to the youth of New York's black community. But between the lines of Hamilton's alternation of thanksgiving and remembrance were serious revisions of the pantheon of America's founding fathers. Washington and Jefferson were no longer seen as the progenitors of liberty and freedom. Their legacies marked the contradiction that undergirded U.S. society. He turned then from these figures to the members of the New York Manumission Society (referring to the 1799 legislation that led to the eventual abolition of slavery in New York state). In his view these persons were the true defenders of liberty and freedom.

Hamilton's revision occurred against the backdrop of an interesting inversion. For Hamilton and others, slavery was the definitive feature of American society. The idea of individual dignity and equality in the United States could not be understood apart from an extreme form of servitude. In other words, the meaning of individual dignity and equality in the United States had to be grasped in the light of slavery. By placing slavery at the center of American life, Hamilton was then able to claim the benevolent legacies of U.S. society. Proponents of slavery had betrayed the spirit with which the nation was born. Only those who defended the natural rights of every individual could claim the ideals of the nation as their own. So he invoked the spirit of '76 and the memorable words of the Declaration of Independence to claim victory over prejudice and oppression in the United States.[33] The ideals of democracy were now part of his, *our*, legacy.

This reimagining of America was a crucial element of the major celebrations. The New York Abolition celebrations incorporated within their liturgies a rereading of the ideals of the America. Sections from the Declaration of Independence were often read, or the spirit of the Revolution was invoked to ground the participants' claims to liberty. As notions of a national community were consolidated through the ritualized activity of commemoration, the ideals of the American nation provided participants with a vocabulary of dissent.[34] The idea of America, then, was critical to the construction of a national black identity.

Austin Steward's address on July 5, 1827, in Rochester, New York, illustrates this point. Steward employed, as did most keynote speakers, the same rhetorical mode of thanksgiving and remembrance. He gave thanks to God and then remembered the afflictions of the past. His remonstrations against the horrors of slavery were tempered, however, by his sophisticated rereading of the greatness of America's democratic principles. For him, the sharp edges of slavery were blunted by the opportunities democracy offered.

> Although Almighty God has not permitted us to remain in the land of our forefathers and [to experience in] our own land, the glories of national independence, and the sweets of civil and religious liberty, to their full extent; but the strong hand of the spoiler has borne us into a strange land, yet has He of His great goodness given us to behold those best and noblest of his gifts to man, in their fairest and loveliest forms; and not only have we beheld them, but we have already felt much of their benignant influence. Most of us have hitherto enjoyed many, very many of the dearest rights of freemen. . . . It is the dictate of sound wisdom, then, to enjoy without repining, the freedom, privileges and immunities which wise and equal laws have awarded us—nay proudly rejoice and glory in their production, and stand ready at all times to defend them at the hazard of our lives, and of all that is most dear to us.[35]

The blessings and hardships of slavery were revealed in the encounters with the principles of democracy and the precepts of the Christian gospel. Democracy offered manifold possibilities. And, for Steward, we only have such possibilities because of the curse of slavery.[36]

There is an irony in Steward's remarks. It lies in his juxtaposition of the greatness of democratic principles in the United States and the enslavement of black Americans. Even as he reconciled the enslavement of Africans and God's benevolence, Steward highlighted the existence of un-

freedom and freedom in U.S. society. He turned at the moment of ex-
pounding the greatness of America's ideals to the narrative of Exodus and
placed in the foreground the untold sorrows that framed the joy of deliverance and democratic possibility.

> Like the people of God in Egypt, you have been afflicted; but like
> them too, you have been redeemed. Your are henceforth free as the
> mountain winds. Why should we, on this day of congratulation and
> joy, turn our view upon the origin of slavery? Why should we harrow
> up our minds by dwelling on the deceit, the forcible fraud and
> treachery that have been so long practiced on your hospitable and
> unsuspecting countrymen? . . . Why should we remember, in joy
> and exuberance, the thousands of our countrymen who are today,
> in this boasted land of civil and religious liberty, writhing under the
> lash and groaning beneath the grinding weight of Slavery's chain?
> . . . But away with such thoughts as these; we will rejoice, though
> sobs interrupt the songs of our rejoicing, and tears mingle in the
> cup we pledge to Freedom.[37]

In this passage Steward consistently infringed on the borders of his inter-
dictions. The remarks that should not be spoken at a celebration were
stated over and over again. They focused on the contradictions that undergirded the country's ideals of liberty and freedom. More important,
Steward's use of Exodus and irony placed African Americans at the fore-
front in the retrieval of the true meanings of democracy. These efforts
yielded a specific black identity, one forged out of the struggles to acquire
freedom in the "wilderness of North America." Such an identity generated a recognition of one's fellows and a sense of duty to one's community:
individual action became linked to a broader community of concern.

Up to this point I have emphasized the content of the speeches delivered at the freedom celebrations. I have also highlighted two of the three
distinctive features of this ritual activity. But what of the activity itself?
What of the ritualized coming together of fellows and the self-expression
such activities allowed? These gatherings not only remembered the horrors of slavery and translated the prevailing concerns of the day into the
terms of the ritual, they also enacted the moment of jubilee with festivals,
processions, and cookouts. Indeed, they celebrated as an act of self-
recognition and national solidarity.

In these activities ordinary black folks engaged in the construction of community. The speeches delivered at the celebrations or at the rites themselves were not passively received. The celebrants actively absorbed the meanings of the orations and refracted the rites' and speakers' intentions through the common practices of the everyday. The culinary rituals of eating barbecue and drinking whiskey to excess, as well as the traditions of singing, dancing, and playing games,[38] called forth memories of the South and the slave experience. These memories lodged, as it were, in acts of enjoyment, aided in the organization of the consciousness of the group while basic bonds of kinship and community were established as persons exchanged toasts, foods, and jokes.

But many of the northern elites rejected the idea of processions and cookouts. Samuel Cornish and John Russwurm, editors of *Freedom's Journal*, argued that processions betrayed the solemnity that should be present at the freedom holidays. They suggested that the celebrations were moments of profound thanksgiving for the blessings the community had received. Public processions were simply inappropriate:

> On the subject of public parades, we have never concealed our sentiments, and the recent one at Brooklyn compels us once more to denounce them. If we except the commission of crime, nothing serves more to keep us in our present degraded condition than these foolish exhibitions of ourselves—it is a fact that they profit none of us—many a hard day's earnings being expended to prepare and purchase the cast off garments of some field officer, or the sash and horse trappings of some dragoon serjeant—that we may appear as Generals or Marshals, or Admirals, on these occasions complete and appropriate laughing stocks for thousands of our citizens, and to the more considerate of our brethren, objects of compassion and shame.[39]

Yet these processions were an intricate part of the July 5 and August 1 celebrations. They allowed the celebrants to strut their wares. The symbolic act of "firing gun salutes, the display of banners and community dinners . . . expressed the mood of jubilation"[40] and became a basis for the expression of the nation within each person.

The fact that these events were occurring outdoors more frequently did not help the arguments of Cornish and others. The number of celebrants increased during the observances of New York Abolition Day and West Indian Emancipation, and black churches were no longer the only sites for the events. The buildings simply could not hold all of the participants. Instead the open spaces of northern cities and towns became the main sites for the expression of national solidarity.

The debate over parades and cookouts is an important area in which the varying interests within the black community evidenced themselves. Black northern elites had as their principle concern the creation of common interests and the social uplift of their fellows—what I call, following Evelyn Brooks Higginbotham, a politics of respectability. For them, the commemorations were solemn events to give thanks for the blessings that the community had received and to reaffirm their dedication to the betterment of African Americans. On the other hand, the everyday practices of black folks constituted an array of interests that changed from time to time according to the circumstances. These interests were grounded in their own particular, local involvements. The terms of their participation, then, were somewhat ambiguous and complex, and frequently they put the intended aims of the celebrations and its elite organizers to unintended uses—making the idea of a common interest all the more implausible.

The ritualized activity of commemorations negotiated these tendencies and yielded a dynamic sense of community and personal identity, primarily because the rites had the capacity to mediate both local attachments and the imagining of national community. While local and particular attachments shaped the form of the celebrations, a "grammar" of sorts imposed on the varying activities a strong linkage that constituted a coordinated story among otherwise different accounts—providing the participants with a general notion of their shared past and creating what can be called a tradition.

FREEDOM CELEBRATIONS, TRADITION, AND THE BLACK ATLANTIC

This notion of tradition, I maintain, differs quite starkly from the static conceptions of tradition that inform most nationalist projects (as they are presently understood). To be sure, the celebrations constructed monumental histories of African achievement and even mythologized and romanticized Africa as home, but their primary aim was prospective. That is, they presupposed certain connections and relations as constitutive of African American experiences and inferred from those experiences (in the organization of liturgy and in the detail of the rituals) standards and norms that could help blacks as they struggled in the future. In short, the celebrations and the idea of tradition they generated were as much about projection and anticipation as they were about recollection and memory.

Paul Gilroy begins the last chapter of his text *The Black Atlantic: Modernity and Double Consciousness* with a discussion of the role and function of tradition in the countercultures of racialized communities. He highlights the tendency within these countercultures to burden the concept of tradition with the weight of being a counterdefensive against the logics of white supremacy. Tradition, in this account, becomes the crucible for conceptions of historical pasts that stand opposite the universalizing narratives of modernity. As Gilroy states: "In these conditions where obsessions with origin and myth can rule contemporary political concerns and the fine grain of history, the idea of tradition can constitute a refuge. It provides a temporary home in which shelter and consolation from the vicious forces that threaten the racial community (imagined or otherwise) can be found."[41] This conception of tradition exists in spite of slavery, for slavery is viewed as the site of black victimhood and the place for the intended erasure of tradition. Slavery is then replaced by the continuity between the great African civilizations of the past and the people of African descent in the world. The view reduces tradition to a static conception, "outside of the erratic flows of history."

In contrast to this understanding of tradition, one Gilroy associates with forms of black nationalism, the text offers a more modest conception of the ways in which tradition functions. In this account, tradition is not read as a polar alternative to the inroads of modernity. Rather, Gilroy attempts to demonstrate that "the articulating principles of the black political countercultures . . . grew inside modernity in a distinctive relationship of antagonistic indebtedness."[42]

The desire to constitute (force) a fixed conception of tradition and, subsequently, a pure African identity stemmed from the different registers of time that were experienced in the black diaspora. For Gilroy, the ruptures of the middle passage and the dreams of freedom transformed the way modernity was periodized. This different time register was accentuated by the constant fear that marked the slave experience as well as the consistent efforts to acquire emancipation, citizenship, and autonomy. These experiences, temporal and historical, played themselves out in public spaces such that communities of sentiment and interpretation were constituted. But to read these elements as evidence of a static tradition, in Gilroy's view, is to miss the complicated interplay between tradition and the modern, an interplay that requires a shift in our understanding of modernity itself.

Gilroy offers a different conception of modernity that emerges from the relation between tradition, modernity, temporality, and social memory. The horrors of the middle passage and the constant reinventions of black identities that emerged and emerge as a result of "an incompletely realized democracy that racializes" have generated specific modes of expression that foreground death and suffering. These preoccupations are the basis, as it were, of a black countertradition. Such a turn to death and suffering emphasizes the narratives of loss, exile, and journey that organize a sense of consciousness of the racial group. These stories which, find their content in the horrors of slavery, become constituting narratives and define the borders of a community of sentiment and interpretation. In light of these claims, Gilroy then offers a view of tradition: "an irreducibly modern, ex-centric, unstable, and asymmetrical cultural ensemble that cannot be apprehended through the manichaean logic of binary coding."[43] Tradition is now the living memory of the changing same, not a home for the articulation of the desire for cultural and racial purity.

As Gilroy challenges particularistic conceptions of black identity, the specificity and dynamism of black life return. He attempts to find a point of mediation between two extreme ways of thinking about black cultural practices: static essentialism and free-floating universalism. Neither of these views can provide an adequate account of the centrality of black experiences in shaping the modern world. One loses sight of the ebb and flow of historical encounter that constitutes hybrid cultures. The other obscures the very specific experiences that, in some significant way, differentiate peoples. In the case of black people in the United States, the terror and suffering of slavery and racial subjugation are lost in the fog of universalism.

But how do we think about this diverse but central set of black experiences that helped shaped the modern world? How does Gilroy stave off the driving force of narrow and vulgar nationalisms? He offers his concept of the black Atlantic. In his discussion of black cultures, Gilroy emphasizes the roots and routes of exchange in the production of black cultural practices. He discusses how the dualistic structures that put Africa in opposition to the Americas are no longer viable given the two-way exchanges that mark the diaspora. In this view, to talk about black American music, for example, as if it grows indigenously (without influence) on the soil of the United States is to slip into a purist conception of the cultural artifact.

Black cultures are the result of untidy intermixtures that betray attempts to ground them in any authentic source.

The idea of the black Atlantic requires, then, a different conception of tradition. In light of the claim that all black cultures result from the crossroads that is the diasporic experience, tradition can no longer function within the narrow boundaries of a specific territory. "It may make sense to try and reserve the idea of tradition for the nameless, evasive, minimal qualities that make these diaspora conversations possible. This would involve keeping the term as a way to speak about the apparently magical processes of connectedness that arise as much from the transformation of Africa by diaspora cultures as from the affiliation of diaspora cultures to Africa and the traces of Africa that those diaspora cultures enclose."[44] In this passage, the ambiguities of tradition are transferred onto "apparently magical processes"—processes that are unnamable and evasive. The passage also fails to provide some clue as to how we return to specific places in the diaspora that have determinate traditions that speak of specific or particular experiences.

In the effort to hold off what he calls ethnic absolutism, where the boundaries of black culture are hermetically sealed, Gilroy seems to overstate his case or, at least, lose sight of the specificities within the roots and routes of black cultural exchange. His emphasis on the "untidy elements of hybridization" that constitute black cultures does not necessarily lead to an abandonment of talk of traditions within specific territories. It does not follow from the recognition of the fact that cultures are hybrid that talk of traditions must be displaced onto a magical field of diasporic conversation. This does not amount to a harsh criticism of Gilroy. It stands only as a caveat that we must make room within our formulations for a return to the local. Put simply: most people don't live diasporic lives. They live locally through traditions that refract the varieties of influences into specific identities.

The freedom celebrations used tradition "neither to identify a lost past nor to name a culture of compensation that would restore access to it."[45] Yet, through the public reenactment of stories of bondage, suffering, and deliverance, a specific community—dare I say a national community— was constituted. One could read these events in light of broader discussions of modernity and, subsequently, as illustrations of the circulation and mutation of meanings in the black Atlantic. But the one point pressing itself onto the page is that these celebrations produced a specific community with a particular set of concerns.

Speakers at the August 1 celebrations acknowledged the explicit exchange of meaning between the West Indies and the United States. These meanings were, however, reconfigured within the stories that called forth memories of slavery and deliverance in the United States.[46] The memories which produced sentiments of solidarity that enabled the production of vocabularies of desire linked to emancipation, citizenship, and autonomy did not rely on a static conception of tradition. The dramaturgy of the communal performance, the tension between American and black identity (what I have called a structure of ambivalence), and the practices of the everyday seemed to revel in the problematized, transformative character of blackness (understood here as a social [and real] matter, not a biological fact). The discussion of tradition in this context does not necessitate the turn to the broader canvas of the black diaspora. Rather, its use in these celebrations directs our attention to a fungible and more mobile conception of nation language and black identity, one based in a pragmatic notion of racial solidarity.

PART TWO

Exodus Politics

Away back in the days of bondage they thought to see in one divine
event the end of all doubt and disappointment; few men ever worshipped
Freedom with half such unquestioning faith as did the American Negro
for two centuries. To him, so far as he thought and dreamed, slavery was
indeed the sum of all villainies, the cause of all sorrow, and the root of
prejudice; Emancipation was the key to a promised land of sweeter
beauty than ever stretched before the eyes of wearied Israelites.

W. E. B. DU BOIS

When it is acknowledged that under the disguise of dealing with ultimate
reality, philosophy has been occupied with the precious values embedded
in social traditions, that it has sprung from a clash of social ends and
from a conflict of inherited institutions with incompatible contemporary
tendencies, it will be seen that the task of future philosophy is to clarify
men's ideas as to the social and moral strifes of their own day. Its aim is
to become so far as is humanly possible an organ for dealing with
these conflicts.

JOHN DEWEY

6

→←

The Initial Years of the
Black Convention Movement

By the early 1800s the fervor of the revolutionary age was waning, and Americans groped for some sense of national cohesiveness. The fourth of July became the day to rekindle the patriotism of the Revolution and to tell the story of America's commitment to freedom and liberty. Ironically, the celebration of the fourth called attention to the contradiction inherent in the practice of America's ideals. Free blacks were not allowed to participate in most of the celebrations. Even as distant spectators, their presence called into question the very meaning of America's past and present. The fourth became one of the most menacing days of the year for free blacks in the North,[1] and it is precisely in the convergence of developing racialized and national identities that this racial violence took on so much force during the 1830s and 1840s.

The "July Days" of 1834 in New York City provide a case in point. A mob of merchants attacked an integrated Fourth of July gathering at Chatham Street Church. Amid rumors that the church condoned "amalgamation" by not segregating its pews, violence erupted and the church was burned to the ground. The mob refused to stop there. Reverend Peter Williams, pastor of St. Philip's African Episcopal Church on Center Street, had been accused of officiating at an interracial marriage. The raucous crowd invaded the church, destroying everything in sight and subsequently spilled over into the streets of Five Points. In an odd allusion to

Passover, the mob "demanded that white families illuminate their windows so that their race might be identified and their homes passed over; the mob would attack homes with darkened windows only."[2]

The fear of "amalgamation" fueled this violence, and this fear made sense in light of the developing science of race. By the first half of the nineteenth century, a number of racial theorists in the United States were prepared to defend the claim, pace environmentalism, that there were inherent, unchangeable differences between races. A source of this shift lay in the preoccupation of many nineteenth-century writers with national identity and uniqueness, an interest that would come to dominate Europe and the United States in the 1850s. The idea of a white national subject, distinct in kind from blacks, provided the discursive backdrop, differentiating the races in terms of biological essences rather than environmental accidents, and this gave the threat of amalgamation its power. This convergence of violence and science during the July riots spoke directly to efforts to consolidate an American national character, for the elaboration of national character during the fourth of July celebration was in lock step with the classification of races.[3] The threat of amalgamation then was a not-so-coded way of constituting national identities through difference and, if necessary, violence.

The specter of violence and its relation to death and suffering is crucial if we are to understand the distinctive uses of nation language in the political rhetoric of early nineteenth-century black Americans. The violence of persons and knowledge circumscribed the life chances of free blacks in the North while traditional forums of political and legal redress remained, for the most part, unavailable. Violence and its potentially deadly consequences were constitutive of the horizons within which African Americans produced and reproduced political and social identities. No one could escape the potential threat: black skin linked one inextricably to modes of expression that drew on what Cornel West[4] describes as the "ur-text" of black cultural expression—guttural moans and cries for home and recognition grounded in the persistent violence of antebellum America.

This threat of violence—along with what Paul Gilroy describes as the turn to death and suffering—places in the foreground particular narratives within which notions of solidarity and moral obligation are critical. As Gilroy notes, "the turn towards death points to the ways in which black cultural forms have hosted a dynamic rapport with the presence of death and suffering."[5] This rapport generated specific modes of expression that were antagonistic to what Gilroy sees as Enlightenment assumptions informing much of American public life. Because death and suffering were so integral to the stories of "loss, exile and journeying" that pervaded African American life, they served what Gilroy calls a mnemonic function, "directing the consciousness of the group back to significant, nodal points in its common history and its social memory."[6] As such, reiterative reference to these stories, Gilroy maintains, "plays a special role, organizing the consciousness of the racial group socially and striking the important balance between inside and outside activity—the different practices, cognitive, habitual, and performative, that are required to invent, maintain, and renew identity."[7] For him, this mnemonic function points to the "non-traditional tradition" that undergirds the black Atlantic: the site for the flux and flow of the living memory of the changing same (what Gilroy sees as a more acceptable understanding of tradition).

In chapter 5 I argued that Gilroy's use of the black Atlantic to block the essentialism and ethnic absolutism of local nationalisms was a bit premature. I suggested that the local produced and reproduced fungible and mobile conceptions of national identity that complicate how we understand tradition and the boundaries of the "racial" community. In short, the local, even in the hands of black nationalist ideologues, constitutes a more complex site for the production and reproduction of political and social identities. I take this issue up in more detail in chapter 7, where I explore the raging debate within the black community about the political efficacy of race language. But here I want to extend Gilroy's discussion of the turn toward death and suffering not in order to locate an idea of diaspora that avoids the pitfalls of essentialism, but instead to examine and illuminate a specific and quite different way in which nation language took hold in early nineteenth-century black political culture.

The looming presence of violence, suffering, and death transcodes broader discourses of national belonging. This transcoding is usually examined as simply a mirroring or an inevitable inversion of dominating discourses: African Americans either draw on the language of American democracy to articulate their notions of freedom, or they simply imagine a context in which whites are not relevant or in power. Although this mirroring actually occurs, a singular focus on either often obscures the different and transformative ways dominant discourses are transcoded. The turn toward death and suffering in black political languages highlights the violent disjunction between the ideals of America and its practice. Even though the use of ideals of democracy within the political articulations of African Americans recasts American ideals, the presence of violence, suffering, and death in the lives of blacks distinguishes, generally speaking, their use of the ideals from America itself. The origins of the difference lie in the inflamed condition of collective terror.

Let me be polemical for a moment to make the point clearer: To live under the threat of violence, to be subjected daily to various forms of humiliation, and to know that only those who look like you, regardless of class, experience this kind of humiliation and suffer this form of brutality create feelings of terror and uncertainty that necessitate forms of solidarity—cultural solidarity grounded in the experience of a violent, racist culture, not in any deep (and disturbing) ontological commitment to "the race." This solidarity often brought a sense of self-respect repeatedly denied in antebellum America and, for the most part, provided a ballast for African Americans' sense of their own moral and national identity: the sense of being a person and community of a particular kind, who lives and exists by some values rather than others.[8]

This is a critical point. The moral identity constituted under the conditions of violence, suffering, and death differentiate in real terms, in spite of the sameness of the rhetorical form, black America and white America. It points to the persistent and, in some cases, intractable gap between their form of life—one hostile to black Others—and African Americans' desire for freedom. Moreover, the relation of this violence and suffering to notions of solidarity and obligation are critical to the narratives that, to some degree, made antebellum black American practices intelligible. These stories, in particular Exodus, drew on the persistence of violence (that of Pharaoh and Egypt) to shore up the importance of thanksgiving, remembrance, and duty. They often provided the existential resources to answer the questions Why go on? What's the use? What is it all for?[9] In short, they defined the boundaries of inside and outside activity, of them and us.

This distinction has a direct bearing on the way we think about "black" publicity in the nineteenth century, particularly about the way antebellum blacks were able to engage in public deliberation about the matters that confronted them. I have maintained, following John Dewey, that publics are not simply spaces for the development of discursive opinion, but are formed in the problem-solving activity of securing some consequences and avoiding others. I have also suggested that they are sites for the formation and enactment of particular identities. Publics and participation in them, then, are not simply a matter of being able "to state propositional contents that are neutral with respect to a form of expression."[10] Rather, public participation and deliberation entail being able to give voice to one's experiences (one's doings and sufferings) and thereby construct and express a cultural identity—that is, a sense of solidarity with others who face similar problems and who struggle to overcome them.

Of course, biblical narrative, particularly Exodus, provided a large portion of the public vocabulary for African Americans of the period: the covenant, Egypt, the wilderness, and the promised land were tools in black public life that disclosed the violence, suffering, death, and hope so indicative of African American experiences. Reiterative reference to these stories helped organize a black American national public to confront the racial violence of the early nineteenth century. I call this effort a form of Exodus politics because the story, by direct or indirect reference, gave expression to what can be call the soul of the nation.[11] Its languages and images aided in the articulation of a tragic-comic disposition toward life in that the invocation of the story announced an ongoing struggle, with the help of a transcendent God active in history, against the realities of existence. Moreover, the story told of black America's sojourn and directed the consciousness of the group back to significant points in its common history, enabling, as it were, a constant renewal of community through social memory. Exodus politics, then, was based in a form of common complaint against oppression, a "hope against hope" for deliverance, a sense of obligation to and solidarity with those similarly situated, and the knowledge that the true test of American democracy rested with the nation's darker sons and daughters.

Exodus politics can be thought of as a form of criticism that pressures a given society to live up to its ideals. In effect, it is an appeal to principles announced at the nation's inception that somehow have been compromised by the choices of people. Such criticisms of the internal arrangements of the community (be they of the socioeconomic order or the manner of inclusion or exclusion, and so on) attempt to define the nature of the moral community and the kind of life to which it aspires. For antebellum African Americans, whose political languages were tied to a black Christian imagination, Exodus politics as common complaint stemmed from the idea that God ordered things and that his promised deliverance and grace mandated moral standards that stood in accordance with his law and action. As such, a deep-seated moralism characterized African American Exodus politics in the early nineteenth century, a politics that assumed, as Cornel West rightly notes, "that some ultimate morally grounded sense of justice ought to prevail in personal or society affairs."[12]

And, of course, this sense of justice, as many antebellum black leaders noted, could be found in the principles of American democracy.

Even as critique was brought to bear on various forms of social evils and visions for a more just society were offered, the prevalence of violence and suffering in African American life required an idea of hope (within Exodus politics) that could be sustained in spite of the persistence of evil. If this hope was to be based only in the actions of men and women then surely the road to despair would not have been long. Instead, a form of what can be called eschatological hope[13] was necessary for Exodus politics in black America. This "hope against hope" captured the commonsensical understanding that a radical transformation of American society was implausible and that "the nation might well succumb to the moral slobbism that has always threatened its existence from within."[14] Eschatological hope was grounded, then, in a regulative ideal toward which we aspire but which ultimately defies historical fulfillment. One hoped not for a heavenly kingdom on earth but, rather, that men and women would assume a prophetic stance—with an eye toward that kingdom beyond history—in which the evils of the world are seen as part of the exigencies of life, as challenges to confront and, with the help of God, overcome.

In this light, suffering could not overwhelm the spirit. Instead, it necessitated a response because suffering produced discernible hurt and pain in the lives of God's children.[15] Early nineteenth-century African American uses of Exodus politics commanded solidaristic efforts to resist suffering (to reject what David Walker called the habit of servility). It also imagined a future that did not consist in the violent subjugation of African Americans but, rather, one in which the principles of democracy extended to all.[16] Such a politics required ongoing conversation and critical reflection on the conditions of black collective life, and no other institutional effort in early nineteenth-century black politics filled this need more than the National Negro Convention Movement.

PHASE ONE: THE EARLY YEARS, 1830–1835

In 1804 and 1807 the Ohio legislature passed what came to be known as the Black Laws. These laws demanded that blacks entering the state prove that they were freemen and required them to post $500.00 bond to guarantee their lawful (good) behavior.[17] The laws were seldom enforced. But due to the exponential increase of the black population in Cincinnati between 1810 and 1820,[18] white Cincinnatians demanded that the laws on the books be enforced. Bowing to this pressure, the leaders of the city announced their intention to enforce the codes. The black population asked for a delay and petitioned the Ohio legislature to repeal the acts. The white citizens of Cincinnati, however, had little patience with delay, and a crowd about three hundred in number launched an attack on black neighborhoods, businesses, and persons. The riot lasted for three days, leaving one black person dead and numerous others injured. Blacks fought back, however, killing one white rioter and wounding several others.

After the attack on "Bucktown" in Cincinnati and in view of the persistent violence against free blacks in the North, many thought it time to convene a national meeting to address the escalating issues facing the community. Blacks throughout the North rallied in support of the roughly twelve hundred to fourteen hundred persons[19] who fought the white mobs of Cincinnati during the three-day attack. It could not escape the attention of most that the nation was becoming uneasy: that the pangs of national adolescence increased racial tensions. Many African Americans, a number of them from Cincinnati, sought to leave the country. They looked to Haiti. Some found a suitable place of refuge in Canada. All, if they remained in the United States, faced the unenviable task of being black, "living black," in the Age of Jackson.

The first stage of the national black convention movement began here—in between the racial terror of Jacksonian mobs and the expressed desire to "do something" about the circumstances of free blacks in the North. So, on September 20, 1830, the first national black convention was convened in Philadelphia (the site of a relatively mild racial riot on November 22, 1829). On the agenda were emigration, opposition to the American Colonization Society, and issues of education and self-help.

The 1830 convention was, to some extent, the first national forum for civic activity among northern free blacks in the United States. Although members of the AME and AMEZ churches[20] competed over the convention, religious denominations did not determine who would participate. Local black leaders of any ilk attended. This is not to diminish the significance of independent black churches and the kind of civic activity they generated. Far from it. In fact, the convention movement stood as a secular adjunct of the black church,[21] an extension into a broader public space of the black religious impulse of self-reliance and social uplift. Its uniqueness, though, centered around the very democratic process of debate and repeated exchange that the convention formalized—that flood of talk, argument, and analysis so central to Exodus politics.[22] For on the floors of these conventions, ordinary, and some extraordinary, men (and this was a decidedly male endeavor) debated the future of black America, and that conversation became the principal agency for black activism from 1830 up to the Civil War.[23]

There were two distinctive features of the conventions in the first stage: (1) an initial consideration of emigration as a viable political option and (2) the embrace of a politics of respectability. Both of these features reflected an outside-and-inside approach (within the convention movement) to the problems facing the free black community. The conventions consistently held, except for a brief period between 1836 and 1842, a political stance in relation to the broader racial policies of the state. I want to call this the convention's outside approach. The delegates explicitly condemned the racist practices and laws of the state, and under certain conditions opted for emigration as a response to such practices yet under other circumstances vigorously pursued the franchise. In any case, a politics in relation to the American nation-state was a constitutive part of the convention movement's efforts.

The inside approach focused more on the development of group solidarity and sustained self-critique and improvement. Issues of education, temperance, and economic self-sufficiency were considered key elements in the fight against social misery and racism. Thus, each convention concerned itself with a politics of respectability, that is to say, a strategy of reform directed at the members of the black community and an effort to sustain conversation among themselves about the problems facing them. Of course, these approaches overlap. In the case of the former, the politics is about us but is principally concerned with state power. The insider orientation, however, is all about us and only secondarily about the state.

Such a distinction is necessary,[24] I believe, because most traditional histories of black nationalisms tend to focus only on the politics as they related to the state. According to these stories, uses of nation language are best understood in the context of an opposition to the practices of the U.S. nation-state or as an effort to form a separate political state for blacks. Even the narratives that focus on the importance of the cultural retrieval of a buried national identity assume this process as a politics in the traditional sense of the word, that is, as a ground for a challenge to state power. By my reading of the convention movement, however, there is another way of understanding African American uses of nation language: as a cultural notion that draws its power from efforts to generate a conversation among black Americans about the problems facing them. It is not so much a nationalist politics in the sense of a challenge to political power by a nation with an explicit and peculiar character as a commonly held sense of group distinctiveness—an ambiguously rich notion of "we-ness." I distinguish the two approaches, then, only to call attention to the different registers at which ideas of we-ness and we-intentions operate.

THE OUTSIDE-INSIDE . . . THE STATE AND US

Because the convention movement began as a response to the precipitous violence of white mobs, the first convention's principal preoccupation was with the issue of emigration to Canada. This was made abundantly clear in the preamble to the constitution of the first national meeting:

> In conformity to a resolution of the Delegates of Free persons of Colour, in General Convention Assembled, in the City of Philadelphia, September 20th, 1830, recommending the formation and establishment of a Parent Society in the City of Philadelphia, for the purpose of purchasing land, and locating a settlement in the Province of Upper Canada; and to which all other Societies formed for that purpose, may become auxiliary.[25]

The conventions of 1831 and 1832 also understood emigration as one of their primary concerns. The turning point, however, was the debate over the issue at the convention of 1832.

Thomas D. Coxsin of Gloucester County, New Jersey, introduced a resolution on the floor of the convention. He wanted the delegates to consider the purchase of lands in the Upper Province of Canada as a permanent home for black Americans, if and when they were compelled to move from the United States.[26] The resolution sparked heated debate and was subsequently sent to a committee of seven[27] charged with writing a response to the resolution that represented the arguments on the floor as well as to generate a general policy position for the convention. What resulted was a six-page report that included a brief history of the question before the convention and an interesting revision of the positions of the 1830 and 1831 national meetings.

Both of these conventions had held the view that a colony in the Upper Province of Canada was a viable political option that required the financial and philosophical support of the national meeting. Bishop Richard Allen, the venerable Methodist preacher who forty years earlier had been removed from St. George's Church during prayer, spoke directly to this issue in his address to the African American community: "[T]he formation of a settlement in the British province of Upper Canada would be a great advantage to the people of colour. In accordance with these views, we pledge ourselves to aid each other by all honourable means, *to plant and support one in that country,* and therefore we earnestly and most feelingly appeal to our coloured brethren, and to all philanthropists here and elsewhere, to assist in this benevolent and important work."[28] Clearly the position of the 1830 convention was to found a colony and provide support for those persons who felt compelled to leave the United States. They even solicited the aid of artisans to help erect buildings and advertised the colony as an advantage to large families, to students who desired advancement, and to anyone who sought a future of prosperity. In effect it was an active embrace, due to the violence of law and of persons, of emigration.

The 1831 convention echoed this position. As the group that formally organized the convention movement, the delegates stated unequivocally their support for Canadian settlement. A spirit of persecution was the cause of their convention, they contended; it was that violence which first induced them to seek an asylum in the Canadas. And they were happy to report to the free black community that their efforts were not in vain.

> Our prospects are cheering; our friends and funds are daily increasing; wonders have been performed far exceeding our most sanguine expectations: already have our brethren purchased eight hundred acres of land—and two thousand of them have left the soil of their birth, crossed the lines, and laid the foundation for a structure which promises to prove an asylum for the coloured population of these United States. . . . We therefore ask of you, brethren . . . to assist us in this undertaking. We look to a kind Providence, and to you, to say whether our desires shall be realized, and our labours crowned with success.[29]

Emigration, then, was a real option. The convention laid the foundation. But the debate in 1832 would foreshadow a significant shift in the convention movement's position, and by 1833 the convention would no longer actively seek to establish a colony in the Upper Province of Canada.

The committee of seven began its report with three basic questions: (1) Is it proper for the free people of color in this country, under existing circumstances, to remove to any distant territory beyond the United

States? (2) Does Upper Canada possess superior advantages and conveniences to those held out in these United States or elsewhere? (3) Is there any certainty that the people of color will be compelled by oppressive legislative enactments to abandon the land of their birth for a home in a distant region?[30] The committee recognized the dangerous position of the African American community, slave or free, in the United States. They went as far as to claim that the situation of blacks was more precarious than it had been at any other period since the Declaration of Independence.[31] But they rejected (in principle) the idea of emigration.

The committee argued that to support the founding of a colony would necessitate the end of all of their efforts for intellectual and political advancement in the United States. It would be tantamount to abandoning the possibility—however remote it appeared—of living in the United States as truly free men and women. Moreover, they claimed that "to colonize our people beyond the limits of these United States, tend[ed] to weaken the situation of those who [were] left behind, without any peculiar advantage to those who emigrate[d]."[32] The committee reaffirmed its commitment to address domestic problems and recommended to the convention that a more vigorous effort be made to secure funds for the struggle to advance the interest of the black community in the United States.

The committee agreed, however, that Canada did offer, in spite of the reported cases of prejudice and the efforts of some white Canadians to prevent the general influx of people of color into the province, some advantages to African Americans who wished to leave the United States. Given the racial climate of the country, they could not deny that the Upper Province offered a refuge from the rising tide of violence, particularly since they could not guarantee that the nation would not pass legislation to expel the free black population. The committee ended with a muddled position.

Emigration would not be actively pursued. Instead, all efforts would be made to enhance the life-chances of the black population in this country. And despite claiming it inexpedient for the convention to purchase lands in Upper Canada, they would continue to raise funds to aid those who may choose to emigrate to the province.[33] The 1832 debate marked the beginnings of a significant shift in the focus of the convention movement. They were beginning to direct more of their attention to the other feature of the movement: issues of moral and mental improvement (features of the inside approach).

Alongside the issue of emigration to Canada stood what Evelyn Brooks Higginbotham calls a politics of respectability. This politics stressed the reform of "individual behavior and attitudes both as a goal in itself and as a strategy for reform of the entire structural system of American race relations."[34] Black folk were urged to embrace temperance, to work hard, and, in short, to assume a general sense of self-regulation and self-improvement along moral, educational, and economic lines.[35] This would provide a point of departure for addressing the racial policies of the nation-state. The delegates understood that through moral living, education, and economic self-sufficiency the lives of African Americans would be improved, and thus they would be elevated "to a proper rank and standing among men."[36] They would be, in effect, worthy of respect.

But over and beyond the issue of how black people were perceived by the larger public was the effort to sustain a conversation among blacks about their well-being. How do we improve our lot? What must we do to correct the ills in our community? These questions were also at the root of the conventions' politics of respectability. They emanated from a genuine concern about the life-chances of African Americans in a world seemingly arrayed against them. They served as organizing principles in the formation of independent black churches, mutual relief associations, and literary societies. As the 1832 conventional address suggested, such concerns were at the heart of the "awakening spirit in our people to promote their elevation, which speaks volumes in their behalf."[37]

What deserves examination here are the protean features of this politics, particularly its fluid ability to move between ideological extremes, that is, between a conservative and a radical position. This may speak more broadly to the slippery character of a nation-based politics and its tendency to stand on the cusp of a conservative and a progressive vision for "the people." But for my purposes, it speaks directly to two different inflections within the politics of respectability itself: the privatization of racial discrimination and an immanent conversation about racial discrimination and its effects. The former located, as best it could, the problem of racism outside government regulation[38] and placed it in a private domain with public implications. The thinking went something like this: if we changed our attitudes and behavior then we could command the respect of others. In this view, the problems lay with our slothfulness and intemperance. We need only correct this "impoverished" way of living and the difficulties facing the community would inevitably disappear. The latter responded to the problem of racism by accenting the agency of black people, insisting that they were capable of responding, through self-critique and improvement, to the problems facing the black community. This immanent conversation constituted a call of sorts for solidaristic efforts to reject white paternalism and to alleviate the condition of black people in general.

Michael Walzer's view of political education and civic participation in Exodus politics illustrates the need to make this distinction within a politics of respectability. He suggests that it is in the wilderness that the Israelites acquired some sense of the rights and obligations of citizenship and actually used their newly acquired civic tools. For Walzer, these activities extend in somewhat different directions. Political education begins prior to the formation of the covenant. Civic participation occurs afterwards—and rightly so. Prior to the covenant, the Israelites were not properly aware of themselves as free and equal moral agents. They remained, in spite of their massive resistance, caught in the moral and psychological webs of Egyptian oppression.

The slavishness learned in Egypt takes two forms. First, the Israelites internalized a view of themselves as defeated. They were passive toward, or better, subservient to their Egyptian masters. Indeed they were weighed down by oppression, crushed and frightened.[39] This is not to suggest that Egyptian slavery was successful in obliterating any Israelite desire for freedom. "They still possessed some idea of themselves as free or potentially free men and women."[40] But it does acknowledge the fact that the legacies of Egyptian bondage hindered the development among the Israelites of certain qualities necessary for freedom and citizenship.

Second, the Israelites had what can be thought of as an Egyptian idea of freedom.[41] Freedom was understood in terms of a lack of responsibility that was a part of their existence as slaves: slavery required nothing but work and servile obedience. As such, "[t]he Israelites could become free only insofar as they accepted the discipline of freedom, the obligation to live up to a common standard and to take responsibility for their own actions."[42] Most feared this responsibility and resented the demands of the law and of mutual obligation.

Walzer describes two sorts of responses to these two forms of slavishness. One states that the liberation of the oppressed will require an act of God or the heroic energy of a vanguard group. The other believes that liberation will be achieved, to some degree, by the oppressed or "at least be the work of the oppressed themselves.[43] The vanguard view holds that the people are too enamored of their masters to be capable of liberating

themselves. They need in effect a revolutionary cadre who will lift them
up out of their condition and show them the true path to liberation and
freedom. The latter reading, what Walzer calls a social-democratic reading, stresses the indirection of the march itself and the educative role of
the wilderness, that is, the back-and-forth process of the spiritual and political escape from Egypt: The "people's simultaneous willingness and un-
willingness to put Egypt behind them" makes the achievement of liberty
a more gradual process, requiring ongoing education that culminates in
the formation of the covenant.

   This distinction between a vanguard and a social-democratic reading
of Exodus helps us, I believe, understand the difference between the two
inflections within a politics of respectability. Proponents of one view seek
racial uplift but see the people as downtrodden, incapable of liberating
themselves. The other understands that freedom requires a cooperative
effort and a stern discipline among fellows if they are to take on responsibility for the community (recall David Walker's urgings in chapter 2). But
neither is possible without the initial commitment to take charge of themselves. There is a sort of "secular" refusal: an attempt to define themselves
apart from the gaze of Egypt. That is to say, the Israelites—read black
folk—engage in self-determining acts to live up to a common standard
and to take responsibility for their actions. These two features within Exodus itself, then, distinguish two kinds of politics despite their underlying
similarity.

   For example, both tendencies within the politics of respectability took
the issues of education, temperance, and economic self-sufficiency to be
crucial steps toward eventual freedom. Indeed the convention movement's embrace of each of these elements, in a context that characterized
black people (with the authority of science) as biologically inferior, was
truly subversive and, to some extent, a necessary feature of the movement's politics.[44] The delegates were well aware of the scientific assaults
on black intelligence and black beauty (on black humanity in general) and
quite cognizant of the way impoverished and illiterate blacks were pointed
to as evidence for such claims. Mere ignorance, the convention argued,
was no just criterion for the intellectual capacity of a people. "[I]t has
actually been seen, in various remarkable instances, that the degradation
of the mind and character, which has been too hastily imputed to a people
kept, as we are, at a distance from those sources of knowledge which
abound in civilized and enlightened communities, has resulted from no
other causes than our unhappy situation and circumstances."[45] Educa-

tion, temperance, and self-help, then, were understood as weapons against racial science. And as features of a politics of respectability, they signified the need for self-esteem and racial solidarity if "the people" were to overcome social misery and racism.[46]

Yet, this same politics stood as a complicitous embrace of American society's norms of manners and morals, disclosing, as Higginbotham suggests, class and status differences within the group.[47] On this reading, the black elite espoused a politics of respectability to secure its place as a middle class. Here moral reform, particularly temperance, took on symbolic value: a way of distinguishing a proper middle and a degraded lower in which religious piety, order, and cleanliness were the critical terms of differentiation.[48]

This emphasis on moral reform also defined the roles of black men and women in the work of elevating the race, for certain conceptions of gender roles informed this middle-class ideology of racial uplift. I have already mentioned that the convention movement did not allow women to participate. Not until the 1840s were women allowed to engage in public deliberation in this particular arena. Instead, black women's efforts were located in what Carla Peterson calls the domestic sphere of black society.[49] Their obligations defined them as laborers in the household and as bearers and nurturers of the nation's future. Here we see early on the trope of the woman as the nation and her sanctity as central to a particular kind of national imaginary. In fact, for some proponents of the politics of respectability, the ideas of black manhood and moral reform were crucial components of any effort to acquire freedom. Black manhood, of course, characterized those who were self-assertive and independent, capable of leading and protecting their families and, if need be, the nation. Think of Walker's passionate cry: "Are we men!!—I ask you, O my Brethren! Are we men?!" The values of manhood emanated from a comportment with what can be seen as a set of bourgeois values indicative of civilized Christian living. Manhood and moral reform disciplined the activities of black women with such notions as "protection" and "true womanhood."

Even when black women embraced the politics of respectability, their public activities were circumscribed by the actions of black men. Black men somehow had to sanction women's efforts in order for their voices to have public meaning. But as Maria Stewart and many anonymous church women engaged in reform, creating institutions for the indigent, their activities constituted another public. Indeed, the participation of black women in the politics of respectability challenged implicitly and sometimes explicitly how black men's imaginings of the community and their attendant conceptions of moral obligwation constrained the differences (even at the level of terror) within the community itself. Maria Stewart's justification for her public activity, for example, not only indicated her divine calling to act in public but also implicitly critiqued black men for their failure to act courageously on behalf of black people. She told of her calling: "Who shall go forward and take off the reproach that is cast upon the people of color? asked a voice from within, "Shall it be a woman?" And my heart made this reply—"If it [be] thy will, be it even so, Lord Jesus!"[50] But, for the most part, early nineteenth-century black women (even Stewart) embraced the politics of respectability and reproduced the middle-class norms of gender, the body, and sexual behavior that helped distinguish a proper middle and a degraded lower.

It is important to note, however, that the totalizing tendency of America's racist discourse lumped all black people together regardless of class or gender. Black skin was the mode of identification. And racial science did not give any attention to wealth or the manner of comportment among black elites: all were naturally inferior. Given this context, the desire for respectability of an aspiring black middle class demanded that the entire race make itself respectable. Thus, black middle-class aspirations were couched in a discourse of racial uplift and solidarity,[51] accenting the private dimensions of racial discrimination.

Nothing could make clearer the close connection between this bourgeois aspiration and respectability than the convention movement's position with regard to the public processions of the freedom celebrations. The early conventions' policies did not favor public parades at any time because they saw them as embarrassments, shameful displays, as it were, of the backwardness of the race.[52] The delegates to the 1831 convention went as far as to state in their rules and regulations: "the Convention recommends to the People of Colour throughout the United States, the discontinuance of public processions on any day, considering it as highly injurious to our interests as a people."[53] In light of the widespread popularity of these public gatherings it's not difficult to discern a slight tension between "our interest" and "the people."

As Samuel Cornish and John Russwurm had four years earlier, the delegates to the early conventions observed the behavior of the "common" folk at these public festivals and feared the ultimate demise of the race.[54] The unnecessary expenditures on costumes and, of course, the drinking and dancing made the community, in the words of Cornish and Russwurm, objects of shame as well as the laughing stock of the country. For these men, thrift and morality were set aside at these festivals, and a sort of contagion of decadence threatened to infect all free black people.

There seemed to be one moment of disagreement. During the morning session of the 1834 convention in New York, a strong denunciation of public parades was placed before the delegates.

> Whereas, it is the duty of this Convention, to guard the general interest of the coloured community of this country; and whereas, it is conceived that all vain expenditures of time and pomp in dress, are deleterious in their effects, inasmuch as they tend to impoverish us, and to increase the prejudice and contempt of the whites. Therefore, Resolved, That we disapprove, will discountenance and suppress, so far as we have power or influence, the exhibition and procession usually held on the fifth day of July annually, in the city of New York; and all other processions of coloured people, not necessary for the interment of the dead.[55]

A spirited debate ensued during the afternoon session in which, apparently, one Mr. Brown (probably Joshua Brown of New York) defended the parades. But by the end of the debate Mr. Brown changed positions, stating magnanimously that he recognized, after extended conversation with his colleagues, the error of his participation in public processions and would have nothing more to do with them. The resolution passed.[56]

The public parades continued. I suppose the common folk preferred their amusement. The parades grew in size and, during the West Indian Emancipation celebrations, were one of the more important features of the day. The failure of the convention movement to stop the festivals points to the disjunction between their interests as black elites aspiring to the middle class and the everyday expression of group solidarity and uplift.[57] They attempted to impose on all black folk their vision of racial improvement, a vision tied to a quest for respectability. And under such circumstances, it makes sense that their efforts to end the parades remained, for the most part, on an exhortatory level, for the festive parades were potent, ritualized populist critiques of white supremacy, a use of the carnivalesque in the solidaristic effort to fight racism.[58]

To distinguish this aspect of the politics of respectability from the demand for an immanent conversation is not easy. The call for racial solidarity and the rejection of white paternalism has served the ends of an aspiring elite class, whether those elites desired entree into mainstream American society or, full of *resentment,* aimed to establish a nation-state apart from the United States. Indeed, proponents of a politics of respectability and its ideology struggled to hold together their quests for freedom for all African Americans and their desires for bourgeois living. As Kevin Gaines rightly notes, the ideology of uplift "reflected popular and elite tensions: black folk religion and group aspirations for emancipation, landownership . . . and the suffrage contended with an elite, missionary culture of Christian evolutionism."[59]

But I believe this politics can be read another way: as a form of cultural politics that assumes the importance of self-determination. In the context of a people stigmatized by the institution of slavery and racial prejudice, the call for them to debate and analyze the issues facing them, regardless of the content of the call itself, directs our attention to black agency and the struggle of these folk to live in the world on their own terms (as complicated as that may be).[60] I have attempted to locate this cultural politics in the discourse of respectability because, in some ways, I am attempting to rethink the status of moral uplift talk in black historiography. It ought not to be understood only as a bourgeois politics or an imitation of white middle-class manners and morals. Instead, respectability can be seen as a form of "common sense"[61] that presupposes the need for racial solidarity in the face of overwhelming problems. The values of respectability, then, are to be seen as tools for problem-solving. Beyond that, I think, the other concerns are absolutely necessary. But if we focus only on the bourgeois dimensions of this politics, we lose sight of the very fluid conceptions of obligation and solidarity that inform much of its use in nineteenth-century racial politics. For slaves, former slaves, and "third-class" interlopers, respectability constituted a serious politics: the activity of a new nation composed of members willing to take care of themselves. Michael Walzer claims that "in Egypt, the Israelites are a 'people' insofar as they share the experience of oppression."[62] Pharaoh was the first to lump them together and identify them as a people. Their identity prior to liberation, then, was something that happened to them. Walzer maintains that it is "only with the covenant do they make themselves into a people in the strong sense, capable of sustaining a moral and political history, capable of obedience and also stiff-necked resistance, of marching forward and of sliding back."[63] Once the covenant is made the nation is set to fight against injustices, to right a historic wrong, and to strive for a better way of living. In short, the people are mobilized to pursue the covenantal promise. This promise, however, is contingent on the manner in which the people conduct themselves in their day-to-day lives (their ethical stance): "If ye will obey my voice indeed, and keep my covenant, then ye shall be a peculiar treasure unto me" (Exod. 19:5).Voluntary consent is crucial to this covenantal convening of the nation. It limits the role of elites, for consent must be obtained from ordinary people. If follows from this, in Walzer's view, that the individuals committed to the covenant are moral equals who take on the responsibility for the continuity of the covenant.[64]And this continuity requires ongoing debate, continued interpretation and reinterpretation through imaginative reenactments by all the people as individuals and as the nation.[65]

The convention movement's call for black people to address their problems extended the covenantal convening of the nation that began with the emergence of the independent black church. Like the children of Israel, they had lived and were living through Egypt, and the experience had constituted them as a peculiar, perhaps chosen, nation.[66] They were set to fight injustices, to right a historic wrong, and to strive for a better way of living. Now, the challenge they faced was with the direction of their struggle: would it be led by a vanguard group or would it be defined by an ongoing process—the back and forth efforts of all—to escape the spiritual and political legacies of Egypt?

7

⇥⇤

Respectability and Race

1835–1842

A fter only two years of national organization, the convention move-ment began to turn its attention away from emigration and focused almost exclusively on issues of moral reform, economics, and education. By 1833, the delegates rejected outright emigration to Canada as a viable political option, recommended the formation of temperance societies, en-couraged the pursuit of the "mechanical arts," and considered the estab-lishment of a high school on the manual labor system as well as a college in New Haven, Connecticut. During these years, the "outside" politics of the convention extended only to vague demands for universal liberty and downplayed efforts to acquire the franchise or found a colony. Instead the delegates focused on the evil of slavery and their messianic mission to purge the nation of this wrongdoing. The Declaration of Sentiment of the 1834 national meeting clearly stated the convention's position. It framed the convention's efforts in moral terms: "we rejoice that we are thrown into a revolution where the contest is not for landed territory, but for free-dom; the weapons not carnal, but spiritual; where struggle is not for blood, but for right."[1] For some of the convention's participants, the battle for religious and civil liberty and equality among men amounted to a moral struggle between good and evil in which every American citizen and Christian, regardless of color, should fight. African Americans, in particular, played a special role in this spiritual battle.

[I]f our presence in this country will aid in producing . . . a desirable reform, although we have been reared under a most debasing system of tyranny and oppression, we shall have been born under the most favourable auspices to promote the redemption of the world; for our very sighs and groans, like the blood of martyrs, will prove to have been the seed of the church; for they will freight the air with their voluminous ejaculations, will be borne upwards by the power of virtue to the great Ruler of Israel, for deliverance from this yoke of merciless bondage.[2]

The analogy to the Israelites remained. America was still Egypt. But the delegates' primary focus was now on the internal dimension of the struggle: the moral character of the community, black and white.

By 1835 this focus was the official policy of the convention. The issue of moral reform was embraced as a strategy for the improvement of all human beings regardless of "complexional distinctions." The 1835 convention recommended that "as far as possible, . . . our people . . . abandon the use of the word 'colored,' when either speaking or writing concerning themselves; and especially to remove the title of African from their institutions, the marbles of churches, etc."[3] This turn to moral reform and rejection of racial language led to the controversial transmutation of the convention movement, for after 1835 and up until 1842, it would be known as the American Moral Reform Society (AMRS).

The AMRS provides a critical example of the difference between the reduction of racial discrimination to the private sphere and the call for an immanent conversation about racism. The society, like the earliest conventions, took the issues of education, temperance, and economic self-sufficiency as its rallying points. A politics of respectability, then, was at the heart of its efforts. The society also rejected any use of complexional distinctions in the determination of its policies. The delegates saw themselves as working for universal liberty and the moral elevation of human beings in general. This rejection of race language resulted in a complicated and somewhat muddled set of responses to the condition of African Americans in the mid-1830s and 1840s, making it almost impossible to call for an immanent conversation among black people about issues facing their community.

But the society used racial designations in 1836. In fact, most of its efforts were directed toward the "colored population."[4] The delegates called for auxiliaries to adopt efficient measures to educate black children.

They supported the Gerrit Smith, Esq., school. Like the participants in the early conventions, they condemned processions by black people generally, including funeral processions. The delegates also asked "colored" persons who were servants to aid in the elevation of all by cultivating in their employers an "obliging disposition" toward the race. Why then this apparent contradiction? Why reject "complexional distinctions" when the society's primary concern was with people of color? One answer lies in the AMRS's effort to respond to the new science of race.

RACE AND SCIENCE

During the 1830s and 1840s a significant shift occurred in scientific discussions of human difference. The hegemony of eighteenth-century environmental accounts of human variation was widely attacked by a number of racial theorists who were prepared to defend the notion that racial differences were inherent and unchangeable. This shift was tied not only to the emergence of a proslavery defense in the face of abolitionism, to the processes of industrialization and the class tensions they unleashed, but also to a differentiation between theological or religious discourse about nature and the sedimentation of a nontheological, empirical knowledge of nature. What resulted was a removal of moral questions from the soon-to-be "value-neutral" claims of science.[5]

The notion that human difference was inherent and unchangeable challenged the orthodox Christian conception of the unity of man. In the Christian view, God had created Adam and Eve, our original and common ancestors. The human race had descended through the family of Noah. And from this, biblical scholars calculated the approximate beginning of Creation. Defenders of polygenetic accounts, however, refused to believe that the different-looking peoples of the world in their different stages of civilization could have the same ancestors. The roots of this refusal lay in eighteenth-century developments in scientific classification—that is, in "taxonomies in the form of tables, catalogs, indexes, and inventories which impose[d] some degree of order or representational schema on a broad field of visible characteristics."[6]

In the first half of the nineteenth century, particularly with the emergence of the American school of ethnology, these classificatory categories provided new data to justify claims of the separate origins of the races and, in particular, the inherent inequality of all races in comparison to the white race. The publication of Dr. Samuel Morton's *Crania Americana* in

1839, for example, offered a theory of the permanent difference between the races by classifying the various sizes of human skulls. According to Morton, no significant variation existed between the ancient crania of a given race and its modern descendants. Skull size and, by implication, mental capacity for any given race remained constant.[7] Of course, proponents of slavery and racism interpreted Morton's conclusions as evidence for the inherent inferiority of black folk and, for some, his conclusions even pointed to the existence of pre-Adamite races.

To get a sense of the popular currency of racial classification in the first half of the nineteenth century one must turn to the popularization of phrenology and the ascendancy of statistics in the United States. Phrenology originated in the work of Franz Joseph Gall and was later developed by Johann Gaspar Spurzheim in the early nineteenth century. Both argued that the brain was separated into different faculties and that each had a specific function. Some controlled our emotions, others our capacity to reason. These faculties, they contended, could be assessed by an examination of the skull. Depending on the size of one's head, a trained phrenologist could determine human tendencies toward criminality, abstract thinking or, possibly, eroticism.

In the 1820s and 1830s phrenology was widely accepted in the United States. George and Andrew Combe and the *Phrenological Journal*, founded in Edinburgh in 1823, helped popularize the field in the United States.[8] They argued for the importance of genetic inheritance, stressed the different "cerebral development" of the races, and upheld the Caucasian race, particularly the Anglo-Saxon branch, as an example of perfect cerebral organization. By the 1840s, however, most of the findings of phrenology were widely disputed. Dividing the brain into separate spheres to determine mental characteristics was no longer an acceptable practice. But the belief that racial classifications told us something definite about the inherent differences between the races remained a central feature of racial science.

What's interesting about phrenology is not so much its sudden rise and fall within the discourse of science but, rather, what happened to it once it fell into disrepute. After the 1840s most phrenologists wrote for popular audiences, and these writings were a vehicle for the mass dissemination of the assumptions of racial classification. Practical phrenology became a fad in the 1840s, and those interested in its commercial potential exploited for profit the field's assumptions of innate racial differences.[9] This "science" flourished as a micro-industry. Phrenological handbooks, lecture tours, charts, and in some places examination houses extended the basic terms of phrenology to a common language about racial difference.

The ascendancy of statistics serves as another example of the common currency of racial classification and difference during this period. More specifically, the census of 1840 and its conclusions about free blacks in the North provide an excellent illustration of the role of classification in racism. Prior to the 1820s and 1830s, the use of statistics was quite rare. But during the Age of Jackson a number of different types of quantitative documents and materials suddenly appeared. Americans saw themselves as a peculiar people with an innate skill with numbers, and the 1840 census was viewed as a task that would unite this calculating people in proud contemplation of their country.[10]

As it turned out, the census was an absolute failure. Patricia Cline Cohen and others[11] have noted that the census was fraught with errors and difficulties from the moment of its inception. In its nationalistic fervor, Congress had expanded the scope of the census to capture the grandeur of American progress and made it almost impossible to complete the task successfully. Moreover, people in the different parts of the nation refused to answer the census questions. They were suspicious of the aims of the census-takers. Printers also haggled over the publishing rights to the final document. But the most controversial problem was the finding that the black population in the North suffered epidemic rates of insanity, leading some to conclude, with the authority of scientific tables and figures, that freedom for blacks led to insanity.[12]

The errors of the census were hotly debated until the 1850s. Nothing came of the exchanges, however. Proslavery ideologues such as John C. Calhoun drew on the census to counter domestic and foreign arguments for abolition. The census provided scientific evidence against black emancipation, and in the minds of many the numbers could not lie. Few challenged them.[13] At the root of the census errors lay the inability of Jacksonians to think or move beyond racism. Their own racial identities prevented them from asking any critical questions about their science.[14]

But the appeal to quantitative arguments marked a significant shift in the slavery debate and the issue of race. Cohen notes that "in the 1830s, abolitionists and their opponents for the most part stood on moral and emotional grounds in their arguments, with personal testimony about slavery the backbone of their proof."[15] After the early 1840s, however, numbers were increasingly the weapon of choice, so much so that "the growing use of statistics to defend or attack slavery paralleled the emergence of slavery as a central and acknowledged political issue."[16] Moral arguments were now opposed by the authority of science and its numbers, and the task of many black leaders of the period was to keep the moral issues in the foreground. They had to stand in the way of the redescription of moral matters into matters of physiology and into a value-neutral numbers game.

THE AMERICAN MORAL REFORM SOCIETY AND RACE

In his 1837 address to the American people, William Whipper, a participant in the early conventions and principal spokesman for the AMRS, spoke directly to the issue of racial science and what can be called early nineteenth-century "race-based" politics. He bluntly condemned those who viewed blacks as inferior and argued that all human beings were made in the image of God: "If there be those who doubt that we are made in the image of God, and are endowed with those attributes which the Deity has given to man, we will exhibit [to] them our hands and side."[17] He then echoed the sentiment of the 1835 convention—that all racial and geographic distinctions should be rejected in the effort to respond to the new racial science and its prejudices. Subsequently, Whipper and the AMRS relied on appeals to the Christian conscience of fellows for social and political reform.[18] In fact the appeal to Christians and the principles of Christianity became the major features of the society's politics.

Whipper's 1837 address, an explanation of sorts for the existence of the AMRS, captured all of these elements. He maintained that any "general assertion that superiority of mind is the natural offspring of a fair complexion, arrays itself against the experience of the past and present age, and both natural and physiological science."[19] Whipper confronted the new racial science with the environmentalism of the eighteenth century and with the idea of Christian benevolence so common to reformers of the early and mid–nineteenth century. For him, race was merely an effect of conditions of living and indicated little about the worth of human beings. Having placed their institutions on the ground of natural laws and human rights, Whipper and the members of the AMRS "buried in the bosom of Christian benevolence all those national distinctions [and] complexional variations that have hitherto marked the history, character and operations of men; and now boldly plead for the Christian and moral elevation of the human race."[20] Matters of racial prejudice, then, were not the purview of science and its numbers but instead questions of human rights and natural law. As such, the notion of human difference, particularly racial and national differences, had to be abandoned, for the idea of benevolence or love for man demanded it if God's grace were to be obtained.[21] As Whipper understood it, the organization's aim was "to procure the abolition of those hateful and unnecessary distinctions by which the human family has hitherto been recognized, and only desire that they may be distinguished by their virtues and vices."[22]

If we follow Whipper's arguments, the AMRS rejected race language for two distinctive reasons: (1) out of devotion to the universality of Christian principles and fellowship and (2) for pragmatic reasons. On one hand, Christian brotherhood collapsed all spurious distinctions between human beings into one fundamental notion: that all persons were children of God, made in his image. The nation needed only to return to its professed beliefs and escape "the evil in which she has fallen."[23] On the other hand, racial language, in their view, was becoming part of the problem, a tool for those who sought to do evil in the world by separating human beings into types rather than seeing them all as children of God. Thus, racial language had to be avoided; it no longer could address the problems facing people of color because "complexional" language was a major part of the problem of racism.

A vicious irony stood at the heart of the AMRS's position, however. Some of the major proponents of proslavery ideology (not necessarily defenders of racial science but certainly proponents of the natural inferiority of blacks) were white Christian clergymen, particularly the Congregationalists of New England. Threatened by the fervor of abolitionism, some of these clergymen laid a foundation for the proslavery positions that dominated the 1850s.[24] Joseph Tracey, a Congregationalist minister from Vermont and an avid supporter of colonization, rejected the idea that all men were created equal and argued that serious misunderstandings of this notion were at the heart of the traumas of modern man. The immediatism of the abolitionist, for Tracey, was equivalent to the French misreading of America's grand principles and, like the French revolution, would only lead to bloodshed. Charles Hodge, a Presbyterian minister and an influential figure at Princeton Theological Seminary, joined Tracey's condemnation of abolitionism as a threat to the republic. But he also extended the argument to include biblical sanctioning of the peculiar institution. For Hodge, the Bible did not condemn slavery as sinful; in fact, to argue that any defense of slavery was necessarily sinful directly contradicted the word of God.[25]

The delegates to the 1836 AMRS meeting were well aware of such positions among their fellow Christians. In response to these views the society commissioned a committee to draft a letter to the "professed followers of Jesus Christ."[26] The letter stands as a significant expression of the society's policies and a strident critique of the Christian community's complicity with regard to the evil of slavery.[27]

> We know that among the professed disciples of Christ, "the great majority"—to the reproach of the Christian name—do regard color as a material fact in estimating the moral quality of actions, or in deciding upon the merit of the doings of their fellow creatures; a fact so material that it is not infrequently known to weaken the cogency of an argument, invalidate the claims of suffering humanity, metamorphose truth into falsehood, cruelty and injustice into mercy and benevolence.[28]

Christian hypocrisy, then, aroused the committee's ire. No one could be a true Christian and hold the beliefs of the new racial science.

The letter refused the option of an environmentalist defense in which the hue of an individual's skin and his or her mental capabilities were determined by conditions and habits of living. Such a move was almost necessary, since many environmentalist accounts had conceded the fact that black inferiority was irreversible. The authors of the letter turned instead to the Bible, "to the infallible standard by which we are to ascertain the moral quality of the prejudice of which we have great cause to complain."[29] They argued that the new racial science, along with the practices it justified, was "contrary to the declared will of God, essentially repugnant in its nature to the mind that was in Christ (and which should be in us), and glaringly at variance, in the practice to which it necessarily leads to the course of conduct enjoined by the Savior."[30] White clergymen were then asked to live up to the dictates of the golden rule. If they could not or would not do this, the letter asked demandingly, would it not be sinful? The authors answered affirmatively.

> It is sinful because it cannot but work ill to its neighbour;—it is sinful because it unrighteously withholds, or violently wrests, from the colored man, his inalienable right to enjoy life, liberty, and the pursuit of happiness, on the same conditions that are claimed for the white man—it is sinful because it has created and fostered, both

in church and state, invidious distinctions founded upon physical peculiarities.[31]

This invocation of sin drew attention to the subjective character of Christian complicity in America's racial hierarchy. For the members of the AMRS, racial prejudice and slavery were not merely social sentiments and an economic institution. Rather, these were examples of "evil in the world," an evil that corrupted the souls of a redeemer nation. Ending slavery and rejecting racial designations, then, were not merely objective concerns for political and social policy makers but a subjective act of casting off sin.[32] In short, the problems of racism and slavery were basic moral problems: the failure of individuals (particularly Christians) to rise above self-interest and racial chauvinism to live in accordance with the laws of God.

The basic strategy to end this evil was one of conversion. Through the example of others who had already experienced God's sanctifying grace, individuals and, perhaps, the nation could see in their actions their failure to live up to the example of Christ. For without the Gospel and its examples, the nation continued to live in sin, sick and morally degenerate. The task was to revitalize American public life by (re)introducing Christian principles in the private lives of its citizenry. These principles demanded that we purge ourselves of the evil of slavery and race that set brother against brother. And this applied to white and black Americans.

IMMANENT CONVERSATION AND THE AMRS

The society consistently rejected (whenever possible) the use of racial language in talking about issues facing the African American community.[33] For them, race was understood as part of the evil of racial prejudice; it was the justificatory language for slavery and the denial of citizenship rights. Any use of such language only reinforced its insidious hold on the moral imagination of Americans. Moreover, if the society condemned white Americans for their use of racial designations on the basis of the moral law, it simply followed that they would urge "people of color" to reject the language as well. As William Whipper argued, "to prove consistent in the advocacy of moral principles, the basis of our institution should be as broad and universal as the moral law."[34] Such a position required a notion of universal brotherhood, an embrace of persons without regard for complexional distinction. The "color-blind" policy of the AMRS, however, was a source of extended debate among African Americans until

the 1840s—with both sides offering pragmatic arguments for the use or rejection of the language.

Most of these debates occurred, ironically, in the pages of *The Colored American,* a black newspaper founded in 1837 and the main organ for most literate African Americans during the late thirties. Samuel Cornish, co-founder of the short-lived *Freedom's Journal,* edited the newspaper and, from the beginning, voiced his disagreement with the society's stated purpose. He accused the AMRS of evading specific programs for reform. In its rejection of racial distinctions in particular, he saw the society's views as insufficient to address "the condition and wants of our people."[35] After attending the 1837 convention, Cornish plainly stated his opinion: "We found a Purvis, a Whipper, and others, (of whose Christian benevolence and cultivated intellect, we have so many and such strong evidences), vague, wild, indefinite and confused in their views. They created shadows, fought the wind, and bayed at the moon for more than three days."[36] Needless to say, the editorial sparked a series of heated exchanges between members of the AMRS, specifically William Whipper and defenders of a "race-based" politics such as Samuel Cornish.

Sterling Stuckey, in his book *Slave Culture,* analyzes these exchanges in the context of the controversy over names. That is to say, at the heart of the debate about complexional distinctions was the issue of identity, individual and collective, and this issue of how people of color identified themselves—either as colored Americans or simply Americans—in Stuckey's view "provided the occasion for the emergence of important figures in the contest between nationalists and integrationists."[37]

A key element in Stuckey's account is the relation of these various figures to the cultural reality of Africa in the New World. He contends that the debates of the 1840s enable him to assess the commitment of those he views as nationalists to Pan-Africanism as well as their overall consciousness of African ethnicity.[38] And, of course, by extension he is able to judge the relative assimilation of other figures who do not necessarily identify or embrace a "larger Africanity."[39] Thus, the first portion of Stuckey's account is the fall from grace of the term *African* and the emergence of the terms *brown* and *colored.*[40] This fall signaled a shift, in Stuckey's view, from the efforts at self-determination of the early part of the nineteenth century to what he calls the strong integrationist sentiment of the mid-1830s. This sentiment dominated the debate into the 1840s, and its principal proponent was William Whipper.

According to Stuckey, Whipper was a complicated figure and canno

be easily characterized as a "pure integrationist or nationalist."[41] Like
most of his contemporaries, Whipper struggled to address the retrenched
racism of American society and, subsequently, drew on a number of resources to formulate his strategy. But Whipper's refusal of any use of racial
language leads Stuckey to judge him anyway. He is an integrationist,
ashamed of his African ancestry and anxious to prove the right of people
of color to remain in America.[42] In contradiction of his earlier warnings,
Stuckey even characterizes Whipper's views as probably the first example
of a true black integrationism. Whipper argued "that there should be no all-
black institutions, because such arrangements reinforce prejudice against
blacks and militate against racial justice; that black people should depend
on the benevolence of whites for their liberation; and that they should not
seek to preserve any form of cultural distinctiveness about themselves."[43]
Whipper, then, was the archetypal integrationist of antebellum America,
and it seems—at least for Stuckey—that any opposition to Whipper represented a nationalist counter.

But all of this seems a bit forced. Nationalism and integrationism are
rather blunt tools with which to assess the ambiguities of early nineteenth-
century black political culture and, in particular, the positions of William
Whipper. Only one of Stuckey's characterizations can be attributed to
Whipper: that there should be no all-black institutions because such arrangements reinforce prejudice against blacks and militate against racial
justice. The rest are positions of Stuckey's integrationist straw man. Whipper never claimed that black people should only depend on the good will
of those in power. Such a position would tend to obviate his implicit racial
messianism. Moreover, Whipper never claimed that blacks had no values
worth maintaining. He only questioned the utility of describing those values as black. Stuckey admits that Whipper was a complex person whose
views changed over time. Yet he finds it difficult to avoid the conclusion
that Whipper was ashamed of his African ancestry. As he put it,

> His urging his people to set aside color considerations in a society
> based on white supremacy was a doomed strategy, for it meant the
> surrender of blacks in America to prevailing standards of power re-
> lationships and thus uncontested triumph of Anglo-Saxon values.
> This was the deeper significance of his call to remove the word Afri-
> can from the marbles of churches and other institutions. He might
> just as well have advocated the rejection of all things African in his
> people's culture, had he been aware of them, for he feared that any

suggestions of difference between blacks and whites was undesirable not simply on political grounds but in and of itself.[44]

The fact remains, however, that Whipper never advocated the rejection of all things African in his people's culture. He simply rejected the use of racial language by all Americans.

Stuckey's analytical tools blind him to the subtleties of these exchanges in the 1830s and 1840s. Indeed, the debates had implications for black self-identification, and the shift in terms represented the distance between the autobiographical memories of Africa and the emergence of Americans of African descent. But these debates were also about processes of identification. The language of race underwent a fundamental transformation during this period. Environmental and monogenetic accounts of human difference no longer held the imagination of most white Americans. In fact, the new racial science and its numbers aided the emergence of "the white American" as distinct in kind from racial Others. Whipper's rejection of racial language must be understood in this light: as a search for the explanatory tools to engage in problem-solving. Those opposed to him must be understood in this light as well.

Whipper contended that the use of racial language by people of color only reasserted, in all of its guises, the value of a language that assumed the observed differences between human beings to be a priori. In the context of the prevailing beliefs of most of the nation, the language of race devalued the lives of people of color. In a pragmatic gesture, Whipper argued that the language no longer provided sufficient means to address the moral sickness of the nation; indeed, it was a critical feature of that sickness. He maintained that God made of one blood all nations, and that complexional distinction imposed no form of obligation on us. For Whipper, we were all men and Americans and should engage in public conversation with each other as such. He went on to say that under a republican form of government, equal rights should be guaranteed to every citizen and that attention to color only impeded our progress toward this end. For Whipper and the AMRS, race could only serve the purposes of evil, for it obscured the commonality that resides in each of us. But more poignantly, he accused the proponents of a "race-based" politics of committing the same evil as recognized racists. He wrote that "the colored people are equally guilty, by aiding in perpetuating these distinctions, because they cultivate a spirit of selfishness, at war with their dearest interests, and the spirit of common humanity—while they render themselves inconsistent by repudiating in others the practice of principles they themselves support and sustain."[45] Both whites and blacks failed to see our common humanity. Both ignored the dictates of God, and both needed to cast off the sin of race.

Samuel Cornish responded to Whipper by appealing to the specific circumstances of blacks in the United States. He was at pains to see how the issues surrounding racism and slavery could be addressed without reference to the color-based character of that oppression, an oppression that bound each one, by way of common experiences, to his fellows. Cornish argued that "our condition in the community is a peculiar one, and that we need SPECIAL EFFORTS and special organization, to meet our wants and to obtain and maintain our rights." This effort was not necessarily chauvinistic, nor did it compromise any claim to American citizenship. Instead, race language was a useful tool to explain and to respond to specific problems. Cornish asked, "what has the admission of our being American citizens, to do with exonerating us from those definite duties we owe to our brethren, growing out of our peculiar relations to them?"[46] For him, race-based politics did not compromise a commitment to universal principles: God did create all nations out of one blood. As Cornish wrote, "we are as much opposed to complexional distinctions as brother Whipper, or any other man; yet we are one of an oppressed people, and we deem it alike our privilege and duty, to labor especially for that people, until all their disabilities are removed."[47] For Cornish, race talk drew attention to the specific circumstances (not the distinct biology) of blacks in the United States: to a people subjected to the operations of racism and slavery. These practices alone provided sufficient reasons for the use of racial language.

What's interesting here is the pragmatic basis of Cornish's use of complexional distinctions. He does not argue that the use of race commits us to "generalizing about observed differences between human beings as if these differences were consistent and determined, a priori."[48] Instead, he argues that the language of race is the most fruitful way to explain the historic and present wrongs facing the community, wrongs that in fact created a community of experience. How else should we read the last sentence of his response to Whipper? "[W]e deem it alike our privilege and duty, to labor especially for that people, until all their disabilities are removed." Once the disabilities are removed, once the barriers of racism are brought down, the language of race, one would presume, might no longer be beneficial.

This pragmatic view of race is best seen, I believe, in William Watkins's letter to the 1838 convention. The letter was suppressed by the leadership of the convention and subsequently surfaced in the pages of *The Colored American.* Watkins argued that language acquired its meaning in context and sedimented in the practices of everyday life. For him, the assumption that doing away with racial language—burying it, as it were, in some Christian bosom of benevolence—would somehow end racial prejudice missed the significance of race in organizing daily experiences and betrayed a peculiar view of how language worked. Watkins perceptively argued:

> Words are used as the signs of our ideas, and whenever they perform this office, or are truly significant of the ideas for which they stand, they accomplish the object of their invention. In vain do we carp at some supposed inapplicability of a term as applied to a certain object, when imperious custom or common consent has established the relation between the sign or word. . . . This is the case with the word in question. Custom has fixed its meaning in reference to a particular people in this country, and from this decision, however arbitrary, there is, I am sure, no successful appeal. Again, to decry the use of the word, colored, on account of some questionable inaccuracy in its applicability to us, is an argument, which if successful, would blot out from our English vocabularies certain words of established usage.[49]

Race was not a matter of essential or natural differences between human beings. It was instead a language deeply embedded in the customs and habits of American society that played a powerful role in organizing relations with regard to people of color in the country. A simple abandonment of that language would do nothing to alleviate the condition of African Americans or uproot the "imperious custom" of racial difference and prejudice in the United States.[50]

Watkins's critique of the AMRS was particularly devastating. He was one of the early organizers of the society and a firm believer in the importance of moral reform. But, like Cornish and others, he concluded that the "color-blind" policy of the AMRS could offer nothing by way of improvement for the African American community, slave or free. For Watkins, the dichotomy between race-based politics and Christian benevolence was a false one. The use of racially specific forms of redress did not necessarily militate against principles of Christian benevolence. In fact, they were reconcilable: we extend help to people of color because they are despised and neglected for being colored.[51] Yet the society held steadfast to its position, and by 1841, after four more national meetings, remained opposed to "complexional distinctions" of any kind.[52]

Perhaps the most elaborate response to Whipper came from a writer known only as "Sidney." In a series of four letters to *The Colored American*, Sidney offered arguments for the usefulness of race-based politics. He understood race pragmatically and appealed to the history of nations and of the black American struggle to ground his claims. He did not decry the aims of the AMRS. The convention, like Sidney, desired the abolition of slavery and racial prejudice. They disagreed, however. Sidney maintained that the differences did not "resolve themselves into what we shall do, neither for whom we shall do." As he put it, "the condition of our people . . . incites us to effort, and for the upraising of wronged, and pent up, and straitened humanity, as seen in the persons and condition of the colored people of this country." The difference was one of method, "the mode of operation—the how of the matter."[53]

Sidney's refusal to frame the issue of race-based politics in terms of "whats and whos" signals his reluctance to invest race with any meaning outside of the social relations that provided its content. American racism demanded a response, a course of action. Thus, for him, the debate about racial language was one not of racial types but, rather, of how an oppressed people acquires an identity from their oppression and then creatively transforms that identity through struggle. He argued that race language was necessary in light of their circumstances, and that Whipper's failure to recognize this resulted from his own preoccupation with color. Sidney's argument was straightforward: "Whenever a people are oppressed, peculiarly (not complexionally) distinctive organizations or action, is required on the part of the oppressed to destroy that oppression. The colored people of this country are oppressed; therefore the colored people are required to act in accordance with this fundamental principle. If Mr. W[hipper], for a few minutes, get [*sic*] clear of the idea of color, perhaps he will then be able to understand."[54] For Sidney and others, the issue was not one of a commitment to color or the concept of race. Not at all. The question was a methodological one: what were the best means or words to speak to the problems of slavery and racism? Given the social relations of the nation, race language provided a useful tool to single out and account for the distinctiveness of their oppression.

Here Sidney evades the fundamental point of Whipper's argument. For Whipper, race language acquired its meaning only within the context of American racism, so any use of it merely reinforced its hold on people's moral and social imaginations. The distinctiveness of the oppression inflicted on people of color, then, had to be presented in different terms if they were to avoid self-defeat. Sidney eventually addressed this argument by discounting Whipper's understanding of the way words worked. In his view, words were not the source of prejudice. "Prejudice is a moral phenomenon, a wrong exercise of the sentiments and sympathies, a disease of the will."[55] To discontinue the use of the word, then, would not rid us of the evil, for the word itself was not the source of the problem.[56]

Sidney's arguments for "complexionally distinctive" organization, however, went beyond the tiff about the way language works. He believed that without racial terms black people were denied the possibility to fight for themselves. This was a critical feature of Sidney's complaint against Whipper's position. He argued that no people acquired freedom by denying the particular features of their experiences. Those experiences shaped the nation's conscience and prepared it to strike the blow for freedom. Thus, any effort to acquire freedom demanded "a keen sense of actual suffering and a fixed consciousness that it is no longer sufferable."[57] Each of these elements, in Sidney's view, served to unite persons who suffer in feeling and action as well as awaken the sympathy of those in power. Sidney added, however, that the presentation of the wrongs and injustices a people may face must be revealed by them. In a passage reminiscent of David Walker's *Appeal*, he claimed:

It is absolutely important that there should be such a presentation of wrongs as may reveal to the power-holding body the enormity of their oppression; and at the same time, acquaint them that their outrages have so proved the vital seat of suffering, as to arouse the deepest feelings and most inflexible determination of their insulted victims. Now, from the nature of the case this statement of grievance in all its fulness and power, can come from none other than those conscious of suffering. How is it possible, we ask, for men who know nothing of oppression, who have always enjoyed the blessedness of freedom, by any depth of sympathy, so fully and adequately express the sense of wrong and outrage, as the sorrowful presence and living desire of us who have drank the dregs of the embittered chalice?[58]

For Sidney, the oppressed are their best representatives.[59] Their voices are required to truly capture the horrors of American slavery and racism. But, more important, the voice of the oppressed gives life to them. It vindicates their character in light of the brutality of their experiences, and no sympathetic advocacy can achieve this. "The oppressed themselves," Sidney argued, "must manifest energy of character and elevation of soul. Oppression never quails unless it sees that the downtrodden [are] outraged."[60] Drawing on the imagery of Exodus, he claimed that even if the abolitionists redoubled their efforts and descended on Pharaoh like a "pitchy cloud of locusts" the condition of African Americans would remain the same. Even the plagues brought by God on Egypt would not deliver the children of Israel. Interracial solidarity could only go so far. They, the slaves of Egypt, had to awaken to a responsibility for themselves and manifest it by "giving it actuality," that is, by actively struggling for their liberation.

Sidney's defense of racial language was bound up in his conception of black struggle. His arguments consistently compare black America to other oppressed nations of Europe as well as to the struggle of the American nation itself. These were examples of groups striking the blow for freedom for themselves. Such examples provided the blueprint for black Americans. Sidney maintained that the early conventions were born out of this effort, but that the American Moral Reform Society had strayed from its path in the name of "heaven-born truth." He had no sympathy with that cosmopolitan disposition which "tramples upon all nationality, which encircles the universe, but at the same time theorises away the most needed blessings, and blights the dearest hopes of a people."[61] The particular experiences of black folk necessitated specific activity "that white men could not assume,"[62] not even those who stood in solidarity with blacks. For Sidney this was not evidence of his "colorphobia," as Whipper contended. He argued that he was quite satisfied with the color God had given him. Instead, it was more evidence of the colorphobia of the nation. As he put it in his final letter: "We are afflicted with colorphobia, and it is going to work wonders with us—wonders like those Moses wrought in Egypt—of fearful nature, and destructive tendency; unless the right means are used to effect a radical cure, so that henceforth, neither the fact, nor the term indicative of it, shall excite convulsions, nor create a MONOMANIA."[63]

"Pharaoh's on Both Sides of the Blood-Red Waters"

Henry Highland Garnet and the National Convention of 1843

The national conventions of the 1840s were, to a large degree, an out-growth of the debates about complexional distinctions. Many black leaders were torn between a color-blind appeal for moral reform and a race-based politics that addressed the specific social and political circum-stances of people of color. The state conventions partly settled the matter.[1] Much to the dismay of some white and black abolitionists, these meetings were organized around specific issues facing people of color and stood as alternative forums to the American Moral Reform Society and white antislavery organizations. The New York State Convention of 1840, for example, embraced the language of a common humanity in the context of an argument for black voting rights. The delegates maintained that without the franchise colored people would remain "nominally free."[2] They also contended that without the political power to effect change, the community would remain in darkness and further be denied access to education and jobs.[3]

The state conventions combined the language of the AMRS with a more direct, what I've called "outside," political program. The franchise was seen by the delegates to these conventions as a vehicle for the im-provement of the conditions of African Americans. Yet, they used the moral language of the AMRS and of general abolitionism. The complicity of Christians with the evil of slavery continued to be denounced, and the contradiction of the founding principles of the nation—the betrayal of America's civil religion—was consistently exposed.

But more important, for my purposes at least, the state conventions served as a training ground for a new generation of African American leaders.[4] One in particular would greatly influence the timbre of the national conventions of the 1840s: the incomparable Henry Highland Garnet. I want to examine Garnet's "Address to the Slaves of the United States of America" at the National Negro Convention of 1843 in Buffalo, New York, because his speech represents an early example of the pressing pessimism that developed among blacks of the mid–nineteenth century, an outgrowth, as it were, of entrenched racism and the pragmatic view of race of the late thirties. For lingering on the borders of the call for an immanent conversation among the oppressed was the specter of violence: the raging swell of despair in the face of repeated indifference and the demand "to strike the blow for freedom." Indeed, because of this, Garnet's address can be characterized as an example of what Michael Walzer calls political messianism.

MICHAEL WALZER AND POLITICAL MESSIANISM

In *Exodus and Revolution,* Walzer interprets the Exodus story as "a paradigm of revolutionary politics." *Paradigm* here is understood loosely, for Exodus is not to be taken as a theory of revolution. Instead, Walzer reads the story as a broad narrative in which a range of political events can be located.[5] In his view the classic story line of Exodus—it's a story with a beginning, a middle, and an ending—makes it susceptible to a number of uses. Contemporary militants, for example, tie the story's linearity to ideas of progress and the hope of redemption. The story provides the model for a once-and-for-all struggle, a confrontation that, in the end, leads to the transformation of the world.[6] Walzer identifies this politics as millenarianism, or political messianism, and claims that his reading of Exodus is an alternative to it. For him, political messianism is, to say the least, a worrisome politics.

Three characteristics of political messianism trouble Walzer. The first is its extraordinary sensitivity to and longing for apocalyptic events.[7] This may take the form of the expectation of an imminent and inevitable end brought about by an act of God or, in its more secular guises, the fated movement of historical events: a terminus in which the people "win at last the political version of eternal life."[8] The second feature of political messianism is its eagerness to force the End. What's problematic here is not the recognition of agents ready to act politically but rather that action is understood as having an ultimate purpose. As Walzer claims:

> Men and women who force the End take deliverance into their own hands, and it is not from any particular evil but from evil in general that they would deliver themselves and all the rest of us. They claim divine authority for their politics and effectively rule out the requirements of both morality and prudence. When the stakes are this high, it is implausible to demand any sort of restraint. Force itself is sanctified when it is used to bring about the end of days, and so it can be used without guilt.[9]

Moral and prudential constraints, then, are cast aside, and force is sanctified by the ultimate purposes of struggle.

Finally, political messianism lays claim to unconditionality. Victory is final. No arguments to the contrary are allowed. Subsequently, the fulfillment of the messianic mission leaves no regard for losers or any moral obligation to designated enemies. Once victory is declared, the argument, so to speak, is foreclosed.[10] Unconditionality, then, along with the other characteristics Walzer lists, points to a crass politics of winners, quite intolerant of dissent, in which a single vision or truth grounds actions, and only those with access to that truth are capable of leadership. Authoritarianism is justified, and we end up with a worrisome politics indeed.

Walzer counters political messianism with Exodus politics: "an account [of struggle] that does not require the miraculous transformation of the material world but sets God's people marching toward a better place within it."[11] For him, the authentic prophetic voice of Exodus does not reside in a utopian refusal of limits, that is, in a longing for the apocalypse, a readiness to force the end, and the unconditionality of victory. Instead, the story's propheticism is found in the recognition of our actions as occurring within history and the limitations that reality forces on us. The crucial struggle, then, is "in the wilderness—extended into the promised land itself—to create a free people and to live up to the terms of the covenant."[12]

"AN ADDRESS TO THE SLAVES OF THE UNITED STATES"

Henry Highland Garnet's address of 1843 poses an interesting challenge to Walzer's conception (and by extension my conception) of Exodus politics and political messianism. Garnet rejected Exodus as a model for political action, claiming that it induced in slaves and freemen a passive gradualism in which the group, like the children of Israel, waited for providential deliverance. His speech also contained all of the characteristics of messianism that Walzer finds troublesome. But Garnet's address entailed a possible attraction of messianism that Walzer, to some extent, ignores: the existential pain that drives people to force the End. This drive is not so much the result of a longing for the apocalypse or an unconditional victory as it is the outcome of psychical and physical scars and bruises resulting from repeated indifference—people simply refusing to suffer any longer (and this need not be imagined in terms of ultimate purposes, but may be the source of the messianic attraction).

Garnet's readiness to force the End—that is, his call for a general slave rebellion—was based on a pragmatic view of race shaped by an ironic use of moral reform that took seriously the cycle of existential pain and unrest that penetrated deeply the lives of African Americans, slave or free. Each of these features can give us a better understanding of Garnet's address, particularly in relation to the prevailing issues and themes of the moment. Like most of the black men and women around him, Garnet was pessimistic with regard to America's willingness to end slavery and racism. The peculiar institution thrived, proslavery arguments were everywhere, and the new science of race was fast becoming hegemonic. But unlike most of his fellows, Garnet was ready to force the End in the face of white America's indifference to black suffering and its support of the evil of slavery.

Yet, just one year before his address in Buffalo, Garnet disavowed the use of violence to end slavery. Before the National Liberty Party's convention in 1842, Garnet stated:

> I cannot harbor the thought for a moment that [the slave's] deliverance will be brought about by violence. No, our country will not be so deaf to the cries of the oppressed; so regardless of the commands of God, and her highest interests. No, the time for a last stern struggle has not yet come (may it never be necessary). The finger of the Almighty will hold back the trigger, and his all powerful arm will sheath the sword till the oppressor's cup is full.[13]

There seemed a glimmer of hope that the nation would live up to its stated ideals. But what would bring Garnet to the "militant despairing" of the black condition in 1843? Why would he lose faith in America's ability to hear the cries of the oppressed and become pessimistic about the possibility of American democracy flourishing?

Several factors probably influenced Garnet's pessimistic outlook. In the previous chapters I mentioned the growing acceptance and influence of the new science of race in American life. Many proponents of slavery embraced the language of science to justify the peculiar institution and their entrenched racial prejudices. Such views were becoming hegemonic in the 1840s, and by midcentury they were the accepted norm. The value-neutral domain of science, in effect, legitimized the institution of slavery and the widespread belief of innate differences between the races. Another factor was the 1842 Supreme Court decision in *Prigg v. Pennsylvania,* in which the Court upheld the fugitive slave law of 1793, clearly stating that the government had the right to maintain slavery. Coupled with the expulsion of U.S. Congressman Joshua Giddings from the House of Representatives in 1842 for his antislavery stance[14] and the growing rift between white and black abolitionists over political tactics, the national climate for racial redress was decidedly hostile. Apparently, the oppressor's cup was full, and the country would move only with agitation, in particular the resistance of millions of slaves locked in the dark prison of oppression. This became the basis of the 1843 address in Buffalo.

A pragmatic view of race—the recognition that social and political conditions make racial solidarity an important political and social strategy—frames the 1843 address. Garnet opened with an acknowledgment of such bonds and a deep sadness over the persistence of slavery: "Your brethren of the North, East, and West have been accustomed to meet together in National Conventions to sympathize with each other, and to weep over your unhappy condition."[15] For Garnet, the occasion of the address or, more generally, the convention movement, was the result of the disaster experienced by all African Americans, the experience of slavery and the dark shadow the institution cast over the nation. These individual experiences justified imagining those who have lived them as members of a nation, as a collective audience with interests and aims.

This imagined community was strengthened by the recognition that so-called free men and women in the North were slaves as well. Like the concurrent freedom celebrations, Garnet understood freedom as partially proleptic, a description of circumstances to come. Blacks in the North could not claim freedom for themselves, for an identification between the slaves in the South and the quasi slaves in the North, through the social heritage of slavery and the persistence of discrimination, bound them together. "Years have rolled on, and tens of thousands have been borne on streams of blood and tears, to the shores of eternity. While you have been oppressed we have also been partakers with you, nor can we be free while you are enslaved. We, therefore, write to you as being bound with you."[16] Finally, national solidarity was cemented with reference to familial bonds, for many blacks in the North were connected to slavery by relations of blood. Their parents, wives, brothers, and sisters were still enslaved in the South. For some, something personal or individual[17] that paralleled other personal or individual stories constituted their relation to those in slavery. As Garnet acknowledged: "Many of you are bound to us, not only by the ties of a common humanity, but we are connected by the more tender relations of parents, wives, husbands, children, brothers, and sisters, and friends. As such we most affectionately address you." Only after these levels of solidarity were acknowledged by Garnet did he venture to exhort the slaves to seek freedom. Each level gave voice to the experiential basis of the community, to the parallel histories among fellows who did not know each other but in whose minds lived the image of their communion.[18]

I want to suggest that such a conception of the black community relies on a pragmatic understanding of race, not a biological one. Three years before his speech in Buffalo, Garnet delivered an address before the American Anti-Slavery Society in 1840. He spoke of the ties that bound him to the slave:

> There is, Mr. President, a higher sort of freedom, which no mortal can touch. That freedom, thanks be unto the Most High, is mine. Yet I am not, nay, cannot be entirely free. I feel for my brethren as a man—I am bound with them as a brother. Nothing but emancipating them can set me at liberty. . . . For although I were dwelling beneath the bright skies of Asia, or listening to the harp-like strains of the gentle winds that whisper of freedom among the groves of Africa—though my habitation were fixed in the freest part of Victoria's dominions, yet it were vain, and worse than vain for me to indulge in the thought of being free, while three millions of my country-men are wailing in the dark prison-house of oppression.[19]

This acknowledgment of ties was not premised on any conception of the "racial self" as authentic or natural, that is, as a stable identity connected with similarly biologically constituted racial selves. Instead, Garnet spoke of the conditions and experiences of people of color. Slavery and pervasive prejudice bound each one—whether slave or free—to his fellows. The invocation of common experience, sympathy, and, in some cases, "spilt blood" called individuals to speak out against slavery and to struggle for its ultimate demise. They were not the tools to hermetically seal a racial identity.

Garnet's address to the Liberty Party Convention of 1842 illustrates this point. Garnet rejected explicitly the new racial science and its conception of inherent differences between the races. He stated:

> It is maintained by many that we are to judge men by their complexion, and not by their moral worth. This spirit of caste the friends of freedom have trodden under foot; but it is not dead; it too often shows itself in our country, exerting a withering influence on those who cherish it, and chilling the heart's blood of those against whom it is exerted. But he who is considered so offensive for the complexion his Creator has given him, has the assurance that God "is no respector of persons": and those who make this distinction are to be pitied for their ignorance of the works of God, and of the attributes of His character.[20]

Race as a biological essence was not what Garnet had in mind when he spoke of the community of people of color. That position belonged to proponents of the new science. For Garnet, race marked the effects of environment or the work of God, and its invidious use to justify slavery and racism had to be rejected. It is important to note, however, that this rejection of racial science did not lead Garnet to discard racial language altogether. Unlike William Whipper, Garnet saw the usefulness of race-based politics in a society so completely structured by the concept. But it was a pragmatic understanding of race, not an essentialist one, that guided Garnet's use of the language and his embrace of "complexionally distinct" organization.

Garnet supported the New York State Convention in 1840 and its stand for complexionally distinct organizations. He led the convening and was the principal writer of the two published addresses of the meeting: an address to the people of the state of New York and an address to the colored community. Both provide insight into Garnet's use of race. The former rejected the new racial science, appealed to the humanity of all citizens of the state, called attention to the blood shared on the battlefields for freedom, and demanded that the state live up to the republican ideals of the nation, all of which were framed by descriptions of black achieve-ment. For in spite of racial restriction, Garnet argued, the black commu-nity sustained itself and, in some cases, flourished. This alone satisfied any requirements for civic responsibility.

The address to the black community took a different tone. It appealed to the community to take responsibility for its condition and to act for itself.

> Colored men of New York! Are you willing that your people should longer constitute the proscribed class? Are you willing ever to be deprived of one of the dearest rights of freemen? Are you willing to remain quietly and inactively, political slaves? . . . O no! . . . Breth-ren, by united, vigorous, and judicious and manly effort, we can redeem ourselves. But we must put forth our own exertions. We must exert our own powers. Our political enfranchisement cometh not from afar.[21]

The black community of New York was encouraged to exert itself in the name of its own liberation.[22] The basis for this action was not racial essen-tialism but rather the choice of black persons to act distinctively in the hope that such measures would find their vindication in beneficial conse-quences.

In typical Garnet fashion, the address turned to historical example to buttress this point. Oppressed nations always fought for themselves. Their allies joined them in the fight, but the battle was theirs. And like the many men who sacrificed for the liberation of their nation, black men were urged to sacrifice for theirs.

> We call upon you, then, for effort; nor for effort alone. We call upon you for sacrifice. Examine the annals of the human race, look over the face of the universe, and you will find, that whenever anything was of great worth to be achieved for man, men have been needed, and men have been willing to sacrifice their every thing—their all—yea, to give up life, for the good of their oppressed people. . . . But, we ask, if in all ages of the world, men, in view of the prostrate condition of their compatriots, and the inevitable heritage of poster-ity, have been willing to sacrifice everything of dear and sacred na-ture for the good of man, is there not enough public spirit, of patri-otic feeling, among us, peeled, stricken and smitten, fleeced and

flayed, as we have been, as we now are, to induce, impel us to some sacrifice of time and money, and labor, in our own behalf?[23]

The striking point of this passage is its appeal to national feeling in black New Yorkers in particular and the black community in general. Here the nation is called to sacrifice, and the people are called to act in the name of patriotic devotion. Like all other nations, the black nation in America had to act for its own freedom in light of its condition and the inevitable heritage of posterity—a theme common to Garnet's speeches.

A biological conception of race did not figure in this formulation, for Garnet's use of the language did not extend beyond the social and political relations that gave race its meaning. In other words, race language acquired its moral and political significance in the context of its use. According to Garnet, one could not step outside of these relations or contexts because one's moral duties to respond to the effects of race were shaped and formulated within them. As such, white people had certain duties with regard to the effects of racism based on their position, just as blacks did. The concept of race simply served as a tool to mark off the distinctiveness of the communities' oppression.

Sterling Stuckey reads Garnet's formulation as a kind of reduction of race to the material circumstances of black Americans: the cause of discrimination against blacks was not the color of their skin but their condition. He suggests that "Garnet's conception of the source of prejudice against blacks—formed before racism in America, some believed, had taken on a life of its own—seems strikingly modern in its possibilities for class analysis but modern also in the degree to which he underestimated racism as a force in its own right."[24] Perhaps so.

Stuckey, however, makes the mistake of separating talk of the condition of black Americans from issues of racism. For Garnet, one could not talk of the liberation and freedom of African Americans without addressing the issue of race: it was a part of the condition. Moreover, most people of color of the period rejected the idea that race alone was the source of their problems. Like the convention movement he participated in, Garnet's efforts for freedom included a politics of respectability with its emphasis on temperance, education, and economic self-sufficiency. These were tools for the improvement of the community and points of departure for addressing the racial policies of the nation-state, but they were not reducible to the problem of racism.

As I discussed in chapter 6, this politics had two sorts of inflections. It assumed a bourgeois aspiration for middle-class respectability, and it called for an immanent conversation about racial discrimination and its effects. The former argued that through education, moral living, and economic self-sufficiency an aspiring black middle class, and thus blacks in general, would improve in "rank and standing among men." The latter called for solidaristic efforts to reject white paternalism and to alleviate, through self-critique and conjoint action, the condition of black people. To some extent, Garnet embraced both. He was an ardent supporter of moral reform but articulated it within a race-based politics and a call for black solidarity to end slavery and racism. In fact, an ironic use of moral reform in his 1843 address was a critical part of his call for a slave insurrection. Garnet spoke directly to the Christian piety of slaves and, in the process, drew on the moral language of general abolitionism. Slavery was an evil, a sin against God: "In every man's mind the good seeds of liberty are planted, and he who brings his fellow down so low, as to make him contented with a condition of slavery, commits the highest crime against God and man."[25] But Garnet did not embrace Christian benevolence as the form of redress for this kind of debasement. It seems he was not very concerned about the souls of white folks.

Instead, Garnet turned religious benevolence on its head: the focus was not on the demand for proponents of slavery to forsake sin and believe in the mercy of Christ but, rather, on the duties of black Christian slaves to forsake the obstacles to obtaining the grace of God. Thus, moral reform for the slave, according to Garnet, might require general insurrection because the slave was still obligated, in spite of his condition, to obey the laws of God.

> TO SUCH DEGRADATION IT IS SINFUL IN THE EXTREME FOR YOU TO MAKE VOLUNTARY SUBMISSION. The divine commandments you are in duty bound to reverence and obey. If you do not obey them, you will surely meet with the displeasure of the Almighty. He requires you to love him supremely, and your neighbor as yourself—to keep the Sabbath day holy—to search the Scriptures—and bring up your children with respect for his laws, and to worship no other God but him. But slavery sets all of these at nought, and hurls defiance in the face of Jehovah.[26]

The invocation of sin drew attention to the subjective character of the slaves' complicity with the peculiar institution: the slaves were partly to blame because they submitted to the evil of slavery. Ending slavery, then, was not merely an objective concern but a subjective act of casting off sin, and, for Garnet, the slave had to do this for himself.

> The forlorn condition in which you are placed, does not destroy your moral obligation to God. You are not certain of heaven, because you suffer yourselves to remain in a state of slavery, where you cannot obey the commandments of the Sovereign of the universe. If the ignorance of slavery is a passport to heaven, then it is a blessing, and no curse, and you should rather desire its perpetuity than its abolition. God will not receive slavery, nor ignorance, nor any other state of mind, for love and obedience to him. Your condition does not absolve you from your moral obligation. The diabolical injustice by which your liberties are cloven down, NEITHER GOD, NOR ANGELS, OR JUST MEN, COMMAND YOU TO SUFFER FOR A SINGLE MOMENT. THEREFORE IT IS YOUR SOLEMN AND IMPERATIVE DUTY TO USE EVERY MEANS, BOTH MORAL, INTELLECTUAL, AND PHYSICAL, THAT PROMISES SUCCESS.[27]

Obviously, the precepts of moral reform and religious benevolence have been used for unintended purposes here. Garnet used the dictum "to cast off sin" as a rallying cry for the ending of slavery by the slaves themselves. He appealed to the Christian fervor of the slaves and criticized them for not living up to the demands of God. Having received, in his view, God's sanctifying grace, Garnet, like moral reformers generally, was obliged to extend to his fellows the means to obtain that grace. Ironically, however, this led to a call, if necessary, for violence.

Some scholars separate Garnet's use of moral reform from his call for slaves to act. In their view, each stands as a distinctive rhetorical strategy in the speech, and, in the case of moral reform, suggests his close affiliation with Garrisonianism. Like Garrisonians, Garnet condemned slavery and slaveholding as a sin. He argued that the entire nation shared the guilt of that sin and that a moral attack would bring about the eventual destruction of slavery. Yet, scholars such as Harry Reed separate these propositions from Garnet's conception of "the slave as an agent in his own liberation," what Reed considers Garnet's unique contribution to nineteenth-century abolitionism. Reed in particular fails to see that through the principles of moral reform Garnet exhorted the slave to act "as an abolitionist and agent of change" on his own behalf.[28] This rhetorical strategy is critical because it makes slave rebellion a moral imperative.

This strategy also exposed an irony in the position of some reformers.[29] For many moral reformers and abolitionists the problem of slavery and racism was a moral one: a failure on the part of individuals who did not live up to the dictates of God because of self-interest and racial chauvinism. The task was obvious: a recognition (for some an immediate one) of the evil of slavery and racism and a commitment to remove this sin by embracing Christian virtue. In this view, faith was placed in the innate moral capacities of the individual, in the infinite worthiness of man.

Garnet agreed with this. But unlike many moral reformers and white abolitionists, he had faith in the inner moral capacities of individuals of color. He believed that black folk must, with the aid of their allies, wrench themselves from their wretched condition—commit themselves, as it were, to cast off the sin of slavery. This shift in focus—from the sinful character of slavery and its proponents to the sinful aspect of the slave's submission—exposed the moral reform movement and immediate abolitionism's strengths as weaknesses, for their boisterous faith in the moral capacities of individuals fell silent when confronted with the agency of people of color.

Moral reform grounded Garnet's exhortations to force the End, and his irony highlighted the agency of slaves instead of the sinfulness of slaveholders. But Garnet's use of moral reform also led him to embrace political messianism. Indeed, for him, there was a short distance between "sanctifying grace" and "sanctified violence." He called for slaves to be true Christians. They had to rebel, and an ultimate order sanctioned such action, for slaves were justified to use any means to end slavery, including violence, because they were struggling to live a Christian life. Prudential constraints, then, were cast aside, and no danger was too great to confront—for "life was not worth having on some terms."[30]

In this vein, Garnet called forth the images of Denmark Vesey, Nat Turner, Joseph Cinque, and Madison Washington. Each of these tragic heroes risked his life, through violent insurrection, for freedom. Garnet skillfully framed this violence, however, within the tradition of revolutionary America. These men simply answered the question, "Is it better to choose Liberty or Death?," in the same manner of America's founding fathers. They were "noble men! Those who have fallen in freedom's conflict, their memories will be cherished by the true-hearted and the God-fearing in all future generations; those who are living, their names are surrounded by a halo of glory."[31] These heroes set examples for the slaves, and Garnet's claim that slaves deliver themselves followed easily from their heroic example, for after he recounted the bravery of these men, Garnet exhorted the slave to freedom: "Brethren, arise, arise! Strike for your lives and liberties. Now is the day and the hour. Let every slave throughout the land do this, and the days of slavery are numbered. You cannot be more oppressed than you have been—you cannot suffer greater cruelties than you have already. Rather die freemen than live to be slaves. Remember that you are FOUR MILLIONS!"[32]

Walzer would readily see a worrisome politics on the horizon here. Garnet grounded his claims in Christian duty: the revolutionary actions of slaves were sanctioned by an ultimate order. Garnet even offered a secular version, still drawing on ultimate ends, by lifting up the example of tragic heroes—men who were courageous for us—to excite bravery among slaves. The stakes, then, were certainly high, and demands for restraint were met with claims of cowardice. But why this sense of urgency on the part of Garnet? Perhaps the sense of suffering in his background, and a consciousness of the suffering of his people, impelled him to force the End.[33] Walzer assumes the presence of this pain and suffering but never really explores its effect on the Israelite struggle.

For Garnet, the pain and suffering of slaves justified his eagerness to force the End. For him, slavery "dirtied" them, not only in the present but in death as well. Slavery robbed the slave of his death. No peace awaited him in paradise, for there was a continuation of suffering from the living to the dead. He stated this unequivocally in a description of slavery: "Nor did the evil of . . . bondage end at their emancipation by death. Succeeding generations inherited their chains, and millions have come from eternity into time, and have returned again to the world of spirits, cursed and ruined by American slavery.[34] Death and heaven were not safe havens from white supremacy nor great liberators from suffering and evil.[35] Instead, slavery extended its shame and burden to past and future generations.

What is interesting for me, though not for Sterling Stuckey, is not the relation between Garnet's formulation of the reciprocity between the living and the dead and traditional African religious beliefs but rather his attempt to redirect the Christian energies of the slave.[36] Stuckey too often burdens his analysis of personalities and themes with claims of continuity with an African ethnos, so much so that his arguments seem strained. For example, he argues that "[s]ince the principle religious ceremonies of the slaves were devoted to the renewal of contact with the ancestors, [Garnet's] references to the continuing responsibility of the slave to them is a brilliant illustration of cultural thought being put to revolutionary purposes."[37] But Garnet's address is best understood in Christian terms, not as an example of African religious sentiments put to political use. His appeal to Christian piety and devotion—what I've called his use of irony—grounded his call for slave insurrection. If the slave loved God, then he had to rebel.[38] Also, Garnet's redescription of death and heaven held off the more accommodating tendencies of slave Christianity: its focus on the other world as compensation for the despondency of slave life.[39] For Garnet, freedom would not be found in death. As long as slavery and racism existed freedom would be understood as proleptic, that is to say, as an anticipated outcome of our actions in the face of such evil. This proleptic conception of freedom, in death or in the North, demanded of each black person a stern discipline to remember those in bondage and required actions to end the conditions that enslaved the entire community. No black person could rest until the scourge of slavery and racial prejudice was destroyed.

In the most stunning moment of his address, Garnet put this formulation to use. He rejected Exodus as a model for black liberation.

> You had far better all die—die immediately, than live slaves, and entail your wretchedness upon your posterity. If you would be free in this generation here is your only hope. However much you and all of us may desire it, there is not much hope of redemption without the shedding of blood. If you must bleed, let it all come at once, rather die freemen, than live to be the slaves. It is impossible, like the children of Israel, to make a grand exodus from the land of bondage. The Pharaohs are on both sides of the blood-red waters![40]

For Stuckey this moment represents Garnet's refusal of moral suasion as a strategy sufficient to end slavery (he only quotes the first part of this paragraph!). He fails to see that Garnet's call for slaves to resist turns on his use of the cycle of existential pain and unrest. The paragraph begins with the formulation of reciprocity, the seemingly endless succession of births and deaths in slavery. The only way to end this cycle was, perhaps, through the cathartic moment of violence, a once-and-for-all struggle that lifted the burden of slavery in the present, into the future, and from the past.

Yet, violence was not the only means to achieve this end. It was a last resort. Garnet stated:

> Think how many tears you have poured out upon the soil which you have cultivated with unrequited toil and enriched with your blood; and then go to your lordly enslavers and tell them plainly, that you are determined to be free. Appeal to their sense of justice, and tell them that they have no more right to oppress you, than you have to enslave them. Entreat them to remove the grievous burdens which they have imposed upon you, and to remunerate you for your labor. Promise them renewed diligence in the cultivation of the soil, if they will render to you an equivalent for your services. . . . Tell them in language which they cannot misunderstand, of the exceeding sinfulness of slavery, and of a future judgement, and of the righteous retribution of an indignant God. Inform them that all you desire is FREEDOM, and that nothing else will suffice. Do this, and forever after cease to toil for the heartless tyrants who give you no other reward but stripes and abuse. If they then commence the work of death, they, and not you, will be responsible for the consequences.[41]

If violence was to occur, the enslaver, not the slave, would be morally culpable; physical force could be used without guilt.

Garnet understood that his call to action, to some extent, cut against the grain of the slave, nay, the black Christian imagination. He turned then to the most important story of this people in bondage, Exodus, and decried its analogical use in the black American context. "It is impossible, like the children of Israel, to make a grand exodus from the land of bondage." This rejection of Exodus spoke directly to the slaves' belief that God was acting, in fact, would act on their behalf as he had acted for Israel. Providential gradualism stood in the way of Garnet's eagerness to force the End, and he attacked it head-on. Garnet stated:

> But you are a patient people. You act as though you were made for the special use of these devils. You act as though your daughters were born to pamper the lusts of your masters and overseers. And worse than all, you tamely submit while your lords tear your wives from your embraces and defile them before your eyes. In the name of God, we ask, are you men? Where is the blood of your fathers? Has it all run out of your veins? Awake, awake, millions of voices

are calling you! Your dead fathers speak to you from their graves.
Heaven, as with a voice of thunder, calls on you to arise from the
dust.[42]

A call for confrontation immediately followed this passage. "Let your
motto be resistance! resistance! RESISTANCE! No oppressed people have
ever secured their liberty without resistance."[43] Garnet had set the stage.
He had listed the nationalist ideologues' ultimate horror: the raping of
wives and daughters. He described the enemy as devils, and, in some respects, beyond salvation. And, finally, Garnet challenged the manliness of
the slave and of the black convention movement. He confronted them
with a critical choice: moral suasion or political militancy. Perhaps the
contrast is too sharp. The militancy of Garnet relied heavily on a moral
argument that drew most of its content from an ironic use of general abolitionism. Such arguments had a tremendous political impact on the nation. Still, it makes a difference whether one emphasizes the politics of
the struggle for racial equality or the morality of that struggle, even if the
latter has political effects.

Garnet's address presented before the convention movement a direct
frontal assault on the policies of the nation-state. His speech called for
radical political action by people of color. As such, the inside dimension
of the convention movement—that immanent conversation about the circumstance of black people with the two different inflections that created
a domain of self-determining action on the part of black people—confronted, with a violent posture, the domain of the state. Herein lies the
radicalism of Garnet's address. Out of the dimension of the convention
movement that spoke to cultural identity he attempted to articulate a national politics that violently challenged the nation-state. In other words,
he interpreted the call for an immanent conversation as a call for general
slave insurrection in the South and mass "black" political action in the
North.

Opposition to Garnet came almost immediately from Frederick Douglass and others committed to Garrisonianism.[44] They complained that the
speech advocated excessive force and that such actions would be fatal to
the free blacks in the slave and border states. A great debate ensued on
the floor of the convention. Garnet defended his address, often moving
his audience to tears. Douglass countered with as much emotion, implor-
ing the convention to try "the moral means a little longer."[45] In the end,
the convention rejected Garnet's address by a vote of 19 to 18. The dele-

gates made a choice: that the black nation would remain essentially in the cultural domain. They embraced a race-based politics but rejected any call for violence against the state. Instead, the convention movement turned to the precepts and language of moral reform. The black struggle for freedom, in their view, was a moral struggle, a fight for the soul of the American nation, and violence compromised that fact. Exodus 23:9 dictated a way of living: "You shall not oppress a stranger. You know the heart of a stranger, for you were strangers in the land of Egypt."

Epilogue
The Tragedy of African American Politics

Henry Highland Garnet's 1843 speech brought the two strands of the national convention movement together in an unexpected way. To be sure, the participants in the state conventions[1] were joining the politics of respectability with efforts to secure the franchise for African Americans; they rejected the AMRS's attempt to separate issues of morality from the political realities of their conditions of living. Garnet, however, took a different tack. He used the precepts of moral reform to urge a violent challenge to state power and, in voicing the culturalist notion of racial solidarity as the basis of that challenge, forced participants in the convention to make a choice between identifying, however ambivalently, with this fragile experiment of democracy or defining themselves and their political aims over and against it. Both positions presupposed the idea of racial solidarity: that African Americans ought to organize for themselves on the basis of their common experiences and move to in some way alleviate their situation. Both aimed, then, to improve the lot of the community. One, however, was in effect a soul-craft politics, an argument over the soul of the nation. The other laid the foundation of what we have come to recognize as a black nationalist politics.

Although in 1848 Garnet reprinted the "Address" with the full text of David Walker's *Appeal*, the rhetorical effect of his speech remained quite different from that of Walker's. The "Address," like the *Appeal*, called for slave insurrection and viewed the submission to slavery as sin. But unlike the *Appeal,* Garnet's speech was not a jeremiad. The call for violence was not couched in a prophetic language that warned the nation of the wages of sin. In fact, Garnet explicitly rejected attempts to imagine African Americans as a chosen people who reminded America of its covenantal duty to deal justly with others (particularly blacks). America, for him, was not the issue.

Walker's *Appeal,* on the other hand, in spite of its call for violence, did not force a choice of native identification. He demonized slaveholders and their defenders but, in the end, claimed the country as his birthright and offered it a means for salvation. In fact, African Americans remade in the image of Hebrew slaves, in his view, called the nation back to its principles and made it possible that "we may yet, under God, . . . become a united and happy people."² Nowhere in Garnet's address is this possibility mentioned. He simply ends obliquely, "Labor for the peace of the human race, and remember that you are FOUR MILLIONS."³

I am not claiming that Garnet rejected America outright and that his political aims were the overthrow of the country and the formation of a black nation-state. Such descriptions of his intentions would amount to fantasy. Instead, I only want to show that Garnet's speech, whether he intended it or not, exposed the ambivalence at the heart of the convention's efforts (its simultaneous rejection of American racism and its embrace of an American identity) and forced a choice. His inversion of the languages of moral reform and his radicalization of the politics of respectability (as a politics with an accent on agency-as-struggle) emphasized the plight of African Americans irrespective of the soul of the nation; black folk were addressed not as the potential saviors of the state but as saviors of themselves. The "American ideology," then, did not predetermine the content of the argument. It was beside the point.

But Garnet's efforts cannot be easily assimilated into a crass nationalist project in which our identities are hermetically sealed by some transcendental conception of race. Not at all. Garnet sought rhetorically to mobilize similarly situated selves (let's say men) to act and sacrifice in order to secure some consequences and avoid others. His was not a project in which "the people" could be talked about in primordial terms or in ways in which language, geography, or biology made them unique. Instead, Garnet appealed to the doings and sufferings of these folk: the fact that they had been singled out and were vulnerable to a certain kind of treatment and experience. This pragmatic view of race connects Garnet's speech to the underlying logic informing "race-based" politics in early nineteenth-century black political culture, that is, the idea of we-intentions based in the problem-solving activity arising in a violently racist society.

I have attempted throughout this book to trace, however vaguely, the outlines of a specific tradition of racial advocacy that presupposes this cultural logic—what I have described as a peculiar use of nation language. I have located it in two domains: the analogical uses of the Exodus story and the politics of respectability. Through biblical typology, particularly uses of Exodus, African Americans elevated their common experiences to biblical drama and found resources to account for their circumstances and respond effectively to them. By my reading, Exodus history sustained hope and a sense of possibility in the face of insurmountable evil. The analogical uses of the story enabled a sense of agency and resistance in persistent moments of despair and disillusionment (in light of the fact that the odds of human history were seemingly arrayed against the slaves). The politics of respectability extended this vision. Although complicated by its bourgeois aspirations and gendered presuppositions, this politics asserted the need for African Americans to live up to a common standard and take responsibility for themselves. Its efficacy stemmed from the immanent conversation it required: that African Americans reflect on the conditions of their collective lives. This Exodus politics, I have maintained, did not rely on a utopian refusal of limits; instead its prophetic power was found in the recognition of the historical constraints on blacks' actions and the limits that reality imposed on them. The crucial struggle, then, was and is not in quests for land or in efforts to eradicate demonized enemies. Rather, the struggle lies in the effort to create a free people and to live up to the moral principles that signify the best way of living.

In some ways, my use of nation language to describe all of this has been ironic. We often associate all uses of nation language with the ideology of nationalism. As such, a particular story of black nationalism has a hold over how we understand nation language in black political culture. In this narrative, black nationalism develops out of the desperation of African Americans—where the horrors of racial terror diminish any hope that America will ever be home. Black nationalism finds its initial place in the various schemes of colonization or emigration designed to escape this tyranny and feelings of desperation and alienation. It is assumed that the quest for a different place is linked to a quest for a nation-state. Wilson Moses notes, however, that black nationalism is not necessarily concerned with the quest for a nation-state, though many of its proponents may be.

For him, black nationalism has been nationalism only in the sense that it "seeks to unite the entire black family, assuming that the entire race has a collective destiny and message for humanity comparable to that of a nation."[4]

It can be said, then, that a deep-seated pessimism about American democracy and a desire for black unity animates the political project. To put it bluntly, black nationalists understand American democracy as a modern form of tyranny, a nation consumed by white supremacy.[5] If black folk are to achieve a modicum of sanity and well-being, they must reject this nation. Their allegiance must be to themselves because a necessary condition for the flourishing of American democracy is their subordination.[6] A choice is made. America is not for us, and a certain understanding of nation language becomes the way to articulate this rejection. It captures not only our distinctiveness in relation to the United States; it also anchors the idea of unity in an extra degree of particularity. The black nation, in this account, is predicated on definitions of sameness and otherness grounded in nature.

Most black people in the United States, I believe, do not characterize their actions or practices as nationalist, except those who profess black nationalism as their political project. When my great-grandmother used to tell me, with her Mississippi drawl, "Baby, don't let nobody tell you that you ain't nothing, always remember that you somebody and always act like you somebody," I don't think she had, for example, Molefi Asante's Afrocentricism in mind. Asante is fond of saying that Afrocentrisim is a simple idea: it's simply treating Africans as subjects, not as objects. Mymy, as we called her, consistently professed such simple ideas, but she would have thought Asante's nationalism odd.

Most black people in the United States, I believe, do not deny the existence or relevance of racial solidarity, except those who profess a radical individualism as their political project. When I was growing up in Mississippi people talked about black folks as a group all the time. Mr. Hyde, a black conservative in Moss Point, used to talk about the importance of black people in our town doing for themselves. He used to say, "If we take on responsibility as individuals then the burden of the race will be lifted." He never questioned the idea of solidarity; he merely thought that his kind of politics was best for the people of our community.

I think it an egregious error to leave the talk of racial solidarity to persons who espouse black nationalism as their political project and predicate such actions on a rejection of America, and it is equally problematic to limit responses to this political project to a wholesale abandonment of talk about racial solidarity. I have attempted in this book to tell a different story—one that chooses not to reject America, although doubts remain about the possibility of blacks' flourishing here. I have assumed all along that the organic conceptions of nation that came to dominate the mid- and late nineteenth century represent a second phase in the development of the language in African American political culture. Indeed the Exodus story (and Psalms 68:31) became a vehicle for articulating organic and, by extension, chauvinistic conceptions of the nation. The story lent its images to messianic visions of a promised land and the policing of the boundaries of "blackness" by scorned elites. This does not alarm me.

The different events of the story make plausible a number of different readings.[7] One could emphasize "the mighty arm of God or the slow march of the people, the land of milk and honey, the purging of counter-revolutionaries or the schooling of the new generation."[8] The point to be made is that messianic readings of the story by African Americans find their source in the choice to reject America. As Michael Walzer rightly notes, "messianism [a general way of describing ideological nationalisms] has its origins in disappointment, in all those Canaans that turn out to be almost barren."[9] The constant fight against despair, disillusionment, and defeat can easily lead to a desire for a once-and-for-all struggle where history itself, with its account of blacks' torture, pain and misery, becomes a burden from which the sufferers long to escape. Political messianism answers that longing; it offers a panacea not only for a particular evil but evil in general, and nation language is one of its primary tools.

As I understand its use in the early nineteenth century, nation language grounded common experiences and relationships in the effort to combat American racism. No extra degree of particularity was required, for race was merely an explanation that helped account for certain experiences in order to respond more effectively to specific problems. This view of nation did not fall out of use once organic understandings entered the language. That would have been odd. We need only think more broadly of the competing uses of *nation:* the principle of nationality, organic notions, and Wilsonian conceptions all informed early twentieth-century exchanges about nationalism. Old uses of words do not easily disappear. They often continue on, competing with newer conceptions while serving particular ends. Such was the case with this peculiar use of *nation* as merely an expression of solidarity.

I have described this view as pragmatic because it is grounded in the problem-solving activity of black agents. It is not a vulgar form of practicalism or opportunism; rather, its use has to do with conceiving of ways to promote black agency in and through a particular community of experience (actions that give ethical significance to an open-ended future). In particular, I have maintained that African American uses of nation language in the early nineteenth century did not presuppose a biological notion of race: racial or national identity was not a stable, fixed thing that stood apart from the vicissitudes of actual history. Rather, race language was an explanatory account of certain conditions of living that warranted problem-solving activity. In other words, identity was not about discovery, an archeological project in which blacks uncovered their true selves and inferred from that what they must do. Instead, taken together, the problem-solving activity turned out to be their lives.[10] The Exodus story helped along the way. Its use (and the languages of black Christianity in general) provided a means to describe the extensive, enduring, and serious consequences of white supremacy. I have not emphasized a territorialist reading of the use of the story. I've offered instead an ethical reading in which, as Nathaniel Paul noted in 1827, "righteousness alone exalteth a nation." In short, I have tried to isolate a tradition of racial advocacy, one animated by the idea of racial solidarity, that chooses America.

To choose America, however, is not to efface the evil of white supremacy. No matter how you read the Exodus story it begins with concrete evil. As such, the realities of American racism remain in spite of the choice, and the brutality of bondage is kept alive in living memory to remind us from whence we came. To choose America, then, is not to choose the nation as it is or as it was but, rather, as we hope it to be. The choice is prospective; it is all about a risk-ridden future. But the evil persists.

Sometimes we are at a loss as to how to respond to the disease, the dread, and despair in our lives. Throughout the nineteenth century, public figures grappled with the question of theodicy: how to make sense of African Americans' suffering in light of their conception of God? Some found blacks' condition a result of their own actions—that somehow they had turned their backs to God and were now suffering his wrath. Others, like Daniel Payne, wondered aloud if God was truly just. "Sometimes it seemed as though some wild beast had plunged his fangs into my heart and was squeezing out its life-blood," he wrote. Payne even questioned the existence of God: "If he does exist, is he just? If so, why does he suffer one race to oppress and enslave another?" His doubt weakened, however, as he reflected on his faith: "With God one day is as a thousand years and a thousand years as one day. Trust in Him and He will bring slavery and all its outrages to an end." Black Christianity and its specific accent on the hope of triumph over evil acted on Payne's "troubled soul like water on a burning fire."[11] At this level of abstraction, the Christian view of the tragic made sense of the order of things and, to some extent, empowered African Americans in a God-forsaken world. At this level of abstraction, we can confront "candidly individual and collective experience of evil in individuals and institutions—with little expectation of ridding the world of all evil."[12] But once we stop pondering God's intent or the meaning of the cosmos, once we stop thinking of liberation, say, as an ascent to a messianic kingdom and instead see it as an effort to leave Egypt and secure basic human dignity for ourselves and our children, we are then in historical time and confronted with the tragic choices of fragile human beings. Toni Morrison captures best the tragic sense of choosing America in the pained questioning of Stamp Paid: "What are these people? You tell me, Jesus. What are they?"[13] Stamp Paid's questions acknowledge the fact that even as we choose to identify with this place that choice is made in light of historical experience and the immediacy of evil.

My understanding of the tragic follows Sidney Hook's brilliant account in *Pragmatism and the Tragic Sense of Life* (1974). Hook offers a vision of tragedy, by way of John Dewey and William James, that frames the central themes of pragmatism—an open-ended universe, an accent on human agency, and the importance of critical intelligence—with the vital options, inescapable limitations, and piecemeal losses we all confront as we act in the world. Relying heavily on William James, Hook suggests that "no matter how intelligent and humane our choices, there are real losses and real losers." The reality of our lives, the fact that we live in a dangerous world, and the seriousness that we attribute to life means "that ineluctable noes and losses form a part of it, that there are genuine sacrifices, and that something permanently drastic and bitter always remains at the bottom of the cup."[14]

Tragedy is an inescapable part of the moral exigencies of life. It involves principally the moral choices we make daily between competing and irreconcilable goods, and it entails the consequences we must endure, if we live, and the responsibility we must embrace without yielding to what Toni Morrison calls "marrow weariness." Tragedy, in this view, is not understood as preordained doom; rather, it depends on us and, to some extent, the choices we make; "we become the creators of our own tragic history."[15] As Hook writes:

Every mediation entails some sacrifice. The quest for the unique good of the situation, for what is to be done here and now, may point to what is better than anything else available, but what it points to is also a lesser evil. It is a lesser evil whether found in a compromise or in moderating the demand of a just claim or in learning to live peacefully with one's differences on the same general principle which tell us that a divorce is better for all parties concerned than a murder.[16]

The pragmatic sense of the tragic, then, attempts to make possible living in a world that is inescapably tragic "without lamentation, defiance, or make-believe." We will always be confronted with conflicting moral ideals, and even our best efforts cannot escape this fact. In this light, our task is to enlarge human freedom by way of critical intelligence and a bit of luck in a world shot through with pain and suffering.

With this view in mind, I read Henry Highland Garnet's address as exposing the tragic sense of life at the heart of African American politics: the fact that we are constantly having to choose either to identify ourselves with this fragile democracy, struggling for its soul, or to define ourselves over and against it—and live with the consequences of such choices without yielding to despair. Pharaoh or some such evil is indeed on both sides of the blood-red waters.

I have urged throughout these pages a reading of nation language that simultaneously accents the idea of racial solidarity and identifies with America. My aim has been to give another kind of support, one often associated with black nationalism, to that soul-craft politics which assumes that "by the irony implicit in American democracy, [we] symbolize its most stringent testing and the possibility of its greatest freedom."[17] Garnet's challenge to this view lost by only one vote, and we have been making and remaking that choice ever since.

Notes

1. Lawrence Levine, *Black Culture and Black Consciousness: Afro-American Folk Thought from Slavery to Freedom* (New York: Oxford University Press, 1977), chap. 1, particularly the "Quest for Certainty" section.

2. Theophus Smith, *Conjuring Culture* (New York: Oxford University Press, 1994), 55. Of course, the language of Republicanism was a ready resource for African American conceptions of freedom.

3. Michael Walzer, *Exodus and Revolution* (New York: Basic, 1985), 11.

4. Ibid., 12.

5. Eugene Genovese, *Roll, Jordan, Roll: The World the Slaves Made* (New York: Vintage, 1976), 280–81.

6. Of course, this echoes Benedict Anderson's theory of nationalism. Anderson argues that the nation *is* an imagined community, imagined as both inherently limited and sovereign. It is imagined because members of any nation "will never know most of their fellow members, meet them, or even hear of them, yet in the minds of each lives the image of their communion." It is limited because the nation is finite; it has boundaries outside of which exist other nations. And it is sovereign "because the concept was born in an age in which Enlightenment and Revolution were destroying the legitimacy of the divinely ordained hierarchical dynastic realm." I am not so much concerned here about ideas of sovereignty and national limits as I am about the way different groups imagine national belonging. In the case of African Americans, the reference to biblical narrative, particularly Exodus, served as a critical resource in the construction of the nation. The freedom of the Israelites was linked with the eventual liberation of blacks in the United States. So,

by analogy, blacks in the United States were the children of God, a chosen people and a peculiar (perhaps holy) nation. See Benedict Anderson, *Imagined Communities: Reflections on the Origin and Spread of Nationalism* (New York: Verso, 1993), 6–7.

7. Genovese, *Roll, Jordan, Roll,* 283.

8. Ibid.

9. Ibid.

10. Ibid., 284.

11. Michael Walzer, *Interpretation and Social Criticism* (Cambridge: Harvard University Press, 1987), 43.

12. Walzer, *Exodus and Revolution,* 3.

13. My reading of Walzer is greatly influenced by Jonathan Allen. Jonathan and I were graduate students at Princeton together. He wrote a paper on *Exodus and Revolution* that I believe remains the best explication of the text there is. I am greatly indebted to him.

14. Jonathan Allen, "Exodus and Revolution" (Princeton University, 1991, photocopy).

15. Isaiah Berlin, *The Crooked Timber of Humanity: Chapters in the History of Ideas* (New York: Knopf, 1991), 246.

16. Albert Raboteau, "Exodus and the American Israel," in *African-American Christianity: Essays in History,* ed. Paul E. Johnson (Berkeley: University of California Press, 1994), 246. Also see Raboteau's *Fire in the Bones: Reflections on African-American Religious History* (Boston: Beacon, 1995).

17. Marilyn Richardson, ed., *Maria Stewart, America's First Black Woman Political Writer: Essays and Speeches* (Bloomington: Indiana University Press, 1987), 39.

18. Ibid.

19. John Bracey, Jr., August Meier, and Elliot Rudwick, eds., *Black Nationalism in America* (Indianapolis and New York: Bobbs-Merrill, 1970), xxv.

20. See W. E. B. Du Bois's *Dusk of Dawn: An Essay Toward an Autobiography of a Race Concept* (New Brunswick: Transaction, 1994), 153.

21. Wilson Moses, *Classical Black Nationalism: From the American Revolution to Marcus Garvey* (New York: New York University Press, 1996), 4–5.

22. He also describes this as racial messianism: "the perception of a person or a group, by itself or by others, as having a manifest destiny or a God-given role to assert the providential goals of history and to bring about the kingdom of God on earth." See his *Black Messiahs and Uncle Toms: Social and Literary Manipulations of a Religious Myth* (University Park: Pennsylvania State University Press, 1993), 4.

23. Wilson Moses, *The Golden Age of Black Nationalism, 1850–1925* (New York: Oxford University Press, 1978), 25.

24. Moses maintains that "the black nationalist of the nineteenth century tended to accept the descriptions of the various races and their innate characteristics almost exactly as they had been described by the European philosophers. . . . Racial chau-

vinism therefore often consisted of arguing that nature had actually been kinder to the sensitive and gentle African than to the stolid, frigid European." Ibid.

25. Paul Taylor's brilliant essay "Racialism without Metaphysical Difficulty; Racism without Moral Error" (1994, photocopy) makes this point quite forcefully.

26. Moses, *Black Messiahs and Uncle Toms*, 8.

27. Moses, *Classical Black Nationalism*, 8.

28. Ibid., 6.

29. Of course, Moses would describe this as a form of pragmatic nationalism, a form of solidarity he contrasts with mystical nationalism. My intention is to collapse this distinction, for it really confuses what is a complicated moment, and describe the view of race as pragmatic (in a more technical sense).

30. Richard Rorty, "Solidarity," in *Contingency, Irony, and Solidarity* (New York: Cambridge University Press, 1989), and Wilfred Sellars, "Objectivity, Intersubjectivity, and the Moral Point of View," in *Science and Metaphysics: Variations on Kantian Themes* (New York: Routledge & Kegan Paul, 1968), chap. 7.

31. Rorty, "Solidarity," 194.

32. Ibid., 195.

33. Ralph Ellison, "What America Would Be Like without Blacks," in *The Collected Essays of Ralph Ellison*, ed. John F. Callahan (New York: Modern Library, 1995), 577.

34. Toni Morrison, *Beloved* (New York: Penguin Group, 1987), 244.

CHAPTER TWO

1. Delany went on to say that "prayer is a spiritual means used in conformity to the spiritual law, and can only be instrumental in attaining a spiritual end. Neither physical wants, nor temporal demands of man can be supplied by it" in this serial in *The North Star*, 16 February 1849, 2; 23 March 1849, 2; and 13 April 1849, 2.

2. Theodore Wright, "The Slave Has a Friend in Heaven, Though He May Have None Here," in *Proceedings of the New England Anti-Slavery Convention* (Boston: Isaac Knapp, 1836), 20–22; reprint, Philip S. Foner and Robert James Branham, eds., *Lift Every Voice: African American Oratory, 1787–1900* (Tuscaloosa: University of Alabama Press, 1998), 165.

3. Foner and Branham, *Lift Every Voice*, 165.

4. W. E. B. Du Bois, *Souls of Black Folk*, in *W. E. B. Du Bois Writings* (New York: Library of America, 1986), 499.

5. Cornel West, "Subversive Joy and Revolutionary Patience in Black Christianity," in *Prophetic Fragments* (Grand Rapids and Trenton: Eerdmans and Africa World Press, 1988), 163.

6. Timothy Mitchell, "The Limits of the State: Beyond Statist Approaches and Their Critics," *American Political Science Review* 85 (March 1991): 81. My thinking

in this regard is greatly influenced by the work of Wahneema Lubiano. See her "Black Nationalism and Black Common Sense," in *The House That Race Built: Black Americans, U.S. Terrain,* ed. Wahneema Lubiano (New York: Pantheon, 1997), 232–52.

7. Evelyn Brooks Higginbotham, *Righteous Discontent: The Women's Movement in the Black Baptist Church, 1880–1920* (Cambridge: Harvard University Press, 1993), 8. She draws on the work of Peter Berger and Richard Neuhaus, *To Empower People: The Role of Mediating Structures in Public Policy* (Washington, D.C.: American Enterprise Institute, 1977).

8. This is a shorthand version of Michael Omi and Howard Winant's definition of the racial state in *Racial Formation in the United States: From the 1960s to the 1990s,* 2d ed. (New York: Routledge, 1994), 83–84. They rely on the work of Bob Jessup, *The Capitalist State* (New York: New York University Press, 1982), and Theda Skocpol, "Bringing the State Back In: A Report on Current Comparative Research on the Relationship between States and Social Structures," *Items* 36, nos. 1–2 (1982).

9. Jo Ann Boydston, ed., *John Dewey: The Later Works, 1925–1953,* vol. 2, *1925–1927* (Carbondale: Southern Illinois University Press, 1984), 245–46.

10. *The Doctrines and Discipline of the African Methodist Episcopal Church* (Philadelphia, 1817), 14.

11. Higginbotham, *Righteous Discontent,* 9.

12. Ibid.

13. Boydston, *John Dewey,* 2:314.

14. Matthew Festenstein, *Pragmatism and Political Theory: From Dewey to Rorty* (Chicago: University of Chicago Press, 1997), 85.

15. Boydston, *John Dewey,* 2:328.

16. Will Gravely, "The Rise of African Churches in America (1786–1822): Reexamining the Contexts," in *African-American Religion: Interpretive Essays in History and Culture,* ed. Timothy E. Fulop and Albert J. Raboteau (New York: Routledge, 1997), 136.

17. I am thinking of the work of Albert Raboteau, Will Gravely, Timothy Smith, Lawrence Levine, and a number of other religious historians.

18. I should acknowledge that there is some controversy around this dating. The Gallery incident is now commonly dated sometime in 1792. Albert Raboteau's essay on Richard Allen in *A Fire in the Bones* (Boston: Beacon, 1995) uses the 1792 date. I have chosen to stay with November 1787 because AME church historians have retained this date.

19. I have emphasized *national* here because of the existence of the African Union Church. This denomination tended to be more regional, appearing in Delaware, Pennsylvania, the New York region, and some congregations in the South. But the AME church was the first *truly* national black denomination.

20. Gravely, "Rise of African Churches," 137. Also see John H. Cromwell, "The

First Negro Churches in the District of Columbia," *Journal of Negro History* 7 (1922): 65; *"The Negro Pew": Being an Inquiry Concerning the Propriety of Distinctions in the House of God, on Account of Color* (Boston: Isaac Knapp, 1837); B. W. Arnett, ed., *Proceedings of the Semi-Centenary Celebration of the African Methodist Church of Cincinnati, Held in Allen Temple, February 8–10, 1874* (Cincinnati: H. Watkin, 1874).

21. Christopher Rush, *A Short Account of the Rise and Progress of the African American Methodist Episcopal Church in America* (New York, 1843), 60–73; reprint, Milton C. Sernett, ed., *African-American Religious History: A Documentary Witness* (Durham: Duke University Press, 1985), 151.

22. Gravely, "Rise of African Churches," 138; also see Mechal Sobel, *Trabelin' On: The Slave Journey of an Afro-Baptist Faith* (Westport, Conn.: Greenwood, 1979), 265–66.

23. Preamble of the Free African Society (Philadelphia, 1787); reprint, John Bracey, Jr., August Meier, and Elliott Rudwick, eds., *Black Nationalism in America* (Indianapolis: Bobbs-Merrill, 1970), 19–20.

24. This healthy tension between religious commitments and secular aims exposes perhaps an ambiguity in the term *community*. We can think of communities in a descriptive sense. We can describe a range of communities of individuals banded together to secure and avoid particular consequences. Criminal syndicates, gangs, corporate elites, white racists, nation-states can all be described as communities of sorts. But communities not only have a descriptive sense; they also have what John Dewey calls a normative sense. The term describes not only our associations but also the way we *should* associate. Of course, gangs and criminal syndicates are examples of, on one level, highly social behavior, but they are also highly antisocial in other ways, and it is precisely in our concern with the kind of associations we make and sustain that the moral or normative sense of *community* takes on added force.

25. Gravely, "Rise of African Churches," 139; see also Robert G. Sherer, "Negro Churches in Rhode Island before 1860," *Rhode Island History* 25 (January 1966): 9–25; Julien Rammelkamp, "The Providence Negro Community, 1820–1842," *Rhode Island History* 7 (January 1948): 20–33.

26. Gayraud Wilmore, "The Black Church Freedom Movement," in *Black Religion and Black Radicalism: An Interpretation of the Religious History of the Afro-American People,* 2d ed. (New York: Orbis, 1994), 74–98.

27. David Walker, "Address Delivered before the General Colored Association at Boston," *Freedom's Journal,* 19 December 1828; reprint, Bracey et al., *Black Nationalism,* 31.

28. Bracey et al., *Black Nationalism,* 31.

29. Ibid.

30. Ibid., 32.

31. Ibid., 33–34.

32. Peter Hinks, *To Awaken My Afflicted Brethren: David Walker and the Problem*

of Antebellum Slave Resistance (University Park: Pennsylvania University Press, 1997), 91.

33. Samuel Cornish, *The Rights of All,* 18 September 1829.

34. West, *Prophetic Fragments,* 163.

35. Here I am simply echoing the description of Charles Long. His essay "Perspectives for a Study of African-American Religion" remains a critical guidepost for work in African American religious studies. In some ways, we have yet to come close to what he called for in 1971. Reprinted in Fulop and Raboteau, *African-American Religion,* 21–36.

36. Daniel Coker's sermon is reprinted in Herbert Aptheker, ed., *A Documentary History of the Negro People of the United States* (New York: Citadel, 1969), 77.

37. Albert Raboteau, "The Black Experience in American Evangelicalism: The Meaning of Slavery," in *African-American Religion: Interpretive Essays in History and Culture,* ed. Timothy E. Fulop and Albert Raboteau (New York: Routledge, 1997), 99–102.

38. Du Bois, *Souls of Black Folk,* 501.

39. Raboteau, "Black Experience in American Evangelicalism," 100.

40. I do not want to suggest that Raboteau fails to recognize this point: he says very clearly that "otherworldly symbols reflected thisworldly concerns" (100). My only aim here is to lobby for the elimination of the distinction altogether.

41. Du Bois, *Souls of Black Folk,* 501–2.

42. Ibid., 502.

43. Ibid.

44. Ibid.

45. Ibid., 504.

46. I have adapted this phrase from Hortense Spillers, "Moving On Down the Line: Variations on the African-American Sermon," in *The Bounds of Race: Perspectives on Hegemony and Resistance,* ed. Dominick LaCapra (Ithaca: Cornell University Press, 1991), 39–71. She writes that "if by ambivalence we might mean the abeyance of closure, or break in the passage of syntagmatic movement from one more or less stable property to another, as in the radical disjunction between 'African' and 'American,' then ambivalence remains not only the privileged and arbitrary judgment of a postmodernist imperative, but also a strategy that names the cultural situation as a *wounding*" (54). I take Spillers's aim here to extend what can be considered an analytic term of postmodern theory in the direction of the particular experiences of African Americans. To avoid the need for such verbal gymnastics, I simply join Spillers's notion with that of Raymond Williams (a move I think she makes but never explicitly acknowledges). In *Marxism and Literature* (Oxford: Oxford University Press, 1977), Williams defines what he calls "structures of feelings." He writes: "We are talking about characteristic elements of impulse, restraint, and tone; specifically affective elements of consciousness and relationships: not feelings against thought, but thought as felt and feeling as thought: practical

consciousness of a present kind, in a living and interrelating continuity. We are then defining these elements as a structure: as a set, with specific internal relations, at once interlocking and in tension. Yet we are also defining a social experience which is still in process, often indeed not yet recognized as social but taken to be private, idiosyncratic, and even isolating, but which in analysis has its emergent, connecting and dominant characteristics, indeed its specific hierarchies" (132). *Structures of ambivalence* means, for me, then, a social experience (that is still in process) characterized by a sense of wounding, of being in but not of a nation that structures the experiences of African Americans.

47. Williams, *Marxism and Literature,* 134.

48. This formulation attempts to include what Cornel West calls the triple crisis of self-recognition, that is, the cultural predicament that "was comprised of African appearance and unconscious mores, involuntary displacement to America without American status, and American alienation from the European ethos complicated through domination by incompletely European Americans." *Prophesy Deliverance! An Afro-American Revolutionary Christianity* (Philadelphia: Westminster, 1982), 31.

49. Raboteau, "The Black Experience in American Evangelicalism," 92.

50. Ibid., 95.

51. Daniel Coker, *A Dialogue between a Virginian and an African Minister* (Baltimore: Benjamin Edes for Joseph James, 1819); reprint, Dorothy Porter, ed., *Negro Protest Pamphlets* (New York: Arno, 1969).

52. *David Walker's Appeal to the Coloured Citizens of the World, but in Particular, and Very Expressly, to Those of the United States of America* (New York: Hill and Wang, 1965), 13.

53. Wilson Moses, "The Black Jeremiad and American Messianic Traditions," in *Black Messiahs and Uncle Toms: Social and Literary Manipulations of a Religious Myth,* rev. ed. (University Park: Pennsylvania State University, 1993), 30–31.

54. *Walker's Appeal,* 2.

55. I adapted the concept of critical intelligence from John Dewey.

56. *Walker's Appeal,* 10.

57. See Charles Mills's *Blackness Visible: Essays on Philosophy and Race* (Ithaca: Cornell University Press, 1998), 7.

58. Thomas Jefferson, *Notes on Virginia,* in *The Life and Selected Writings of Thomas Jefferson,* ed. Adrienne Koch and William Peden (New York, 1944), 138, 139. Also see Winthrop Jordan, *White over Black: American Attitudes Toward the Negro, 1550–1812* (New York: Norton, 1977), 438.

59. Jefferson, *Notes on Virginia,* 141–43; Jordan, *White over Black,* 438–39.

60. Hinks, *To Awaken,* 209–10; my reading of Walker is greatly influenced by Hinks, whose reading of *Walker's Appeal* is the single best interpretation of the document available.

61. Ibid., 211.

62. *Walker's Appeal,* 70n.

63. Hinks, *To Awaken,* 214–15.

64. Quoted in *The Public and Its Problems* in Boydston, *John Dewey,* 2:335.

65. Jo Ann Boydston, ed., *John Dewey: The Later Works,* vol.7, *1932* (Carbondale: Southern Illinois University Press, 1985), 162.

66. *Walker's Appeal,* 23–27.

67. Ibid., 23.

68. Hinks, *To Awaken,* 224.

69. *Walker's Appeal,* 25.

70. Ibid.

71. Ibid., 61–62.

72. Ibid., 28.

73. Ibid.

74. Ibid., 74.

75. Ibid., 25–26.

76. Ibid., 59.

77. Ibid., xiv.

78. Walker writes of salvific history early on in the *Appeal:* "But has not the Lord an oppressed and suffering people among them? Does the Lord condescend to hear their cries and see their tears in consequence of oppression? Will he let the oppressors rest comfortably and happy always? Will he not cause the very children of the oppressors to rise up against them, and oftimes put them to death? 'God works in many ways his wonders to perform'" (3).

79. Ibid., 66.

80. Ibid., 69–70.

81. Hinks, *To Awaken,* 247.

82. *Walker's Appeal,* 55.

CHAPTER THREE

1. Theophus Smith, *Conjuring Culture* (New York: Oxford University Press, 1994), 62–63.

2. Ibid., 7, 63.

3. Werner Sollors, *Beyond Ethnicity: Consent and Descent in American Culture* (New York: Oxford University Press, 1986), 41.

4. Ibid., 49.

5. Richard Allen, *The Life, Experience and Gospel Labors of the Rt. Rev. Richard Allen* (Nashville: Abingdon, 1983), 52–53.

6. Sacvan Bercovitch, *The Rites of Assent: Transformations in the Symbolic Construction of America* (New York: Routledge, 1993), 33.

7. Ibid., 33–34.

8. Ibid., 34. In the *American Jeremiad* Bercovitch argues contra Perry Miller that uses of the rhetoric of errand to chastise the faithful of New England sustained a sense of the sacredness of the original errand into the Wilderness. In effect, the sermonic form of the jeremiad, through its continued use from the seventeenth century to the nineteenth century, became the central means for the expression of a broader American ideology. See Sacvan Bercovitch, *The American Jeremiad* (Madison: University of Wisconsin Press, 1978).

9. Bercovitch, *Rites of Assent*, 36. In the mid–nineteenth century, the symbols of errand were reworked as America's Manifest Destiny. America, the Redeemer Nation, was now "popularly conceived as spreading the blessings of democracy, free enterprise, and Protestantism across the continent." The rhetoric of errand laid the foundation for these imperialistic moves, for the story of Exodus, its promise of land, and the idea of chosenness justified, to some degree, the conquest and subordination of other people.

10. Ibid. It was also during this period, according to Bercovitch, that a transformation in the role of the founding fathers (the Puritans, not Washington, Jefferson, and so on) occurred. They were now the stuff of legend, characters in a story of cultural beginnings. The backdrop of this change was the revision of the Puritan errand: Exodus was now the property of all Anglo-American settlers and heralded "one city on a hill." The foundation was then laid for America's civil religion.

11. Ibid., 37.

12. Ibid., 38.

13. Samuel Williams, *A Discourse on the Love of Country* (Salem, 1775), 22; Ebenezer Baldwin, *The Duty of Rejoicing* (New York, 1776), pp. 38–40; Thomas Blockway, *America Saved* (Hartford, 1784), 24. Bercovitch also states that "[w]ith the revolution, the Puritan vision flowered into the myth of America. For errand itself was rooted in biblical myth. However eccentric their interpretations, the Puritans had relied on the authority of scripture. . . . The Revolutionary Whigs took the justification, rather than the tradition behind it, as their authority. No matter how piously they invoked scripture they were appealing not to a Christian tradition, but to the series of recent events through which they defined the American experience." *Rites of Assent,* 39.

14. Ibid., 40.

15. Ibid., 39.

16. Ibid.

17. Vincent Harding, "The Uses of the Afro-American Past," in *The Religious Situation, 1969,* ed. Donald R. Cutter (Boston: Beacon, 1969), 829–40; also quoted in Raboteau's "Exodus and the American Israel," in *African-American Christianity: Essays in History*, ed. Paul E. Johnson (Berkeley: University of California Press, 1994), 9.

18. One of the distinguishing aspects of this concept of "the people" is that the source of individual identity is located within it. The populace is seen as the bearer

of sovereignty, the central object of loyalty, and the basis of collective solidarity. And, for some, this process marks the beginning of modern nationalism, in which its distinctive modern meaning emerged in England in the sixteenth century when the word *nation* "was applied to the population of the country and made synonymous with the word people." Liah Greenfeld, *Nationalism: Five Roads to Modernity* (Cambridge: Harvard University Press, 1991), 6. See also Guido Zernatto, "Nation: The History of a Word," *Review of Politics* 6 (1944): 352–66.

19. Bercovitch, *Rites of Assent,* 44.

20. Ibid., 46–47.

21. Ibid., 43.

22. Ibid., 367.

23. Giles Gunn, *Thinking Across the American Grain* (Chicago: University of Chicago Press, 1992), 30.

24. Bercovitch, *Rites of Assent,* 46.

25. Ibid., 51.

26. Ibid., 49.

27. Michael Walzer, *Exodus and Revolution* (New York: Basic, 1985), 108.

28. Ibid.

29. Nathaniel Paul, "An Address Delivered on the Celebration of the Abolition of Slavery in the State of New York, July 5, 1827," *Freedom's Journal,* 10 August 1827; reprint, Carter G. Woodson, ed., *Negro Orators and Their Orations* (New York: Russell & Russell, 1969), 64.

30. Woodson, *Negro Orators,* 74.

31. Ibid., 74.

32. Ibid., 76.

33. Bercovitch, *Rites of Assent,* 36.

34. See Nathan O. Hatch, *The Democratization of American Christianity* (New Haven: Yale University Press, 1989).

35. C. Eric Lincoln and Lawrence Mamiya, *The Black Church in the African American Experience* (Durham: Duke University Press, 1990), 47.

36. Ibid.

37. Ibid.

38. My concern is not with understanding the black church in the terms of nation-state formation. Instead, I want to direct attention to the ways black national identity is imagined with a *difference,* that is, apart from the usual features of nation formation, and the distinctive role of black religion (as a set of practices and as an institution) in the lives of African Americans is the best place to begin. See David W. Wills, "Exodus Piety: African American Religion in an Age of Immigration," in *Minority Faiths and the American Protestant Mainstream,* ed. David O'Brien and Jonathan Sarna (forthcoming), 19.

39. James Horton and Lois Horton, *In Hope of Liberty: Culture, Community and*

Protest among Northern Free Blacks, 1700–1860 (New York: Oxford University Press, 1997), 207.

40. *Freedom's Journal,* 1827, in *Black Nationalism in America,* ed. John H. Bracey, Jr., August Meier, and Elliot Rudwick (New York: Bobbs-Merrill, 1970), 26.

41. A number of black newspapers emerged in the early nineteenth century. All of them experienced financial hardships. Samuel Cornish was involved with a number of short-lived papers: *Freedom's Journal* (1827), *The Rights of All* (1829), and, the longest running of the early newspapers, the *Colored American* (1837). There were others, such as the *Weekly Advocate* (Charles Ray only published one issue of it in 1837 before he joined with Cornish to publish the *Colored American*). David Ruggles published the *Mirror of Liberty* in New York in 1838; its appearance was quite irregular. See Donald Jacobs, ed., *Antebellum Black Newspapers* (Westport, Conn: Greenwood, 1976), and Martin Dann, *The Black Press, 1827–1890: The Quest for National Identity* (New York: Putnam, 1971).

42. Benedict Anderson, *Imagined Communities: Reflections on the Origins and Spread of Nationalism* (London: Verso, 1993), 33.

43. Ibid.

44. Ibid., 35.

45. Use of Acts 17 poses some interesting problems for my reading of Exodus. How can God simultaneously have made of one blood Pharaoh and the chosen people? The answer, of course, depends on the context as well as the actions of individuals. African Americans used Acts 17 quite often to derail claims of permanent difference between the races. It was one way of getting at a monogenetic account of human beginnings. Moreover, the fact that God made us of one blood does not render irrelevant the actions of human beings. Some of God's children choose to act wrongly. Others follow his word. Exodus, on the other hand, was often deployed to account for the past, present, and future of people caught under certain circumstances. In other words, it was a means to narrate human activity and God's activity in history, particularly God's willingness to act on behalf of those who have given their lives to him.

46. I am thinking about the works of Charles Caldwell, *Thoughts on the Original Unity of the Human Race* (1830), as well as George Calvert's work on phrenology in 1832. Samuel George Morton's *Crania Americana* (1839) and the work of his follower Josiah Nott also come to mind. The important point is that by the "late 1840s the racial question was at the heart of scholarly discussion in the United States. . . . The concept of racial inequality had clearly carried the day . . . [and] the most general disagreement with Nott and Morton was not that they divided the world into superior and inferior races, but that in adopting polygenesis as the original reason for racial differences, they had challenged the Mosaic account of creation." Reginald Horsman, *Race and Manifest Destiny: The Origins of American Racial Anglo-Saxonism* (Cambridge: Harvard University Press, 1981), 133.

47. James McCune Smith, *The Destiny of the People of Color, A Lecture Delivered before the Philomathean Society and Hamilton Lyceum in January 1841* (New York: n.p., 1843), 9. See also *A Dissertation on the Influence of Climate on Longevity* (New York: Office of the Merchant's Magazine, 1846); Frederick Douglass, "The Claims of the Negro Ethnologically Considered," a speech delivered to the Philozetian and Phi Delta Societies of Western Reserve College in Hudson, Ohio, 12 July 1854, in *The Frederick Douglass Papers*, ser. 1: *Speeches, Debates, and Interviews*, vol. 2 (1847–1854), ed. John W. Blassingame (New Haven: Yale University Press, 1982), 505.

CHAPTER FOUR

1. See Hayden White's *Tropics of Discourse: Essays in Cultural Criticism* (Baltimore: Johns Hopkins University Press, 1978).

2. *Oxford English Dictionary*, 2d ed. (Oxford: Clarendon, 1989), 231, 69.

3. E. Ellis Cashmore, *Dictionary of Race and Ethnic Relations*, 2d ed. (London: Routledge, 1988), 235. Also see Michael Banton and Jonathan Harwood, *The Race Concept* (Newton Abbot, U.K.: David & Charles, 1975).

4. Jupiter Hammond, *America's First Negro Poet: The Complete Works of Jupiter of Long Island*, ed. Stanley Austin Ransom, Jr. (Port Washington, N.Y.: Kennikat, 1970), 69.

5. Absalom Jones's Thanksgiving Sermon, Philadelphia, 1 January 1808, in Dorothy Porter's *Early Negro Writing* (Boston: Beacon, 1971), 339.

6. Martin Delany, *The Condition, Elevation, Emigration and Destiny of the Colored People of the United States* (1852; Baltimore: Black Classic, 1993), 209.

7. Raymond Williams, *Culture and Society: 1780–1950* (New York: Columbia University Press, 1983), xiii.

8. John B. Thompson, *Studies in the Theory of Ideology* (Berkeley: University of California Press, 1984), 7.

9. Ibid.

10. George L. Mosse, *Toward the Final Solution: A History of European Racism* (New York: Howard Fertig, 1978), 2.

11. The powerful display of religious sentiment in the rhetoric of the Revolution is important to note here. As Ellis Sandoz suggests, the religious backdrop on which republican claims were made assumed "man as a moral agent living freely in a reality that is good, coming from the hand of God. . . . Among the chief hindrances to this life of true liberty is the oppression of men. . . . Liberty is, thus, an essential principle of man's constitution, a natural trait which yet reflects the supernatural Creator." *Political Sermons of the American Founding Era: 1730–1805*, ed. Ellis Sandoz (Indianapolis: Liberty, 1990), xix–xx.

12. Richard Nisbet, *Slavery Not Forbidden by Scripture. Or a Defence of the West-India Planters, from the Aspersions Thrown out against Them, by the Author of the Pam-*

phlet, Entitled, "An Address to the Inhabitants of the British Settlements in America, upon Slave-Keeping" (Philadelphia, 1773); reprint, Louis Ruchames, ed., *Racial Thought in America,* vol. 1, *From the Puritans to Abraham Lincoln* (Amherst: University of Massachusetts Press, 1969), 145–46.

13. James Otis, *Rights of the British Colonies Asserted and Proved* (Boston, 1764), 29; also quoted in Gary Nash, *Race and Revolution* (Madison, Wis.: Madison House, 1990), 8.

14. Arthur Lee, "Address on Slavery," *Rind's Virginia Gazette,* 19 March 1767, document reprinted in Nash, *Race and Revolution,* 91–96.

15. Samuel Stanhope Smith, *An Essay on the Causes of the Variety of Complexion and Figure in the Human Species. To Which Are Added, Animad-versions on Certain Remarks Made on the First Edition of This Essay . . . ,* ed. Winthrop Jordan (1810; Cambridge, Mass.: Belknap, 1965), 161–64. Also quoted in Winthrop Jordan, *White over Black: American Attitudes toward the Negro, 1550–1812* (New York: Norton, 1977), 443.

16. Hugh Williamson, *Observations on the Climate in Different Parts of America* (New York, 1811), quoted in Reginald Horsman, *Race and Manifest Destiny: The Origins of American Racial Anglo-Saxonism* (Cambridge: Harvard University Press, 1981), 99.

17. See Jordan, *White over Black,* 287; Benjamin Rush, "Address on Slavery of the Negroes," in *Selected Writings of Benjamin Rush,* ed. Dagobert D. Runes (New York: Philosophical Library, 1947), 24–26.

18. Benjamin Rush, "Observations Intended to Favour a Supposition That the Black Color (as It Is Called) of the Negroes Is Derived from the Leprosy. Read at a Special Meeting July 14, 1797," *Transactions of the American Philosophical Society* 4 (1799): 289–97. Also see William Stanton, *The Leopard's Spots: Scientific Attitudes toward Race in America, 1815–59* (Chicago: University of Chicago Press, 1960).

19. Rush remarked that "Dr. Smith in his elegant and ingenious Essay on the Variety of Color and Figure in the Human Species has derived it from four causes, viz. Climate, diet, state of society, and diseases. I admit the Doctor's facts, and reasoning as far as he has extended them, in the fullest manner. I shall only add to them a few observations which are intended to prove that the color and figure of that part of our fellow creatures who are known by the epithet negroes, are derived from a modification of that disease, which is known by the name of Leprosy." Ruchames, *Racial Thought in America,* 218.

20. John Adams, writing under the pseudonym Humphrey Ploughjogger, *Boston Gazette,* 14 October 1765 and 19 January 1767; reprinted in Robert E. Taylor, ed., *Papers of John Adams* (Cambridge, 1977), 181–82, and quoted in David R. Roediger, *The Wages of Whiteness: Race and the Making of the American Working Class* (London: Verso, 1991), 28.

21. Edwin Clifford Holland, *A Refutation of the Calumnies Circulated against the Southern & Western States* (Charleston: A. E. Miller, 1822), v–vi, 7–15, 60–61, 77–

78, 82–87, quoted in Larry Tise, *Proslavery: A History of the Defense of Slavery in America, 1701–1840* (Athens: University of Georgia Press, 1987), 60.

22. Richard Allen, *The Life Experience and Gospel Labors of the Rt. Rev. Richard Allen* (Nashville: Abingdon, 1960). Also see Absalom Jones and Richard Allen, *Narrative of the Proceedings of the Black People, during the Late Awful Calamity, in the year 1793* (Philadelphia, 1794), reprinted in Nash, *Race and Revolution*, 182–83.

23. James Forten, *Letters from a Man of Colour on a Late Bill before the Senate of Pennsylvania* (Philadelphia, 1813), reprinted in Nash, *Race and Revolution*, 192.

24. Ibid.

25. Jordan, *White over Black*, 289.

26. Charles Caldwell, "An Essay on the Causes of the Variety of Complexion and Figure in the Human Species," *American Review of History and Politics* 2 (July 1811): 148.

27. Ibid., 136.

28. As Winthrop Jordan notes, environmentalism was especially attractive to Americans during this period for two reasons: (1) the estrangement from England compelled colonists to "ask what made the child different from the parent, the New World different from the Old, the continent different from island"; (2) "as Americans talked increasingly of the rights of 'man'—natural rights—they were impelled to take an environmentalist approach to the differences among men. For if all men everywhere possessed the same rights and were in this sense really created equal, then distinctions among groups of men stood in another category—created not by God but by 'accidental causes.' " *White over Black*, 288–89.

29. Horsman, *Race and Manifest Destiny*, 102.

30. Webster was an environmentalist. In 1793 he published *Effects of Slavery, on Morals and Industry* (Hartford, 1793). He wrote that "making the usual allowances for the effects of their native climate, all the peculiar features in the character of the African race in America, may be justly ascribed to their depressed condition." He went on to say "that freedom is the sacred right of every man whatever his color, who has not forfeited it by some violation of municipal law, is a truth established by God himself in the very creation of human beings. No time, no circumstances, no human power or policy can change the nature of this truth, nor repeal the fundamental laws of society by which every man's right to liberty is guaranteed. The first act therefore of enslaving men is always a violation of those great primary laws of society, by which alone the master himself holds every particle of his own freedom." Quoted in Ruchames, *Racial Thought in America*, 230.

31. It is during this period that science is conceptualized as a value-neutral domain of knowledge and, thus, as an apolitical, nonmoral arena. "It began to replace theological and moral discourse as the appropriate discourse with which to discuss nature. Science also encroached heavily on political discourse, as many political issues were transposed into the realm of neutral 'nature,' the scientists' province. *The outcome was a narrowing of the cultural space within which, and the cul-*

tural forms by which, the claims of biological determinism could be effectively challenged." Nancy Stephan and Sander Gilman, "Appropriating the Idioms of Science: The Rejection of Scientific Racism," in *The Bounds of Race: Perspectives on Hegemony and Resistance,* ed. Dominic LaCapra (Ithaca: Cornell University Press, 1991), 80, emphasis added.

32. Margaret Wetherell and Jonathan Potter, *Mapping the Language of Racism: Discourse and the Legitimation of Exploitation* (New York: Columbia University Press, 1992), 19.

33. Guido Zernatto, "Nation: The History of a Word," *Review of Politics* 6 (1944): 352–66.

34. Liah Greenfeld, *Nationalism: Five Roads to Modernity* (Cambridge: Harvard University Press, 1991), 6.

35. Eric Hobsbawn, *Nations and Nationalism since 1780: Programme, Myth, Reality* (Cambridge: Cambridge University Press, 1993), 21.

36. Anders Stephanson, *Manifest Destiny: American Expansionism and the Empire of Right* (New York: Hill and Wang, 1995), 5.

37. Samuel Langdon, *The Republic of the Israelites an Example to the American States,* 5 June 1788, in *God's New Israel: Religious Interpretation of American Destiny,* ed. Conrad Cherry (Englewood Cliffs, N.J.: Prentice-Hall, 1971), 98–99, emphasis added.

38. Hobsbawn, *Nations and Nationalism,* 19.

39. Stephanson, *Manifest Destiny,* 20.

40. Sacvan Bercovitch, *The Rites of Assent: Transformations in the Symbolic Construction of America* (New York: Routledge, 1993), 39.

41. One can easily see, then, how Bercovitch's focus could lead him to overlook this point.

42. Barbara J. Fields, "Slavery, Race, and Ideology in the United States of America," *New Left Review* 181 (1990): 101.

43. Bercovitch, *Rites of Assent,* 50.

44. Etienne Balibar and Immanuel Wallerstein, *Race, Nation, Class: Ambiguous Identities* (London: Verso, 1988), 95.

45. Ibid., 96.

46. Ibid.

47. Ibid., 98.

48. Ibid., 100.

49. As Balibar notes in "The Nation Form: History and Ideology," in *Race, Class, and Nation:* "It is possible to suggest (with Hegel and Marx) that, in the history of every modern nation, wherever the argument can apply, there is never more than one single founding revolutionary event (which explains both the permanent temptation to repeat its forms, to imitate its episodes and characters, and the temptation found among the 'extreme' parties to suppress it, either by proving that national identity derives from before the revolution or by awaiting the realiza-

tion of that identity from a new revolution which would complete the work of the first)" (87). The political projects of Afrocentrism and the Nation of Islam can be thought of in these terms.

50. *The Sons of Africans: An Essay on Freedom with Observations on the Origin of Slavery* by a member of the African Society in Boston (Boston, 1808); reprinted in Dorothy Porter, *Early Negro Writing, 1760–1837* (Boston: Beacon, 1971), 26–27.

51. Albert Raboteau, *A Fire in the Bones: Reflections on African-American Religious History* (Boston: Beacon, 1995), 192.

CHAPTER FIVE

1. "Absalom Jones's Thanksgiving Sermon," 1 January 1808, in Dorothy Porter, *Early Negro Writing, 1760–1837* (Boston: Beacon, 1971), 335.

2. Ibid., 339.

3. A lot of work is being done in this area. Maurice Halbwach's *The Collective Memory* (New York: Harper & Row, 1980) is an early example; see also Pierre Nora's work on what he calls "the sites of memory," *Les Lieux de mémoire* (Paris: Gallimard, 1997). The collection of essays edited by John Gillis, *Commemorations: The Politics of National Identity* (Princeton: Princeton University Press, 1994), serves as an excellent introduction to the relation between memory and national identity. Yael Zerubavel's *Recovered Roots: Collective Memory and the Making of the Israeli National Tradition* (Chicago: University of Chicago Press, 1995) is an excellent text in this regard. For works specifically addressing black Americans, see Genevieve Fabre, "African-American Commemorative Celebrations in the Nineteenth Century," in *History and Memory in African-American Culture,* ed. Genevieve Fabre and Robert O'Meally (New York: Oxford University Press, 1994), 72–91, and Toni Morrison, "The Site of Memory," in *Out There: Marginalization and Contemporary Cultures,* ed. Russer Ferguson, Martha Gever, Trinh T. Minh-ha, and Cornel West (Cambridge: MIT Press, 1993).

4. Zerubavel, *Recovered Roots,* 6.

5. In Boston's black community the celebration was held on July 14.

6. Benjamin Quarles, *Black Abolitionists* (New York: Oxford University Press, 1969), 119. Because the celebrations' intended purpose was to celebrate the end of the slave trade and the possible end of slavery in the United States, the continued trafficking of Africans across the Atlantic and the expansion of slave trading in the border states defeated the purpose of the day. Also see William Gravely, "The Dialectic of Double-Consciousness in Black American Freedom Celebrations, 1808–1863," *Journal of Negro History* 67 (winter 1982): 303.

7. The festivals were observed consistently, however, between 1827 and 1834. See Gravely, "Dialectic," 304, and Fabre, "Commemorative Celebrations," 81.

8. Shane White, "It Was a Proud Day: African Americans, Festivals, and Parades in the North, 1741–1834," *Journal of American History* 81 (June 1994): 13–50.

9. Some black communities, such as Baltimore, Cooperstown, and Fredericksburg, chose to celebrate on July 4 instead of July 5. But the desire for a separate black holiday eventually set the 5th as the day. See Gravely, "Dialectic," 304.

10. Prior to the 1820s, July 4 was not widely accepted as a national holiday. There was no consensus as to how America's birth should be recognized. In fact, up until this period the fourth was an occasion of extensive debate about colonization. The ACS used the day to raise money to export Africans from the United States. See John Bodnar, *Remaking America: Public Memory, Commemoration, and Patriotism in the Twentieth Century* (Princeton: Princeton University Press, 1992), chap. 2; see also the *Commemorations,* edited by John Gillis. For discussion of the ACS's use of July 4 see George Fredrickson, *The Black Image in the White Mind* (Hanover: Wesleyan University Press, 1987), chap. 1.

11. From 1834 to 1862, approximately 150 of these observances were recorded, some with crowds exceeding 7,000. Gravely, "Dialectic," 304.

12. *Douglass Monthly* 2 (1959); also quoted in Gravely, "Dialectic," 305.

13. Catherine Bell, *Ritual Theory, Ritual Practice* (New York: Oxford University Press, 1992), 197.

14. Ronald Grimes, *Research in Ritual Studies* (Metuchen, N.J.: Scarecrow and American Theological Library Association, 1985), 8.

15. Meyer Fortes, "Religious Premises and Logical Technique in Divinatory Ritual," in *Philosophical Transactions of the Royal Society,* ser. B, 251 (1966): 410.

16. For a detailed account of the origins of this holiday, see Maulana Karenga, *Kwanzaa: Origins, Concepts, Practice* (Los Angeles: University of Sankore Press, 1977).

17. Kenneth Burke, *The Philosophy of Literary Form* (Berkeley: University of California Press, 1973), 1.

18. Ibid., 84. Bell's use of redemptive hegemony is a combination of Kenelm Burridge's notion of the redemptive process in *New Heaven, New Earth: A Study of Millenarian Activity* (New York: Schocken, 1969) and Antonio Gramsci's understanding of hegemony. See his *The Modern Prince and Other Writings,* trans. Louis Marks (New York: International, 1957) and *Selections from Prison Notebooks,* ed. and trans. Quintin Hoare and Geoffrey Nowell Smith (London: Lawrence and Wishart, 1971).

19. Bell, *Ritual Theory,* 74.

20. Ibid, 220.

21. Ibid., 104. This is a critical point. It allows me to invoke Exodus even when it is not explicitly mentioned, a point William Gravely overlooks. He states that the "freedom celebration's orators seldom directly compared the black and Jewish experiences. Their consciousness of belonging to a distinct people rather de-

pended on two interlocking images of Africa [homeland and romanticized site of memory] and of racially based enslavement against which the struggle for freedom was fought in the New World" ("Dialectic," 307). But to fully appreciate each of these images, I believe, we have to examine them within the broader story of black America: a story full of allusions to and analogies with the Hebrew exodus. So despite the lack of explicit or direct comparisons, Exodus informs and, precisely because of its organization within taxonomic sets, shapes much of the celebrations' content.

22. Bell, *Ritual Theory*, 116.

23. Fabre, "Commemorative Celebrations," 73.

24. Zerubavel, *Recovered Roots*, 221. On this point she quotes Hayden White: "[N]arrative is not simply a recording of 'what happened' in the transition from one state of affairs to another but a progressive *redescription* of sets of events in such a way as to dismantle a structure encoded in one verbal mode in the beginning so as to justify a recording of it in another mode at the end." Hayden White, *Tropics of Discourse: Essays in Cultural Criticism* (Baltimore: Johns Hopkins University Press, 1978), 98, emphasis added.

25. "Order of the Celebration of the Day," January 1, 1808, in Porter, *Early Negro Writing*, 334.

26. Zerubavel, *Recovered Roots*, 216.

27. My discussion draws on Catherine Bell's analysis of the Roman Catholic Mass. See Bell, "Ritual, Change, and Changing Rituals," *Worship* 63 (1989): 36–41.

28. Zerubavel sees the holiday cycle "as a semiotic system that offers a nonhistorical framework of representation of the past. The holiday cycle determines which aspects of the past become more central to collective memory and which are assigned to oblivion; which events are commemorated as highly significant and which are lumped together in a single commemoration, or ignored. Holidays create commemorative narratives about specific events, detaching them from their broad historical context. This inevitable dissociation allows greater flexibility in delineating the narrative boundaries in order to accentuate a desired moral lesson, leaving out those developments that might detract from it" (*Recovered Roots*, 216).

29. *Liberator*, 11 August 1832.

30. The brutalities of American life are read in relation to biblical narratives, and the structures of oppression are viewed in a transformed way. This transformation by way of Christian narrative yields a tragic sense, what Cornel West sees as a kind of "Good Friday state of existence—with the hope for a potential and possible triumphant state of affairs." See Cornel West, *Prophesy Deliverance! An Afro-American Revolutionary Christianity* (Philadelphia: Westminster, 1982), 151 n. 9.

31. Jones, quoted in Porter, *Early Negro Writing*, 337–38.

32. Shane White, "Proud Day," 34.

33. This move is illustrative of black America's peculiar civil religion. It stands in an uneasy relation with the civil religion that Robert Bellah and others talk about.

34. This should not be collapsed into the notion that black Americans were simply caught in America's rites of assent. I want to suggest that conflict is at the heart of what this means. In other words, black folk (among others) are at the heart of the ideology of America. See also David Waldstreicher, "Rites of Rebellion, Rites of Assent: Celebrations, Print Culture, and the Origins of American Nationalism," *Journal of American History* (June 1995): 38 n. 5: "My interpretation differs in emphasis from that of Sacvan Bercovitch, for whom the rites of assent, typified by such rhetorical constructs as the jeremiad, contain all dissent within an overarching Americanism. I want to stress that the contests within and over Americanism have been important, substantive ones and that rhetorics and rituals are always both contesting and assenting and never essentially one or the other."

35. *Austin Steward: Twenty-Two Years a Slave and Forty Years a Freeman,* in *Four Fugitive Slave Narratives* (Reading, Mass.: Addison-Wesley, 1969), 94.

36. See William Gravely's discussion of theodicy in the early nineteenth-century freedom celebrations, "Dialectic," 308–10. Steward, like many others, struggled to reconcile the suffering of Africans with the benevolence of God. Nathaniel Paul, for example, cried out, "Tell me, ye mighty waters, why did ye sustain the ponderous load of misery? Or speak, ye winds, and say why it was that ye executed your office to waft them onward to the still more dismal state . . . ? And, oh thou immaculate God, be not angry with us, while we come into this thy sanctuary, and make the bold inquiry in this thy holy temple, why it was that thou didst look on with the calm indifference of an unconcerned spectator, when thy holy law was violated, thy divine authority despised and a portion of thine own creatures reduced to a state of mere vassalage and misery?" Paul offered only this answer: "Hark! While he answers from on high: hear Him proclaiming from the skies—Be still and know that I am God!" Woodson, *Negro Orators,* 69.

37. Steward, *Twenty-Two Years a Slave,* 96.

38. William H. Wiggins, Jr., *O Freedom! Afro-American Emancipation Celebrations* (Knoxville: University of Tennessee Press, 1987), 35.

39. *Freedom's Journal,* 29 June 1827.

40. Gravely, "Dialectic," 304.

41. Paul Gilroy, *The Black Atlantic: Modernity and Double Consciousness* (Cambridge: Harvard University Press, 1993), 188–89.

42. Ibid., 191.

43. Ibid., 198.

44. Ibid., 199.

45. Ibid., 198.

46. More specifically, the different contexts of the celebrations served the development of national consciousness in different ways. Ranging from local to international concerns, a concept of national identity extended beyond the provincialism of "Americocentrism" but hoped nevertheless to transform America.

CHAPTER SIX

1. *The Colored American*, 15 July 1839. Also see Leonard Sweet, "The Fourth of July and Black Americans in the Nineteenth Century: Northern Leadership Opinion Within the Context of the Black Experience," *Journal of Negro History* 61 (July 1976): 256–75.

2. Linda Kerber, "Abolitionists and Amalgamation: The New York City Race Riots of 1834," *New York History* 48 (January 1967): 33.

3. David Goldberg makes a similar point (not so much about amalgamation but about racial classification and national character) in his text *Racist Culture: Philosophy and the Politics of Meaning* (Oxford: Blackwell, 1993), 30. Also illustrative of this point is a short piece published in the *Colored American* in August 1838. The editors simply reprinted a brief note that was making its rounds in the nation's newspapers about Richard M. Johnson, the vice president who had a slave mistress openly in Kentucky. "Another case of amalgamation has occurred in Indiana. A writer in one of the papers proposed that both parties be skinned alive. A cruel punishment, though the crime was black and horrible.

"It occurs to us that the people of this country, especially the state of New York, have significantly indicated their acquiescence in another mode of punishment for this offence. The criminal in Indiana, by becoming a resident in a slaveholding state, and slaveholder, might possibly commute the threatened punishment of being skinned alive, by consenting to accept the Vice President of the United States!

"Seriously: let us take another view of the matter—Thousands of our respectable citizens and scores of statesmen, scholars, and church members (if not ministers) are openly living in the black and horrible crime of amalgamation, and no one (except the fanatical abolitionists) raises a cry against the abomination. For why? It is done without marriage: in other words in defiance against God's law. But if any one adventures to do the same thing, without any transgression of the sacred decalogue—why then, (unless he will do for a Vice President) he must be skinned alive! Verily, the Americans bid fair to pass for a sensible and discriminating race of Anglo Saxons! No one can doubt the prolific brain of the Anglo Saxon race, and in proof of it, there is no need to quote as our editors have done, the 15,000 authors living in Germany, nor the 20,000 volumes of learned folly and wisdom sent forth every year by them!—Friend of Man."

4. See Henry Louis Gates, Jr., and Cornel West, *The Future of the Race* (New York: Alfred A. Knopf, 1996), 81.

5. Paul Gilroy, *The Black Atlantic: Modernity and Double Consciousness* (Cambridge: Harvard University Press, 1993), 198.

6. Ibid.

7. Ibid.

8. Jonathan Glover, "Nations, Identity, and Conflict," in *The Morality of Nation-*

alism, ed. Robert McKim and Jeff McMahan (New York: Oxford University Press, 1997), 20.

9. Questions asked by Clifford Geertz in *The Interpretation of Cultures* (New York: Basic, 1973), 253.

10. See Nancy Fraser, "Rethinking the Public Sphere: A Contribution to the Critique of Actually Existing Democracy" in *Habermas and the Public Sphere,* ed. Craig Calhoun (Cambridge: MIT Press, 1996), 125. Also see her "Toward a Discourse Ethic of Solidarity," *Praxis International* 5, no. 4 (January 1986): 425–29.

11. My thinking about "soul" follows that of Ralph Ellison in his brilliant essay "What Would America Be Like without Blacks," in *The Collected Essays of Ralph Ellison,* ed. John Callahan (New York: Modern Library, 1995). Ellison writes, "Without the presence of Negro American style, our jokes, tall tales, even our sports would be lacking in the sudden turns, shocks and swift changes of pace (all jazz-shaped) that serve to remind us that the world is ever unexplored, and that while a complete mastery of life is mere illusion, the real secret of the game is to make life swing. It is its ability to articulate this tragic-comic attitude toward life that explains much of the mysterious power and attractiveness of that quality of Negro American style known as 'soul.' An expression of American diversity within unity, of blackness with whiteness, soul announces the presence of creative struggle against the realities of existence" (582).

12. Cornel West, "The Prophetic Tradition in Afro-America," in *Prophetic Fragments* (Grand Rapids and Trenton: Eerdmans and Africa World Press, 1988), 41.

13. I have adapted this phrase from the work of Glenn Tinder, "Politics and the Prophetic Tradition in Christianity," in *Let Justice Roll: Prophetic Challenges in Religion, Politics, Society,* ed. Neal Reimer (Lanham, Md.: Rowman & Littlefield, 1996), 40–43.

14. Ellison, "What America Would Be Like without Blacks," 583.

15. Cornel West, "Subversive Joy and Revolutionary Patience in Black Christianity," in *Prophetic Fragments,* 164.

16. Again, this is not to say that all forms of Exodus politics have this as its aim and end. The reading I am offering is just one among many that can be given of uses of the story.

17. Carter G. Woodson, "Negroes of Cincinnati Prior to the Civil War," *Journal of Negro History* 1 (January 1916): 1–22.

18. The black population increased fourfold between 1810 and 1820 and seemed destined to double again in the third decade of the century. See Leonard Curry, *The Free Black in Urban America, 1800–1850: The Shadow of the Dream* (Chicago: University of Chicago Press, 196), 104.

19. Michael Feldberg, *The Turbulent Era: Riot and Disorder in Jacksonian America* (New York: Oxford, 1980), 38.

20. Howard Bell talks of the rift between the Philadelphia-based African Meth-

odist Episcopal Church and the New York–based African Methodist Episcopal Zion Church as a significant feature of the first national meeting—citing Richard Allen and the Philadelphia cohort as hijacking the idea for their own interests. See Bell, *A Survey of the Negro Convention Movement, 1830–1861* (New York: Arno, 1969), chap. 2.

21. Gayraud Wilmore, *Black Religion and Black Radicalism: An Interpretation of the Religious History of Afro-American People*, 2d ed. (New York: Orbis, 1994), 92.

22. Michael Walzer, *Exodus and Revolution* (New York: Basic, 1985), 88.

23. Jane H. Pease and William Pease, *They Who Would Be Free: Blacks' Search for Freedom, 1830–1861* (New York: Athenaeum, 1974), vii.

24. A good example of the need for this distinction would be the apparent strangeness of the Million Man March in 1995. The march mimicked in an odd way the march on Washington, but the march's participants, for the most part, chose not to speak to the state at that moment but, rather, to the community. The entire event was an insider affair in front of the state. This, of course, made the choice of venue all the more odd.

25. *Constitution of the American Society of Free Persons of Colour* (Philadelphia, 1831), 5.

26. *Minutes and Proceedings of the Second Annual Convention for the Improvement of the Free People of Color in These United States, Philadelphia, 1832* (Philadelphia, 1832), 8–9.

27. They were Robert Cowley, Maryland; John Peck, Carlisle, Pennsylvania; William Hamilton, New York; William Whipper, Philadelphia; Benjamin Paschal, Philadelphia; Thomas D. Coxsin, New Jersey; and J. C. Morel, Philadelphia.

28. Richard Allen's "Address to the Free People of Colour of These United States," in *Constitution of the American Society of the Free Persons of Colour . . . also The Proceedings of the Convention, with Their Address to the Free Persons of Colour in the United States, Philadelphia, 1831* (Philadelphia: J. W. Allen, 1831), 10, emphasis added.

29. "Convention Address," *Minutes and Proceedings of the First Annual Convention of the People of Colour, Philadelphia, 1831* (Philadelphia, 1831), 12–13, emphasis added.

Bell describes this as half-hearted because of the influence of Garrison and the hatred of colonization. But clearly, in light of the above passage, the convention vigorously supported the efforts of the 1830 meeting. See Bell, *Survey of the Negro Convention Movement*, 30–31.

30. *Minutes and Proceedings of the Second Annual Convention*, 15.

31. Ibid., 17.

32. Ibid., 19. This sentiment was closely tied to the resistance of the efforts of the American Colonization Society. I have purposely excluded discussion of this issue because so much good work has been done in this area.

33. The final resolution read as follows: "*Resolved*—That this Convention rec-

ommend the establishment of a Society, or Agent, in Upper Canada, for the purpose of purchasing lands and contributing to the wants of our people generally, who may be, by oppressive legislative enactments, obliged to flee from these United States and take up residence within her borders. And that this Convention will employ its Auxiliary Societies, and such other means as may lie in its power, for the purpose of raising monies, and remit the same for the purpose of aiding the proposed object." Ibid., 20.

34. Evelyn Brooks Higginbotham, *Righteous Discontents: The Women's Movement in the Black Baptist Church, 1880–1920* (Cambridge: Harvard University Press, 1993), 187. Higginbotham uses this phrase in her discussion of the politics of the Women's Convention in the black Baptist church from 1900 to 1920.

35. Ibid., 196.

36. *Minutes and Proceedings of the First Annual Convention*, 5. A relation exists between this aspect of respectability and white abolitionists' responses to the problems facing the black community. They often called on Northern free blacks to embrace self-improvement. In this vein, a writer in the *Liberator* on January 23, 1832, addressed the free black community: "Be industrious. . . . Let no hour pass unemployed. . . . Be virtuous. . . . Use no bad language. Let not foolish jesting be heard from you, but be sober men who have characters to form for eternity. . . . In a word, endeavor to be good Christians, and good citizens, that all reproach may be taken from you, and that your enemies, seeing your good conduct may be ashamed. Thus you will aid your friends in their endeavors for your good." Quoted in George Frederickson, *The Black Image in the White Mind* (Hanover: Wesleyan University Press, 1971), 36. But it is important, I believe, not to reduce the free blacks' sentiments to this.

37. *Minutes and Proceedings of the Second Annual Convention*, 35. John Bracy, August Meier, and Elliot Rudwick, in *Black Nationalism in America* (Indianapolis and New York: Bobbs-Merrill, 1970), would call these sentiments the simplest expression of a form of black nationalism: *racial solidarity*. For them, it "generally has no ideological or programmatic implications beyond the desire that black people organize themselves on the basis of their common color and oppressed condition to move in some way to alleviate their situation. The concept of racial solidarity is essential to all forms of black nationalism. The establishment of mutual aid societies and separatist churches . . . had little justification beyond that of racial solidarity" (xxvi). What they do not explore is whether some conception of nation or peoplehood is essential to *this* concept of racial solidarity, for race takes on a different meaning during this period than after 1850. Black people did not understand it as a biological difference or as an essentialist category.

38. Higginbotham, *Righteous Discontents*, 203.

39. Walzer, *Exodus and Revolution*, 47.

40. Ibid., 53.

41. Ibid.

42. Ibid.

43. Ibid., 49.

44. It's important to note that the sedimentation of the new science of race and its claim of the innate inferiority of black people necessitated a set of counter-claims. Any form of self-improvement would undermine the new racial science and the racism of its proponents. The delegates to the early conventions understood this: "If amidst all the difficulties with which we have been surrounded, and the privations which we have suffered, we presented an equal amount of intelligence with that class of Americans that have been so peculiarly favoured, a *very grave* and *dangerous* question would present itself to the world, on the natural equality of man, and the best rule of logic would place those who have oppressed us, in the scale of inferiority" (*Minutes of the Fifth Annual Convention for the Improvement of Free People of Colour in the United States, Philadelphia, 1835* [Philadelphia: Gibbons, 1835], 26). Of course, the delegates of the convention backed off the implications of these remarks and, in a brilliant rhetorical move, embraced the natural and universal rights of man. Nevertheless, they understood the import of respect (from others as well as for themselves).

45. *Minutes and Proceedings of the First Annual Convention* 14.

46. Richard Allen captured this sentiment in his address: "to obviate these evils . . . with a desire of raising the moral and political understanding of ourselves . . . we cannot devise any plan more likely to accomplish this end, than by encouraging agriculture and mechanical arts: for by the first, we shall be enabled to act with a degree of independence . . . and by the faithful pursuit of the latter, in connection with the sciences, which expand and enoble the mind, will eventually give us the standing and condition we desire." *Constitution of the American Society of Free Persons of Color,* 7.

47. Higganbotham, *Righteous Discontents,* 187.

48. Joseph R. Gusfield, in *Symbolic Crusade: Status, Politics and the American Temperance Movement* (Urbana: University of Illinois Press, 1963), argues that the temperance movement was closely tied to issues of class and status, a symbol, as it were, of middle-class membership. Also see Frederick Cooper, "Elevating the Race: The Social Thought of Black Leaders, 1827–1850," *American Quarterly* 24 (1972): 615. This is a critical point because this language of differentiation affected the convention's response to a number of popular activities.

49. Carla Peterson, *Doers of the Word: African-American Women Speakers and Writers in the North* (New York: Oxford University Press, 1995), 15.

50. Quoted in Marilyn Richardson's introduction to *Maria W. Stewart, America's First Black Woman Political Writer* (Bloomington: Indiana University Press, 1987), 20.

51. Kevin K. Gaines, *Uplifting the Race: Black Leadership, Politics, and Culture in the Twentieth Century* (Chapel Hill: University of North Carolina Press, 1996), 2.

52. Black elites were not alone in this view. Many whites frowned on the "de-

grading" displays of the white lower classes. See David Waldstreicher, "Rites of Rebellion, Rites of Assent: Celebrations, Print Culture, and the Origins of American Nationalism," *Journal of American History* 82 (June 1995): 37–61.

53. *Minutes and Proceedings of the First Annual Convention,* 11.

54. See *Freedom's Journal,* 29 June 1827.

55. *Minutes and Proceedings of the Fourth Annual Convention for the Improvement of the Free People of Colour, in the United States, New York, 1834* (New York, 1834), 14.

56. Ibid, 15. It passed by a vote of 40 to 2. Among the yeas were, oddly enough, William Hamilton and Austin Steward, both of whom delivered keynote addresses at July 5th celebrations. Steward even describes the parades as a magnificent event in his autobiography.

57. Shane White, " 'It Was a Proud Day': African Americans, Festivals, and Parades in the North, 1741–1834," *Journal of American History* 81 (June 1994): 13–50.

58. Isabel V. Hull, "The Bourgeoisie and Its Discontents: Reflections on 'Nationalism and Respectability,' " *Journal of Contemporary History* 17 (1982): 252–53. Also see Mikhail Bahktin's *Rabelais and His World* (Cambridge: MIT Press, 1968) and Peter Stallybrass and Allon White's *The Politics and Poetics of Transgression* (Ithaca: Cornell University Press, 1986).

59. Gaines, *Uplifting the Race,* 4.

60. When its participants are viewed as agents in history, the African American struggle "becomes the story of a gallantly persistent struggle, of a disparate racial group fighting to enter modernity on its own terms. Politically, this struggle consists of prudential acquiescence plus courageous revolt against white paternalism; institution-building and violent rebellion within the segregated social relations of industrial capitalism. . . . Culturally, this has meant the maintenance of self-respect in the face of pervasive denigration." Cornel West, *Prophesy Deliverance! An Afro-American Revolutionary Christianity* (Philadelphia: Westminster, 1982), 70.

61. My use of the phrase *common sense* follows John Dewey. For him our common sense world signifies "that in which we live, with our loves and hates, our defeats and achievements, our choices, strivings and enjoyments." See Dewey's *A Quest of Certainty: A Study of the Relation of Knowledge and Action* (New York: G. P. Putnam's Sons, 1929). Wahneema Lubiano thinks of common sense as "the ideology lived and articulated in everyday understandings of the world and one's place in it." See her essay "Black Nationalism and Black Common Sense," in *The House That Race Built: Black Americans, U.S. Terrain* (New York: Pantheon, 1997), 232.

62. Walzer, *Exodus and Revolution,* 76.

63. Ibid.

64. Ibid., 84.

65. But it is not simply a matter of individuals remembering the Exodus story. A "living memory" is necessary so that in moments of crisis the nation can reaffirm its commitments. As Walzer notes, "these reaffirmations don't have a merely ritual

character, as if their purpose were to regain the magical efficacy of the original covenanting. They are moral acts; their purpose is to sustain personal and collective obligation"—and, perhaps, to ensure the longevity of the nation (*Exodus and Revolution*, 88).

66. Albert Raboteau, *Slave Religion: The Invisible Institution in the Antebellum South* (Oxford: Oxford University Press, 1978), 320.

CHAPTER SEVEN

1. *Minutes and Proceedings of the Fourth Annual Convention for the Improvement of the Free People of Color, in the United States, 1834* (New York, 1834), 29. This focus on the moral aspect of the struggle is seen in the convention's position in relation to the acquisition of citizenship: "Let us not lament that under the present constituted powers of this government, we are disfranchised; better far than to be partakers of its guilt. Let us refuse to be allured by the glittering endowments of official stations, or enchanted by the robe of American citizenship" (29). For these men, the issue was a moral one entirely.

2. Ibid.

3. *Minutes and Proceedings of the Fifth Annual Convention for the Improvement of the Free People of Colour, 1835* (Philadelphia: William P. Gibbons, 1835), 14–15.

4. "Minutes and Proceedings of the American Moral Reform Society, Philadelphia, August 8, 1836," in *The National Enquirer and Constitutional Advocate of Universal Liberty*, 24 August 1836, 9.

5. According to Nancy Stepan and Sander Gilman, this process sedimented between 1870 and 1920. They associate the move to a "value-neutral" science with the emergence of the scientific essay. Stepan and Gilman argue that "[i]t was in the late nineteenth century that the modern scientific text as we know it stabilized to become the standard, accepted form of writing in nearly all branches of the natural sciences." Citing Gyorgy Markus, they argue that "the scientific paper served normative goals, and through its form—its depersonalized authorship, its demand for a peculiarly competent scientific reader—successfully satisfied the expectations of science for constant innovation and accumulation of knowledge." All of this bears on the problem of the findings and responses of scientific racism. See Nancy Stepan and Sander Gilman, "Appropriating the Idioms of Science: The Rejection of Scientific Racism," in *The Bounds of Race: Perspectives on Hegemony and Resistance*, ed. Dominic LaCapra (Ithaca: Cornell University Press, 1991), 79. See also Gyorgy Markus, "Why Is There No Hermeneutics of Natural Sciences? Some Preliminary Theses," *Science in Context* 1 (March 1987): 5–51.

6. Cornel West, *Prophesy Deliverance! An Afro-American Revolutionary Christianity* (Philadelphia: Westminster, 1982), 55.

7. George Frederickson, *The Black Image in the White Mind: The Debate on Afro-*

American Character and Destiny, 1817–1914 (Hanover: Wesleyan University Press, 1971), 75.

8. Reginald Horsman, *Race and Manifest Destiny: The Origins of American Racial Anglo-Saxonism* (Cambridge: Harvard University Press, 1981), 57. The importance of phrenology to the nineteenth century is captured, I think, in the Erwin Ackerknecht's claim that "phrenology was certainly . . . at least as influential in the first half of the 19th century as psychoanalysis was in the first half of the 20th century." Ackerknecht, *Medicine at the Paris Hospital, 1794–1848* (Baltimore: Johns Hopkins University Press, 1967), 172, quoted in Horsman, 56 n. 27. Also see Madeleine Stern, *Heads and Headliners: The Phrenological Fowlers* (Norman: University of Oklahoma Press, 1971).

9. Horsman, *Race and Manifest Destiny*, 143.

10. Patricia Cline Cohen, *A Calculating People: The Spread of Numeracy in Early America* (Chicago: University of Chicago Press, 1982), 4, 177.

11. See Leon Litwack, *North of Slavery: The Negro in the Free States, 1790–1860* (Chicago: University of Chicago Press, 1961), 74–78; William Stanton, *Leopard Spots: Scientific Attitudes toward Race in America, 1815–1859*, 58–81; Albert Deutsch, "The First U.S. Census of the Insane (1840) and Its Use as Pro-Slavery Propaganda," *Bulletin of the History of Medicine* 15 (1944): 466–82. I am well aware that this material has been presented before on numerous occasions. My only aim is to place it in a different setting. I wish not so much to present new facts as to redescribe its importance in the overall process of racial identification and self-identification.

12. Cohen, *Calculating People*, 177.

13. There were challenges to the census. Members of the American Statistical Association, founded in Boston in 1839, challenged the accuracy of the numbers. In particular, Edward Jarvis was the first person to call attention to the possibility of errors in the census. I've stated the claim so baldly because the challenge was not so much a defense of free blacks against the violence of the numbers but a defense of the science of statistics in the United States, which the census jeopardized. See Cohen, *Calculating People*, 191–101. Also see Gerald Grob, *Edward Jarvis and the Medical World of Nineteenth-Century America* (Knoxville: University of Tennessee Press, 1978).

14. Stepan and Gilman, in "Appropriating the Idioms of Science," make this claim about nineteenth-century racial science generally (74).

15. Cohen, *Calculating People*, 195.

16. Ibid.

17. "American Moral Reform Society Address to the American People," in *The National Enquirer and Constitutional Advocate of Universal Liberty*, 28 January 1837, 84.

18. Of course, this stance is part of the general tendency of Garrisonianism. Moral suasion stood as the philosophical backdrop to most of the American Moral

Reform Society's policies. And "complexional distinctions" were rejected outright. But if we only understand this move to color blindness in the face of the popularizing of racial science as a mimicry of Garrison, the significance of the strategy and its residual effect on black politics in the early *and* latter part of the nineteenth century is lost.

19. "American Moral Reform Society Address," 84.

20. Ibid.

21. For a more general discussion of the role of benevolence in the early and mid–nineteenth century, see Clifford Griffin, "Religious Benevolence as Social Control, 1815–1860," *Mississippi Valley Historical Review* 44 (December 1957): 423–44, also included in David Brion Davis's edited volume, *Ante-Bellum Reform* (New York: Harper & Row, 1967), 81–96.

22. "American Moral Reform Society Address," 84.

23. Ibid.

24. Larry Tise, *Proslavery: A History of the Defense of Slavery in America, 1701–1840* (Athens: University of Georgia Press, 1987. See chapter 10.

25. Charles Hodge, "Slavery," in *Essays and Reviews Selected from the "Princeton Review"* (New York: Robert Carter & Brothers, 1857), 473–512.

26. "Address to the Christian Churches, 1836," *The National Enquirer,* 49.

27. Unlike Howard Bell, who seems to view the letter *only* as a call for the golden rule as a principle of living, I think the letter is a significant monument in early nineteenth-century black politics. It stands as a precursor of sorts to Martin Luther King, Jr.'s "Letter from the Birmingham Jail (1963)." See *A Testament of Hope: The Essential Writings and Speeches of Martin Luther King, Jr.,* ed. James M. Washington (New York: Harper Collins, 1986), 289–302. Again, if you read the letter as simply a reflection of Garrison's criticism of organized religion, you miss the direct linkage between these two letters.

28. "Address to the Christian Churches, 1836," 49.

29. Ibid.

30. Ibid.

31. Ibid.

32. To explore this point in relation to the overall antislavery movement see David Brion Davis's "The Emergence of Immediatism in British and American Antislavery Thought," in *Mississippi Valley Historical Review* 49 (September 1962): 209–230. Also in *Ante-Bellum Reform,* ed. Davis, 139–52.

33. An extended debate about "complexional distinctions" occurred on the floor of the first convention of the AMRS. "Frederick A. Hinton charged that the convention had once voted down the attempt to eliminate the term colored: and that on reconsideration, the decision was reversed by the casting vote of the president." See Howard Bell, *A Survey of the Negro Convention Movement: 1830–1861* (New York: Arno, 1969), 50. Also see *The Colored American,* 2 September 1837, 2–3.

34. *The Colored American,* 10 February 1838, 18.

35. *The Colored American,* 15 September 1838, 118.

36. *The Colored American,* 26 August 1837, 2. Also quoted in Bell, *Survey,* 50.

37. Sterling Stuckey, *Slave Culture: Nationalist Theory and the Foundations of Black America* (Oxford: Oxford University Press, 1987), 194.

38. Ibid.

39. Ibid, 198.

40. "The use of the terms colored and brown—more perhaps than that of any other appellations prior to the nineteenth century—reflected a certain disdain on the part of some people of mixed ancestry for the majority of their people, a tendency to look askance at them on grounds of color and class." Ibid., 199.

41. Ibid., 203.

42. Ibid., 205.

43. Ibid., 390 n. 37.

44. Ibid., 211.

45. *The Colored American,* 29 March 1838, 38.

46. Ibid., 39. In a more stark formulation Cornish states the difference between the two men: "Our first duty is to take off disabilities and raise our people to a level with others, then we may justly mete out to them all, the same measure of benevolence. . . . If we find a colored brethren [*sic*] enslaved and trampled upon, *solely because he is colored,* is brother Whipper so simple as to say we must not unbind nor, elevate him, *as a colored man,* or that we must not organize as *colored men* to meet the condition of the millions of our brethren who are in bondage, lest in doing this we be partial, and make *complexional distinctions?* Nonsense!!" Ibid.

47. Ibid.

48. Henry Louis Gates, Jr., introduction to *Race, Writing, and Difference,* ed. Henry Louis Gates, Jr. (Chicago: University of Chicago Press, 1986), 404. Also discussed in Paul Taylor's "A New Negro: Pragmatism and Black Identity" (photocopy, 1995).

49. *The Colored American,* 15 September 1838, 118.

50. Watkins offered this analogy: "On my passage to Philadelphia, two men, the one white and the other colored, fall overboard—five passengers, all white men, and myself, behold the heart-rending scene—the drowning men cry for help—the five white men having contracted a deep-rooted hatred against a sable hue, & actuated by a sympathy of color, and a supposed identity of interest with the drowning man, run en masse, to succor him; I, finding the colored man neglected from an unworthy principle, spring to his rescue, and stretch out, not one hand to the white man (who has already abundant help) and the other to the colored man, but I reach out both hands to him who has none to help him." Ibid.

51. Stuckey, *Slave Culture,* 208. Also see the *National Reformer,* October 1838, where Watkins also rejected the messianism of the AMRS. He stated that "there

was such a thing as propriety" and that "for a people in our condition just emerging from darkness and degradation, to assume the office of reforming the whole country, betrays, to say the least, a want of modesty."

52. Lewis Woodson, secretary of the Pittsburgh auxiliary of the AMRS (an organization that included a young Martin Delany), joined Watkins in opposition to the society's policies. Woodson maintained the belief in moral reform but argued vehemently for a race-based politics to improve the conditions of black Americans. In fact, the Pittsburgh auxiliary was a race-based organization. They fought against the disenfranchisement of blacks and argued for the necessity of economic self-sufficiency.

A pragmatic view of race was a critical feature of Woodson's politics, even as he embraced the aims of the AMRS. He claimed that "the condition in which we have for generations been living in this land, constitutes us as a distinct class. We have been held slaves, while those around us have been free." This condition created, in his view, a "national feeling" and "general character" that had to be drawn upon for the improvement of black Americans.

The tension between Woodson's embrace of moral reform and a "race-based" politics erupted when a call was made by the AMRS for independent black churches to renounce their racial particularity. Writing in *The Colored American* as "Augustine," Woodson argued that black churches should remain independent. He saw them as important spaces for black agency and critical vehicles for moral reform. Unlike the society, Woodson understood moral reform in terms of pragmatic racialism. He called for the moral reform of colored people by colored people: "Our moral elevation is a work in which we may be assisted, and in which we need much assistance, in which much assistance is owed us, but which never can be done for us." *The Colored American*, 2 December 1837, 2, and 10 February 1838, 18. For an extended discussion of Woodson, see Floyd Miller, *The Search for a Black Nationality: Black Emigration and Colonization, 1787–1863* (Urbana: University of Illinois Press, 1975), 94–105.

53. *The Colored American*, 13 February 1841. Also quoted in Stuckey, *Slave Culture*, 216–17.

54. *The Colored American*, 13 March 1841.

55. Ibid.

56. "Mr. W. May says, prejudice is the result of color, and *therefore* we should not use the term 'colored.' But look again at the matter. If it is the result of *color*, then it does *not* proceed from the word; and if *that* (color), is the cause, and Mr. W. desires to act upon the cause, then let him commence his operations upon the color." Ibid.

57. *The Colored American*, 6 March 1841.

58. Ibid.

59. Ibid.

60. Ibid.

61. Ibid.

62. Ibid.

63. *The Colored American,* 13 March 1841.

CHAPTER EIGHT

1. See *Proceedings of the Black State Conventions, 1840–1865,* ed. Philip S. Foner and George Walker (Philadelphia: Temple University Press, 1979).

2. *The Colored American,* 2 January 1841.

3. Jane and William Pease, *They Who Would Be Free: Blacks' Search for Freedom, 1830–1861* (New York: Atheneum, 1974), 183.

4. Figures such as Martin Delany, James McCune Smith, and Charles B. Ray emerged as important personalities during this period. Of course, Frederick Douglass also came onto the scene during this time.

5. Michael Walzer, *Exodus and Revolution* (New York: Basic, 1985), 7.

6. Ibid., 16.

7. Ibid., 138.

8. Ibid., 139.

9. Ibid.

10. Ibid., 140.

11. Ibid., 17.

12. Ibid., 141.

13. *The Emancipator and Free American,* 3 March 1842, 207. Also see Joel Schor's *Henry Highland Garnet: A Voice of Black Radicalism in the Nineteenth Century* (Westport, Conn.: Greenwood, 1977), 52–53.

14. See Schor, *Henry Highland Garnet,* 54.

15. Henry Highland Garnet, "An Address to the Slaves of the United States," in *Black Nationalism in America,* ed. John Bracey et al. (Indianapolis: Bobbs-Merrill, 1970), 67.

16. Ibid., 68.

17. I stress *individual* for two reasons: (1) following Etienne Balibar, "all identity is individual, but there is no individual identity that is not historical or, in other words, constructed within a field of social values, norms of behavior and collective symbols" (Etienne Balibar and Immanuel Wallerstein, *Race, Nation, Class: Ambiguous Identities* [London: Verso, 1992], 94); and (2) by focusing on the individual and the parallels that an individual's history may have with others' I avoid a complaint that my argument suffers from circularity (group *x* consists of people who've had group *x* experiences). "The history in question is not a global property of the group that depends on the group's prior existence, and which members of the group instantiate on account of their group membership. Rather, the history in question is an intrinsic property of individuals—intrinsic in the sense of being non-

global, not in the sense of being innate—a history in virtue of which they can be considered a group." Here I rely on an argument against Anthony Appiah by Paul Taylor in "The New Negro: Pragmatism and Black Identity" (photocopy), 20.

18. Benedict Anderson, *Imagined Communities* (New York: Verso, 1993), 6.

19. Speech delivered at the seventh anniversary of the American Anti-Slavery Society, 1840. Reprinted in Earl Ofari, *Let Your Motto Be Resistance* (Boston: Beacon, 1972), 127–34.

20. Speech delivered at the Liberty Party Convention, Massachusetts, 1842. Reprinted in Ofari, *Let Your Motto Be Resistance*, 144–52.

21. "Convention of the Colored Inhabitants of the State of New York, August 18–20, 1840, Albany, New York," in *Proceedings of the Black State Conventions, 1840–1865*, vol. 1 (Philadelphia: Temple University Press, 1979), 17.

22. Garnet is speaking directly to the efforts to disenfranchise African Americans in the state. Throughout the North, African Americans who once exercised the franchise were losing it. He simply urged black citizens to defend what they had. See James Horton and Lois Horton, *In Hope of Liberty* (New York: Oxford University Press, 1997), 246–49.

23. Ibid., 16.

24. Sterling Stuckey, *Slave Culture: Nationalist Theory and the Foundations of Black America* (New York: Oxford University Press, 1988).

25. Garnet, "Address," 70.

26. Ibid., 71.

27. Ibid.

28. Harry Reed, "The Slave as Abolitionist: Henry Highland Garnet's Address to the Slaves of the United States of America," *Centennial Review* 20, no. 4 (1976): 386.

29. My use of *irony* follows Reinhold Niebuhr's in *The Irony of American History* (New York: Charles Scribner's Sons, 1952). For Niebuhr, "irony consists of apparently fortuitous incongruities in life which are discovered, upon closer examination, to be not merely fortuitous. Incongruity as such is merely comic. It elicits laughter. This element of comedy is never completely eliminated from irony. But irony is something more than comedy. A comic situation is proved to be an ironic one if a hidden relation is discovered in the incongruity. If virtue becomes vice through some hidden defect in the virtue; if strength becomes weakness because of the vanity to which strength may prompt mighty man or nation . . ." (viii).

30. Alexander Crummel captured this sentiment in *Africa and America* (Springfield, Mass.: Wiley, 1891): Garnet's resolve demonstrated "the early set and bias of his soul to that quality of magnanimity which Aristotle says exposes one to great dangers and makes a man unsparing in his life; thinking that life is not worth having on some terms" (300). Also see Stuckey's *Slave Culture*, 164.

31. Garnet, "Address," 75.

32. Ibid.

33. Stuckey, *Slave Culture,* 154.

34. Garnet, "Address," 68.

35. Cornel West alludes to this in a discussion of Toni Morrison's *Beloved* in his essay "Black Strivings in a Twilight Civilization," in *The Future of the Race* (New York: Knopf, 1996), 87.

36. See Theophus Smith, *Conjuring Culture: Biblical Formations of Black America* (New York: Oxford University Press, 1994), 61.

37. Stuckey, *Slave Culture,* 156.

38. Smith, *Conjuring Culture,* 61.

39. Albert Raboteau, in *Slave Religion: The "Invisible Institution" in the Antebellum South* (New York: Oxford University Press, 1978), explores two poles of behavior within slave Christianity: accommodationism and rebelliousness. With regard to the first, the pole Garnet addressed, Raboteau states, "It was otherworldly in the sense that it held that this world and this life were not the end, nor the final measure of existence. It was compensatory to the extent that it consoled and supported slaves worn out by the unremitting toil and capricious cruelty of the 'peculiar institution' " (317). Raboteau quickly dismisses, however, any attempt to read this focus as a lack of concern for this life.

40. Garnet, "Address," 73. Garnet doesn't completely reject Exodus. He seeks instead to open up space within prevailing interpretations of the story for the kind of action he advocates. His denial of the analogy, then, is an effort to transform the Exodus story in order to justify his revolutionary politics.

41. Ibid.

42. Ibid., 76.

43. Ibid.

44. White abolitionists also condemned the speech. Maria Chapman, assistant editor of the Boston *Liberator,* attacked Garnet directly, accusing him of taking bad advice. In commending the convention's vote against the address, Chapman wrote: "It is a matter of thankfulness whenever the spirit of freedom and of good,—of love, forgiveness, and magnanimity—prevails, even in a single heart, over evil, hatred, force, revenge and littleness. It did so, in a measure, at this Convention;—the address to the slaves, of the Reverend H. H. Garnet, expressing the idea that the time for insurrection had come, having been rejected. Bad counsels have the religious and the political bodies of which he is a member given him. We say emphatically to the man of color, trust not the counsels that lead you to the shedding of blood." Chapman refused to believe that Garnet could draw such conclusions on his own. She went on to say that "Little must the man of color have reflected, who does not see that the white man who now stimulates his feelings of revenge or his trust in violence, would be the first to desert and deny him." Garnet saw this response as another illustration of the refusal of white abolitionists to recognize the agency of blacks. He assured Chapman that he had not received any counsel concerning the address. And in a biting retort he stated: "My only crime is that I

have dared to think and act contrary to your opinion. . . . [But] be assured that there is one black American who dares to speak boldly on the subject of universal liberty." See the *Liberator,* 22 September 1843, for Chapman's article, and 8 December 1843, for Garnet's response.

45. *Minutes of the National Convention of Colored Citizens, Buffalo, New York, 1843* (Buffalo: 1843), 13. Reprinted in *Minutes of the Proceedings of the National Negro Convention, 1830–1864,* ed. Howard Ball (New York: Arno, 1969).

EPILOGUE

1. I should note that most antislavery organizations were biracial, particularly at the regional level.

2. *David Walker's Appeal to the Coloured Citizens of the World, but in Particular, and Very Expressly, to Those of the United States* (New York: Hill and Wang, 1965), 70

3. Henry Highland Garnet, "An Address to the Slaves of the United States," in *Black Nationalism in America,* ed. John Bracey et al. (Indianapolis and New York: Bobbs-Merrill, 1970), 76.

4. Wilson Moses, *The Golden Age of Black Nationalism, 1850–1925* (New York: Oxford University Press, 1978), 17.

5. Henry Louis Gates, Jr., and Cornel West, *The Future of the Race* (New York: Knopf, 1996), 73.

6. Ibid.

7. We need only think of the different ways the image of Egypt has been deployed: not simply as the home of Pharaoh but also as an example of a great "African" civilization. Different images from the story such as Mount Pisgah and Canaan, the seven plagues of Egypt, and Moses, of course, have been used in African American political discourse. I have teased out only one strand, but a lot more work is needed.

8. Michael Walzer, *Exodus and Revolution* (New York: Basic, 1985), 135.

9. Ibid., 146.

10. I have adapted this point from a presentation by the political philosopher Alan Ryan. In a political colloquium at Princeton University in 1994, he spoke about John Dewey and a pragmatic conception of social identity. In some ways my intent has been to lay aside the debate about racial essentialism and perhaps get us to see that what really counts is not our filiation but our politics. Accusations of being a traitor to the race, often hurled by black nationalists, lose a bit of their punch. We turn instead to debate the merits of positions and the ethical significance of our choices for the future. We also open up space for critical reflection on other issues that confront the community, such as gender and class.

11. Daniel A. Payne, *Recollection of Seventy Years* (Nashville: Publishing House

of the A.M.E. Sunday School Union, 1888), 28, reprinted in Benjamin Mays, *The Negro's God as Reflected in His Literature* (New York: Atheneum, 1969), 49.

12. Cornel West, *The American Evasion of Philosophy: A Genealogy of Pragmatism* (Madison: University of Wisconsin Press, 1989), 228.

13. Tony Morrison, *Beloved* (New York: Penguin, 1988), 180.

14. Hook is quoting James here. Sidney Hook, *Pragmatism and the Tragic Sense of Life* (New York: Basic, 1974), 5.

15. Ibid., 20. West rightly takes Hook to task for his use of the description "lesser evil." In West's view, Hook's use was essentially the trope of a cold war liberal reformist, concealing his own complicity with brute force and a crass politics of winners. Yet, in spite of West's reading, I think Hook's view has something to offer. It is true that Hook's defense of America calls into question *his* use of *this* conception of the tragic, but it doesn't vitiate the general view, and West seemingly dismisses this view because of the way Hook used it. The merits of the view—the fact that the tragic is not abstracted from our choices—provide us with a useful tool to sort out some incredibly difficult moments. As West rightly notes, "the point is not really who has a tragic sense (i.e., who is wise, sophisticated, and refined) and who does not (i.e., who is unwise, crude, and naïve), but rather what conception of it does one have and to what uses is it put in light of one's interest and purposes." *American Evasion,* 122. The same question can be posed to him in his critique of Hook and Dewey and his qualified embrace of a Roycean view of the tragic. See his "Pragmatism and the Sense of the Tragic," in *Keeping Faith: Philosophy and Race in America* (New York: Routledge, 1993), 107–18.

16. Hook, *Pragmatism,* 19.

17. Ralph Ellison, "What America Would Be Like without Blacks," in *The Collected Essays of Ralph Ellison,* ed. John F. Callahan (New York: Modern Library, 1995), 584.

Index